The world television industry

The world television industry

An economic analysis

Peter Dunnett

London and New York

First published 1990
by Routledge
11 New Fetter Lane, London EC4P 4EE

Simultaneously published in the USA and Canada
by Routledge
a division of Routledge, Chapman and Hall, Inc.
29 West 35th Street, New York, NY 10001

Phototypeset in 10pt Times by
Mews Photosetting, Beckenham, Kent

Printed and bound in Great Britain by
Biddles Ltd, Guildford and King's Lynn

British Library Cataloguing in Publication Data

Dunnett, Peter J.S.
 The world television industry: an economic analysis.
 1. Television broadcasting. Economic aspects Great Britain
 I. Title
 384.55'43

 ISBN 0-415-00162-5

Library of Congress Cataloging in Publication Data

Dunnett, Peter J.S.
 The world television industry: an economic analysis/by Peter
J.S. Dunnett.
     p.   cm.
 Includes bibliographical references (p.).
 ISBN 0-415-00162-5
 1. Television industry. 2. Television industry – United States.
3. Television industry – Government policy. 4. Television industry –
Government policy – United States. I. Title.
HE8700.4.D86   1990
384.55'1–dc20   89-27591
                                                        CIP

For Jan

Contents

Tables

Tables

Figures

Preface

This book examines the fast-growing and rapidly changing television industry. It attempts to explain the complex relationships between viewers, advertisers, governments, owners of the means of distribution, suppliers of programmes, and the other media in this period of transition. I hope the analysis and the comparisons and contrasts I make will be of interest to a wide range of readers. The economic analysis helps explain why things are the way they are. Political scientists, psychologists, sociologists, policy-makers, journalists, and those in the industry should be able to follow at least the gist of the argument. The remaining chapters are largely non-technical and comprise case studies and shorter vignettes.

In writing this book I have been indebted to the Canadian Department of National Defence and the Social Science and Humanities Council for financial support. I received useful advice, inspiration, and encouragement from Colin Jones, Richard Schwindt, James Boutilier, Richard Pomfret, Jim Bayer, Pad Sri, Bob St John, David Marshall, and Claire Inkster. Benjamin, David, Adam, and Barbara gave me their time. Finally I owe thanks to Lori Heimbecker for her efficient help with the word-processing.

P.D.

Chapter one

Introduction

In 1988 over a half a billion households worldwide owned television sets. This compared to under 80 million in 1970. Television sets require programmes, and this book examines the television industry which supplies and distributes the programmes by broadcasting, cable, satellite, and video-cassette recorder (VCR). It examines who supplies the world with programming and why. It examines who demands television, and why consumers get the sorts of programmes they do. It examines who owns the industry and who controls it. It examines recent change in the industry and why it has changed. It examines who benefits from the change and who loses. It examines why governments play a critical role in the industry and how that role is changing. It attempts to identify the social consequences of the economic changes going on in the industry, an industry in turmoil throughout much of the world.

The book is organized into two sections. The first four chapters examine television from a general perspective. Chapter 2 provides a brief economic history of television. Chapters 3 and 4 examine the forces of demand and supply which exist in different countries and how they affect structure and conduct. The analytical tools used are traditional micro-economic theory with applications to a public good and a well tried model of industrial organization. The following six chapters apply the analysis to specific countries and regions.

Television qualifies as a public good on the grounds that it has the characteristics of *non-exclusion* and *non-rivalry*. Non-exclusion means that sellers are unable to limit consumption only to those who pay for the good. Much television meets this requirement. All television meets the non-rivalry qualification. Non-rivalry means that if consumer A consumes a product then consumer B can also consume it, for example a public park. A and B can both enjoy a park at the same time. This is not the case with a private good such as a chocolate bar, which only consumer A or consumer B can eat, nor indeed for most consumer products.

The industrial organization framework adopted throughout the book is one frequently used in industrial organization studies. It is presented diagrammatically in figure 1. How well any industry performs is seen as depending upon its basic conditions of demand and supply, the industry's structure, and the industry's conduct or behaviour. In the case of the media there is an additional performance criterion and that relates to the public interest. The media are expected to serve the public interest. Sometimes, wrongly, that is equated with meeting the government's interests. Sometimes, too, with regard to television, the public interest is equated with a state monopoly of supply.

Figure 1 An industrial organization analytical model

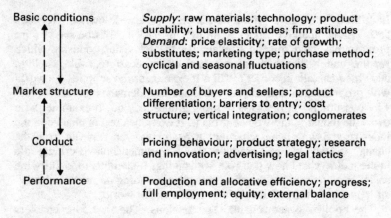

Basic conditions — *Supply*: raw materials; technology; product durability; business attitudes; firm attitudes
Demand: price elasticity; rate of growth; substitutes; marketing type; purchase method; cyclical and seasonal fluctuations

Market structure — Number of buyers and sellers; product differentiation; barriers to entry; cost structure; vertical integration; conglomerates

Conduct — Pricing behaviour; product strategy; research and innovation; advertising; legal tactics

Performance — Production and allocative efficiency; progress; full employment; equity; external balance

Source: F.M. Scherer, *Industrial Market Structure and Economic Performance* (Chicago: Rand McNally, 1976), p. 4

Government policies in all countries have a widespread effect on the structure, conduct, and performance of the media. Government policies are amongst the basic conditions of the industry, and apparently small changes in government policies can have significant, widespread effects on the media in general.

Government policies can influence who may be a television supplier and on what conditions. Foreigners, owners of the other media, telecommunications companies, political opponents, or anybody except the state itself may be excluded. Suppliers may have to pay to supply services or have to meet given standards. Content is bound to be constrained in some way by the government. Usually there are conditions concerning sex and violence. Advertising may be subject to certain limits and conditions. There may be requirements for educational, children's religious, political, or cultural content. Equal time and fairness may be considerations on contentious public issues. Hours of supply may be limited. There may be special labour legislation. Prices and wages may be regulated. There may be special taxes and subsidies. Finally the health of the industry will depend upon the state of the economy, which in turn will be affected by government policies. Rich nations can either directly through licence fees or indirectly through advertising provide greater revenues to finance television programming. For poor nations the scope for government policies to regulate supply is constrained. In general there are limited advertising revenues available, so that commercial television is not a viable option. Television must be state-provided or financed or else subsidized in some other way. If it is state-provided, then there are often more pressing demands on state finances than television programming which then affect programme quality and industry performance.

Using the industrial organization model set out in figure 1, it is possible to examine the effect of any government policy. Usually government policies will affect basic conditions and then have repercussions on industry structure and performance. However, it is quite possible that a government policy will have its initial impact on structure or on conduct. Also this model does not exclude the possibility of performance having feedback effects on basic conditions, on structure, or on conduct. In fact this is likely in the television industry. A government that does not like the way a public sector broadcaster behaves can reduce state funding or cut licence fees. A government that does not like the way a private broadcaster behaves can refuse to renew the licence to operate or, as in the case of South Korea in 1980, take it over.

Governments have played a major role in television, everywhere controlling it in the public interest, however the public interest may be defined. In the past governments had to control the broadcast airwaves, if there was to be order, because the usable airwaves were limited and so a scarce public resource. Chapters 2–4 examine the controlling role of government and how government policy affects industry structure and conduct. The book seeks to cast light upon those issues that determine an optimal policy if the television industry is to contribute to maximum social and economic welfare. To this end it compares and contrasts alternative financing methods including advertising, state finance, licence fees, auctions, lotteries, pledges, and pay systems. Inevitably, however, any conclusions about policy as it affects performance in any industry are constrained by the overall social, political, and economic goals any particular society has set for itself.

Chapters 5–10 are more empirical. They examine and analyse the changing structure of the industry worldwide. Considerable space is devoted to the North American television industry, because it exerts a pervasive influence on many other markets around the world. Serving less than 5 per cent of the world's population, its television industry spends approximately one-third of total world expenditure on programming. These programmes are then exported to a majority of the world's television systems. The chapter on the USA shows how a few media conglomerates play a leading role in determining what much of the world will watch. The same chapter also shows that even in a free-market system the role of government is critical.

Other chapters then examine the changing markets of Britain, Europe, and Japan. Finally the television industry in the Communist world and a variety of industry structures in the fast-growing and quickly changing Third World, or developing world, are examined.

Throughout all the chapters there runs a common theme. All chapters illustrate with examples the problems of market failures and of the externalities associated with the television industry. Television is blamed for contributing to many social and economic problems. It is identified as contributing to the decline in educational levels in the USA, to destroying social activities worldwide, to desensitizing people everywhere, to widespread materialism, and to the rise in violence in many countries. It is accused of destroying cultures, and the USA in particular is often condemned for media imperialism.

Whenever there is market failure, and whenever there are externalities, economics says there is a case for government intervention to try to improve welfare. Intervention may take the form of taxes, subsidies, regulation, or state control. The final chapter attempts to assess the nature and magnitude of the issues involved as they relate to the television industry, an industry in turmoil.

Chapter two

A history of television

In the past the television industry has frequently failed to foresee where lay commercial success and where financial ruin. The history of the industry is littered with accounts of those who failed to anticipate new markets, who anticipated markets which did not materialize, and who failed to see the effects on their industry of new entrants using different methods. Television history is very much a case study in the law of unintended consequences. Notable examples of the industry's failure to see where the future lay include the following.

When John L. Baird, one of the inventors of the disc scanning system which made television possible, demonstrated his invention at Selfridge's department store in London on 27 January 1926 many thought that the new invention would be used to deliver live programmes to theatres. They concluded, therefore, that television would enhance the theatre as an entertainment medium.[1] The fact that television would act as a destructive substitute and decimate both live theatre and movie theatre audiences in Britain was not anticipated. Nobody foresaw that within fifty years television would become for much of mankind the third most time-consuming activity in life, exceeded only by sleeping and working.

In the United States in the 1930s radio manufacturers such as Radio Corporation of America (RCA) foresaw a profitable future selling television sets. At the time a new television set cost $500, as much as a new car. RCA and the other radio-set producers therefore started television networks in order to suply programming for the new products. Fifty years later RCA had made far more from owning a television network than from producing television sets. Similarly when General Electric bought RCA in 1987 they sold off the money-losing television-set manufacturing division to a French company but kept the profitable broadcasting network division, NBC.

A further example of the failure to anticipate the future comes from the president of the Zenith Radio Corporation, E.F. McDonald, junior, in 1947. He said that the revenue from advertising would be inadequate to cover the costs of producing and distributing programmes.[2] This had been the conclusion of the British in the 1930s when they discussed the possibilities of commercial television. The impact of commercial television on programme quality was not then at issue.

Forty years later Zenith was the last American company left producing television sets in the United States, and losing money in the process.[3] Meanwhile advertisers spent nearly $240 dollars a year for each of America's 90 million households in order to get their advertising messages home, and television had become their medium of choice for many sorts of advertising. For nearly forty years advertising had grown at 9 per cent per year, from $5 billion in 1948 to over $100 billion in 1988. Nearly a quarter of this went to television.

A final, more recent example of the inability to anticipate the future comes from UNESCO in1980. In the highly controversial McBride report on the New Information Order there is no mention of video-cassette recorders.[4] The report was concerned that Third World governments were losing their ability to control the information flows into their own countries. The focus of the report was on the press and on broadcast television. Yet within five years it was quite clear that the major threat to any government was not the broadcasting of messages by other governments over the airwaves but the physical transport of small video cassettes. In fact the future was already upon them. In Iran in 1979 video cassettes as well as audio cassettes were a contributing factor to the overthrow of the Shah. Also in Poland in the early 1980s the Solidarity movement used video cassettes to gain strength.

The development of television services.

Television's beginnings can be traced back to 1883, when Paul Nipkow patented a device in Germany that could convert light into electric impulses. It was not until the 1920s that experimentation at the level necessary for commercial implementation took place. In the United States broadcasts were first made at American Telephone & Telegraph (AT&T) in 1922. In London in 1928 John Baird showed colour pictures and made televised movies. In 1928 daily TV tests were made by W2AXD from the laboratories of General Electric (GE) in Schenectady in New York state. In 1931 RCA made experimental broadcasts over 2XBS in New York. In the same year Baird made a television broadcast of the Derby, a top horse race run at Epsom in the south of England. Meanwhile similar broadcast experiments were made in Japan and Germany.

The early experiments showed that television was possible, but picture details remained poor. Signals could be sent only within a radius of about forty miles. Many improvements were necessary if televison was to become commercially viable and more than a novelty and a supplement to the cinema.

Much progress was made in the 1930s. In 1935 RCA began transmissions from the Empire State Building. They also announced a $1 million investment in programme development. RCA were also instrumental in the establishment of uniform standards. With the support of the Federal Communications Commission (FCC) RCA's line cathode-ray tube became the standard in 1941. RCA realized that without uniform standards nobody could succeed in television and therefore shared their technology with their rivals. The standard adopted in the United States in 1940 was a 343 line system. Meanwhile in Britain Baird's 240 line system was dropped by the British Broadcasting Corporation in favour of a 405 line system from Marconi-EMI.

RCA's technology-sharing strategy was a lesson for the future. Nearly fifty years later Sony could have learned it to advantage with its Beta technology for VCRs. In the 1970s Sony's superior technology lost out to the JVC company, which shared the inferior VHS format with other producers, so that by 1988 VHS was the established format. Learning from this in the late 1980s, the Japanese Broadcasting Corporation (NHK) agreed at a conference in Dubrovnik to share its leading high-definition television (HDTV) technology with the world. In the USA and Europe in the late 1980s attempts were under way to stop Japanese standards becoming the norm for high-definition television.

Television has always exploited major events to show off its latest achievements. John Baird chose the Derby in 1931. The coronation procession of George VI was broadcast in London in 1937, the BBC having begun regular transmissions in 1936. NBC began broadcasting in New York in 1939 by showing the opening ceremonies at the New York World's Fair. The Germans televised the Olympics from Berlin in 1936. The Japanese planned to broadcast the 1940 Olympic Games from Tokyo in 1940, until World War II intervened. And in 1988 the Japanese broadcast the Seoul Olympics to fifty public HDTV receivers set up around Japan.

Television, whether spectacular or commonplace, has to be paid for by somebody. Britain and the United States provide a contrast in the two major methods of organizing the television industry in the free world. Britain got off to a faster start in television before the war in part because the British industry was organized as a public corporation financed by licence fees. The United States' initial progress was slow because the industry was left to find its own finances and was organized on a strictly commercial basis without government support. The two basic paradigms for television are public financing and market financing.

Without public finances, the American system turned to sponsorship. The first sponsored show was *Show Business Interviews* in 1939. It was sponsored by the Andrew Geller store in New York. Later in the year Procter & Gamble financed a baseball game and began fifty years of underwriting the costs of television. In 1988 they paid out $1·4 billion to television for advertisements, but in the early years nobody foresaw the dramatic growth in advertising that the industry would enjoy.

Life magazine before the war described television as 'a scientific success but a commercial headache'.[5] Few believed that advertisements would provide sufficient revenue to finance the programmes. It was from the sale of sets that profits would be earned. But if people were to buy the television sets there had to be programmes. The British had discussed the idea of sponsorship and concluded, probably correctly at the time in Britain, that sponsorship was not viable. They therefore adopted the system of a public corporation financed from the sale of annual licences paid for by each owner of a television set. This approach followed the precedent set by BBC radio. It was regarded with envy by the Americans. The New York *Herald-Tribune* compared the smooth-running, relatively intense schedule of the BBC with the American schedule, which it described as hardly out of engineering class.

World War II held up progress in the television industry, which was still an infant industry. In 1936 there were only fifty sets in all of New York. There were 3,000 in London. Even when DuMont produced a set in the US for $200 in 1939, using mass-production techniques, they sold the sets in the carriage-class stores of Bloomingdale's and Abraham & Strauss. Television before World War II was the expensive novelty of the rich, not the entertainment medium of the masses it was to become.

In Britain television went off the air in 1939 with a picture of Walt Disney's Mickey Mouse. It returned with the same picture six years later. By 1946 there were 23,000 sets in Britain. Meanwhile in the United States progress continued throughout the war. The first newscast was broadcast by CBS in December 1941, when the Japanese invaded Pearl Harbor. In the same year the number of lines used for transmissions was raised by the Federal Communications Commission to 525. That is still the United States standard.

Television took off during the decade following the war. The wartime devastation of Germany and Japan halted progress in those countries until the '50s but in London the 1948 Olympics were shown using new camera technology. This helped to raise public consciousness of television throughout Europe. In 1947 in Britain 100,000 licences were issued, despite the fact that a 10 in. television still cost $50, more than three times the average weekly wage. By the time of the coronation of Queen Elizabeth II in 1953 a television aerial mounted on the roof was a familiar status symbol. The impact of the coronation on demand for television in Britain was considerable, and Richard Dimbleby's commentary for the thirteen-hour broadcast set the tone of BBC news and documentary coverage for the next quarter-century.

By 1948 in the United States there were about one million television households. There were thirty-six stations in operation and another seventy under construction. The limited broadcast spectrum could not carry all the stations that had entered the broadcast sector, and by 1948 in the major cities the different stations had begun to interfere with one another. The FCC declared a moratorium on the granting of new licences. When the freeze ended there was a rush to get licences to exploit the economic rents that the owners of licences would almost inevitably enjoy. By 1954 there were 377 stations in operation and 90 per cent of the population had access to television. Television's golden age had begun.

Public financing in Britain had created a monopoly of television broadcasting for the BBC, which it guarded jealously. The monopoly was always controversial. Early radio in Britain had been run by the *Daily Mail*, and as commercial television prospered in the United States lobbying to allow commercial television to meet programme demands not met by the BBC was persistent. In 1954 the Independent Television Act was passed. This established the framework to allow commercial television in Britain.

Meanwhile in the United States commercial television finally became a financial success in the 1950s. There, as in Britain, the structure of the television industry closely paralleled that of the radio industry. Britain had set up the BBC as a public corporation to run radio. Television followed suit. In the United States a system of commercial radio networks across the country had evolved. The same system emerged in television.

The big three networks which have dominated American television for over four decades all developed out of radio. Radio had in its turn languished for many years as a technology without a cause. It was initially thought that it would replace the telephone and the telegraph. It failed for this purpose because it lacked the characteristic of privacy. Everybody could hear what was being said. It was only when a real-estate agent in 1922 had the idea of paying the telephone company AT&T, who owned an early radio station, WEAF, to broadcast a talk discussing the properties he had for sale that radio found a market. In 1923 WEAF linked up with a station in Boston over the AT&T telephone wires for a chain broadcast. By the end of 1924 AT&T had twenty-three stations, which it linked together to form a network.

Other stations, seeing the success and the potential of the AT&T network, attempted to set up their own networks. AT&T wished to keep its monopoly and refused to let the other stations link up over the AT&T telephone wires. One group of radio manufacturers, RCA, began legal proceedings. AT&T knew that under American anti-trust legislation, and given the attitude of the courts at that time to integration, there was little chance of avoiding a conviction for monopolistic practices. They therefore sold their radio interests to a group of broadcasters called National Broadcasting Corporation (NBC) in 1926.

Three years after NBC, CBS was formed in 1929. A cigar company owned by the Paley family was so impressed with the effect of an advertisement placed on radio that it bought the radio station. The Paley family then acquired more radio stations. The third of the network companies, ABC, was spun off from RCA in 1943 when RCA was ordered by the courts to sell off the radio stations it had held before 1926. A confectionery company, ABC, bought them. A fourth network, now defunct, called MBC began in 1939.

AT&T and the other phone companies excluded from the industry by monopoly legislation in the 1920s still have their eye on the industry. Their ambitions to enter were fuelled in 1987 when a telephone company was allowed to own a cable system, for the first time in American history.

There have been several attempts to start new networks. In 1987 Rupert Murdoch launched Fox Broadcasting but even with all the resources of News International found it slow progress attracting sufficient viewers. The reasons for this can be traced back to the basic nature of the radio networks. The key to their success was ownership of the major radio stations in the largest cities of the United States. Out of 901 radio statios before the war the networks owned only twenty-nine. However, those stations dominated the market. Their owners then signed up affiliates. They offered the affiliates expensive programmes at no cost. The programmes could be used to attract listeners, which would make the station more attractive to advertisers. In return the networks were allowed by the affiliates to place national advertisements in the programmes they sent to the affiliates. Part of the revenue from these advertisements went to the affiliates, which were also able to add their own advertisements between network programmes. Free shows from the networks provided revenue and eliminated the necessity to sell and market time on their own station. Once the three networks had control of the twenty-nine major stations in the largest areas of population it was virtually impossible for a new network to be established. Without a licence to broadcast in those areas a new network was unable to attract a large enough audience to finance the quality of programme necessary to attract potential affiliates of major sponsors. Finally the networks used a strategy to create audience loyalty. In 1928 the radio show *Amos and Andy* began. Audiences tuned in weekly to follow the show. The soap opera, named after the soap company Procter & Gamble, sponsor of many soaps, was born.

Television was much more expensive to programme than radio. Having rejected the British model of a public corporation funded by licence fees, the Federal Communications Commission had little option but to encourage networks along the lines of the radio networks. Only a network could conceivably carry the costs of producing television programmes. In order to exercise some control over the networks, the networks were at first restricted to owning just five stations each. This created an incentive for them to sign up affiliates, and until the 1980s the vast majority of successful stations were affiliated.

By the early 1950s television in Britain had ceased to be an entertainment medium just for the more affluent upper and middle classes. Still, an examination of the daily programmes on the BBC television service showed a clear lack of supply of the sort of programmes that the average Briton of the day would have wished to watch.[6] Education, culture, and self-improvement dominated straightforward entertainment. The reasons for this were the perverse incentives built into the structure of the BBC. They are examined in chapter 6. Meanwhile in the United States a lack of funding meant that educational and cultural television was very limited. Both systems, therefore, could borrow from the other to serve the consumer better. Britain began commercial television, strictly supervised by the Independent Broadcasting Authority (IBA), whilst educational television was given some support in the United States.

Around the world other countries began television. In the 1950s most European countries and Japan began regular television broadcasting. By and large most governments were no more willing to give up control of the new medium to the market than they had been with radio. More important, no economy apart from the United States' was large enough even to contemplate creating sufficient advertising to cover the costs of television.

Regular broadcasting began in Mexico in 1950, in Canada in 1951, in Italy in 1953, in West Germany in 1952, in Japan in 1953, and in Australia in 1956. In the late 1950s television was introduced in the Communist bloc. The first African television station was set up in Nigeria in the 1950s but most of the Third World waited until the 1960s and '70s to start television. Then, with satellites to distribute programmes, there was explosive growth in the number of viewers. The 1985 *Live Aid* concert claimed that 2 billion people worldwide watched part of the show.

Colour television was introduced in the 1960s into many countries. Additional stations were started, and many publicly run television systems introduced limited advertising to help defray costs. Basically, however, the economic structure of the television industry until the 1970s in most countries of the world was fairly straightforward. Either the government itself or some sort of public body monopolized television programming and distribution. The only means of delivery was broadcasting. Consequently, directly or indirectly, governments could control what and when their citizens could view.

For fifty years from the early 1920s to the '70s therefore, radio and later television were organized along much the same lines. Then in the mid-1970s everything changed. Television entered a new era. New technologies made possible a variety of new means of delivering programmes. Supply was no longer limited to the broadcasting spectrum. The structure of the industry was transformed worldwide.

In the late 1980s it is still not clear what the final outcome will be. The law of unanticipated consequences is still very much operative. For the state it means a loss of control. For the consumer it means an increase in choice and control. Yet although the change is exciting in many ways, particularly from a technological viewpoint, the fact remains that the viewer in the Western world watches very much the same material that he watched thirty years ago: news, game shows, soap operas, movies, sport, and a smattering of cultural, educational, and self-improvement-type programmes. These make up the daily television diet of the typical viewer. Once the novelty has worn off, few people really care whether the programme they watch comes by traditional broadcasting or by one of the new technologies: cable, satellite, video cassette, or some mix of them all.

To date, therefore, the television revolution has by and large brought more of the same programmes. Leadership from a technical point of view, on the other hand, has passed to the Japanese. At the 1988 Seoul Olympics it was the Japanese who used satellites to transmit high-definition television whilst the European and American governments sought to impose regulations to frustrate Japanese technology becoming the world standard.

Innovation and the new technology

Neither satellites, nor cable, nor video-cassette recorders were new in the late 1970s. In 1963 a satellite was used to cover John F. Kennedy speaking in Europe and in 1964 there were forty hours of satellite television. One of the most notable satellite link-ups in 1964 was between doctors on two continents to observe a heart operation at Houston, Texas. In 1976 the ATS-6 and the ISAT satellites were launched to carry educational television. Relay cable had been used to carry radio to areas blocked by mountains from reception for several decades in Britain and elsewhere. Even coaxial cable had been developed by Bell Laboratories as far back as 1936. Nor were VCRs new. In the early 1970s Sony recorders meant for television studios were popular in the Middle East as a means of enjoying material not available on limited and tightly controlled local broadcasting.

In the late 1970s these new technologies all became commercially viable as a means of distributing television to billions of people, not just a select few. It was a familiar pattern of product development. An invention becomes a practical innovation and a commonplace item because of a number of small modifications and improvements and a significant lowering of costs. In television what had been technically feasible for some time became commercially viable.

The first transmissions of television by satellite were made on satellites launched by the telecommunications industry and meant primarily for carrying telephone messages. Intelsat is the international body made up of over 100 members which handles that traffic. Over the years Intelsat allowed the satellites' spare capacity to be used to transmit images for television rather than for their primary intended use of transmitting sound signals.

The large geographic area of the United States meant that distributing programmes by broadcast microwave transmitters or physically sending tapes to affiliates had always been unsatisfactory. Satellite technology speeded up distribution and lowered costs. Distance no longer mattered. The original intention of those transmitting programmes by satellite was to send them to affiliated stations so that the affiliate could rebroadcast the programmes to their viewers. However, once the networks put their signals in the air for satellite transmission the signals were there for anybody who had a receiver dish to pick them up.

At first the dishes were very expensive, and only a wealthy or very enthusiastic viewer in an isolated district would find it economic to intercept the signal. However, as the price of dishes fell more and more viewers found it worthwhile to intercept signals. Hotels, motels, and apartment blocks could buy one dish and then retransmit the programmes received. As an increasing number of signals were sent up to the satellites, purchasing a dish became ever more worth while.

For most people in the United States, particularly all those who lived in a large urban area with free access to a number of channels by broadcasting, the purchase of a dish was an inappropriate way to gain access to more television. First, three networks, a public television channel, and several local channels meant that for most people there was plenty of free choice. There was little reason to spend extra money on a dish, since for most people diminishing returns to additional stations set in early as they added channels. Second, America was being provided with cable, which offered a prospect of television abundance at much lower cost.

Improvements in cable technology and lower costs meant that by the 1970s cable television appeared to be a commercially viable proposition. Particularly in fairly isolated medium-sized communities where the broadcast choice was perhaps one affiliated station and one local station there was demand for additional television. By hanging a coaxial cable along with the telephone wires past individual houses it was possible for a cable company to offer to sell each household a wide range of television services. With the cable in place, the cable company used a satellite to pluck signals from the air. It then offered to hook up individual houses to the cable system. There was no need for each house to buy its own satellite dish.

A further refinement for the cable television companies was to offer packages of services. For a basic monthly fee the household would receive the local stations it could receive in any case by broadcasting plus other affiliates and network stations from close by, plus a local teletext bulletin board, plus perhaps a so-called superstation like Ted Turner's. Then for an extra payment the cable company would offer to send out a station that just showed old movies, cultural programmes, children's quality programmes, and the like. These the cable company would receive via satellite. They would agree to share the hook-up costs to the household with the original supplier of the signal.

This was the basic technological advance of the 1970s, although the full repercussions would not be felt until the late 1980s in much of America and in the rest of the world. Whilst most people were still limited to receiving a few signals via broadcasting, it was increasingly practical and economic to receive programmes either straight from the satellites with an individual satellite dish, or more cheaply, in America, from a cable passing the dwelling place and connected to the cable company's satellite dish. By the late '80s America was heavily committed to cable.

In Japan and much of Europe cable was much less established in 1988. Either cable, individual satellites, or a mix of both could come to dominate the markets. Both methods deliver abundant television. The dominant technology for delivering television will depend upon quality, costs, and government policy. However, once one method is established another method has to offer a clear superiority if it is to replace it. For cable and satellites there is a race to become the established technology. Basically, the more powerful and expensive the satellite the smaller the dish required to receive the satellite signal. If technology can make satellites more powerful, then dishes can be smaller and cheaper. Direct broadcast satellites' (DBS) commercial prospects in Europe are based on the idea of more powerful satellites allowing individual households to own their own affordable satellite dish.

The structure of the industry in the new television era will be determined largely by the economics of distributing programmes. Broadcast wavelengths are finite and inadequate. They must be supplemented by the new technologies. In 1988 the United States and Japan were at the forefront of the technical development and the market applications of these technologies. What has happened and will happen in the future in those two countries will set the pattern for the rest of the world.

Finally there is another simple means by which programmes can be delivered. By 1989 the VCR had had a devastating effect on pay television and dramatically altered the film industry in both the First and the Third

Worlds. The VCR both complements and substitutes for video received by broadcasting, satellite, or cable. The future of the television industry will be determined by the interaction between all these different methods of delivery and the technological improvements in each of them.

Table 1 VCR penetration of households in US and Europe, 1984 and 1986 (%)

Country	1984	1986
Austria	7	12
Belgium	12	19
Denmark	17	29
Finland	14	28
France	13	26
Greece	5	11
Irish Republic	28	50
Italy	3	6
Netherlands	23	38
Norway	20	32
Portugal	23	36
Spain	9	22
Sweden	23	30
Switzerland	18	27
UK	38	54
West Germany	25	39
USA	22	46

Note: There can be no reliable figures for the Communist and Third Worlds because many VCRs are imported illegally.
Source: *Screen Digest*.

The nature of future technological change is uncertain. High-definition television provides a far superior picture. The technical feasibility of HDTV is well established. Superior picture quality will be enjoyed in the 1990s. For the Seoul Olympics the Japanese set up some fifty public HDTV sets around the country so that the public could see the incredible detail available with high-definition television.

However, it is worth noting that in 1988 Sony subsidized the production of a show by the Canadian Broadcasting Corporation that could be seen in high definition. This was the first HDTV show produced for broadcasting to the general public. *Fools' Gold* was shown on Canadian television but since there were no HDTV sets available it appeared on the usual 525 lines rather than with 1,150 lines. Critics lambasted the $11 million production to make the point that even on HDTV a poor programme is a poor programme.

It is also worth noting that high-definition television is much more expensive than traditional television, and sets will cost ten to twenty times as much as a basic colour set. HDTV is also incompatible with the hundreds of millions of television sets currently in use, requiring much more bandwidth space to broadcast. This means that DBS is the way by which HDTV will likely be delivered in the 1990s.

In the late 1980s there was considerable controversy over how many lines to include in the standard for high definition. The ideal is about 1,700 lines, the Europeans want 1,250 lines, whilst the Japanese want 1,150 lines. The Europeans, particularly the big consumer electronics firms such as Thomson of France and Philips of Holland, believed that a world standard of 1,150 would give the Japanese a world monopoly in the manufacture of HDTV sets. Meanwhile RCA in the United States was working on a system that would be compatible with the current 525 line system. Without compatibility some 200 million television sets in North America would become obsolete.

Whilst the 525 line system of North America is inferior to the systems used in much of Europe, and some upgrading is definitely desirable, the market will determine how that upgrading will take place. The use of digital techniques can improve the quality of the picture with fewer lines. Thus it is not clear that HDTV will be worth the cost, given the technology of the late 1980s. However, technological advances come rapidly and, one way or another, a significant improvement in picture quality for consumers is inevitable.

Not all technical marvels in the field of television find widespread market applications. Three-dimensional television appeared in 1988 in North America. Viewers had to use special glasses which could be obtained from Coca-Cola. Three-dimensional movies have been around since the 1950s, but only as a curiosity. Three-dimensional television could also remain a curiosity. Likewise video-cassette recorders were initially slow movers in the late '70s because of their relatively high price but also because consumers failed to appreciate the variety of functions that a VCR can perform. With more channels available because of satellites and cable there was more reason to record programmes for viewing at a more convenient time. With more and more movies available on video cassette at lower and lower retail and hire prices VCRs became an attractive alternative to going to the cinema to watch a movie. In the mid-1970s these virtues of the VCR were not clearly apparent. This reflects how difficult it is to predict product success and product failure, and how small changes in technology or price can create a dramatic increase in demand for a video product. In contrast to VCRs, videotext and video conferencing were two products with apparent widespread appeal which had achieved little commercial success by 1989.

Many of the technical innovations either already available or promised for the near future will not realize market success. Pocket VCRs are available to allow the consumer to watch movies and recorded television programmes anywhere at any time. Liquid crystal television screens create the possibility of wall televisions only a few millimetres thick and even screens covering all the walls, floors, and ceilings to envelop the viewer completely. Smaller, flatter home satellite dishes are anticipated for the 1990s. The critical question is not whether these products can be demonstrated to the public but whether the public will be willing to pay for them in a world of increasing competition for the consumer's money. For many consumers there may be diminishing returns to video gadgetry to receive basically what are still the same programmes.[7]

Notes

1 Rick Marschall, *The History of Television*, London: Bison, p. 23
2 ibid., p. 31.
3 A small company called Curtis-Mathis still made a line of luxury-class television sets costing considerably more than the standard portable set.
4 The McBride report created a storm of protest from the Western press because the UNESCO report adopted the position, under the influence of the USSR, that states should control information. This contrasts with the Western view that information should flow freely, and that state control of information is a form of censorship.
5 Rick Marschall, *The History of Television*, London: Bison, p. 18.
6 For Saturday 6 June 1953 there was an old movie at 3.15 p.m., followed by the children's show *Whirligig* at 5.00 p.m. The broadcasting was then interrupted, no doubt for tea. At 8.00 p.m. there was a half-hour review of the news, followed by a half-hour show on how to make a cricket bat. Then came a half-hour episode in a detective series, followed by an hour-and-a-half-long Commonwealth talent show.
7 At the time of writing there were already split screens, stereo televisions, digital televisions, 3-D televisions, miniaturized VCRs, VCRs capable of feeding several television sets, and in Japan HDTV.

Chapter three

Demand and supply

Far from being a passing novelty for the rich or remaining a supplement to the live theatre, television has become an ingrained habit for a rapidly increasing number of people around the world. Table 2 shows the growth in the number of receiver sets around the world since 1965. People wake to breakfast television and fall asleep to a late-night show. In India taxi drivers watch television as they wait for fares. In Vancouver people watch television as they wait for aeroplanes. Once aboard a Northwestern plane they can watch television on a screen on the seat before them. By 1988 the average trend-setting American household had the television set operational for nearly eight hours per day. The average individual in America watched over four hours of television and in Japan over three hours.

An examination of the nature of supply and demand for television explains much about the performance of the television industry worldwide. Economics explains why so many viewers are apparently able to enjoy programmes which cost $1 million per hour to produce at no cost. Economics explains why state-run and publicly owned television systems are able to purchase programmes that cost so much to produce for a small fraction of their cost. Economics explains why so much of the world watches American programmes rather than producing its own. Economics provides an explanation of the phenomenon called media or cultural imperialism. Economics also explains why in the view of many critics so much programming is 'mindless trash'.

Similar groups in every society have an interest in the provision of television programmes to the consuming public: (1) the consumers themselves, as the viewers; (2) the advertisers who wish to sell goods and services to the public. They see television as the medium of choice by which to inform consumers about their products; (3) the government, who wish to channel messages of an informational, educational, cultural, and propagandistic nature to their citizens; (4) other assorted groups who wish to propagate some sort of cause or ideology; (5) the suppliers themselves, who create, produce, and distribute the programmes.

Table 2 Growth in the number of television receivers in the world, 1965–86, selected countries (million)

Country	1965	1970	1975	1980	1986
Argentina	1·6	3·5	4·0	5·1	6·6
Australia	1·9	2·8	4·6	5·6	7·5
Brazil	—	6·1	15·0	—	26·0
Chile	—	0·5	0·7	1·2	2·0
Czechoslovakia	2·1	3·1	3·7	4·3	4·4
France	6·5	11·0	14·1	16·0	18·2
Germany, East	3·2	4·5	5·2	5·7	6·1
Germany, West	11·4	16·7	19·2	20·8	23·1
India	0·1	0·5	0·9	4·0	10·5
Indonesia	—	0·1	0·3	3·0	6·6
Iran	0·1	0·5	1·7	—	2·6
Italy	6·0	9·8	12·1	13·3	14·6
Japan	18·8^a	22·9^a	26·4^a	63·0	71·0
Korea, South	0·1	0·4	1·9	6·3	7·9
Malaysia	0·1	0·1	0·5	1·2	1·8
Mexico	1·2	—	—	3·8	9·5
Philippines	0·1	0·4	0·8	1·0	2·0
Poland	2·1	4·2	6·4	7·9	9·7
Romania	0·5	1·5	2·7	3·7	4·5
Spain	—	4·1	6·6	9·4	12·5
UK	13·5	16·3	17·9	18·5	19·5
USA	70·3	84·6	121·0	155·8	195·0
USSR	15·7	34·8	55·2	—	90·0

Note: *a* Licences issued.
Source: UNESCO (1988).

The nature of consumer demand

One reason why people watch so much television is that most of it is supplied free. Other things being equal, the lower the price of any good or service the greater the quantity that will be demanded. Even where consumers pay for television over cable or through licence fees the cost of an additional programme is zero, except for the very few opportunities to date for pay-per-view television.

Figure 2 shows the demand curve for any particular television programme. It shows that, if a positive price had to be paid to watch the programme, then some viewers would still demand the programme. It shows that as the price rises, then, other things being equal, fewer and fewer consumers would buy it. From figure 2 it can be seen that most viewers who watched the show would have been willing to pay a positive price. For example, *ON* viewers would have paid *OP*. All but the *n*th viewer, the marginal viewer, would have paid more than *OP* to watch the show. All but the marginal viewer earn a consumer surplus when television is free.

A consumer surplus is defined as the difference between the total value that consumers place on all units consumed of a commodity and the actual payment they make to purchase the same amount of the commodity. In

The world television industry

Figure 2 The demand for television, showing consumer surplus

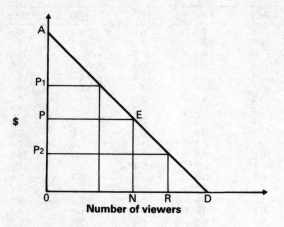

Note: The nth viewer puts a value of *OP* on the programme. The jth viewer puts a value of OP_1 on the show. The rth viewer puts a value of OP_2 on the programme and therefore does not buy it at price *OP*, even though it would give him some utility. Booz Allen & Hamilton (*Subscription Television*, p. 151) estimate consumer surplus as £1,104 in 1977. They estimate costs as £514 and net consumer benefit as $590. They note that a licence fee system should attempt to maximize net consumer benefit and argue that in Britain a higher licence fee and better programmes would increase net benefit.

figure 2 when the price is zero the consumer surplus is represented by the whole area under the demand curve *OAD*. Although the programme came free it was worth *OAD* to all the viewers combined. This concept is important for a theoretical understanding of the economics of television.[1]

Watching television may be without price but it is not without cost to the viewer. Even where the consumer watches a free show at no monetary cost he must sacrifice the opportunity of doing something else with his time. Television is a time-intensive activity and it competes for the limited time in the day with other activities. The opportunity cost of free television, therefore, is the next best alternative use of that time. For somebody who is bored that opportunity cost may be very low. For somebody who could be earning a high income in that time the opportunity cost is high.

After they have worked and slept most people worldwide have some time left for leisure. Television is a strong competitor for the individual's leisure time in many of today's societies. For the sick and the tired television can be a wonderful escape, a form of mental pablum, but it must also compete with other leisure-time activities.

Amongst the close competitors for an individual's entertainment leisure time are the other media, such as newspapers, magazines, and

20

Figure 3 The dimensions of competition for a specific television programme

Dimension of competition	Print medium	Broadcast medium	Electronic medium
Hard news	Newspapers Magazines	Television Radio	Data banks
Advertising	Billboards, magazines Newspapers Flyers, freesheets	Radio Television	
Entertainment	Books, magazines Newspapers	Radio Television	Video-films

Note: Any leisure activity – sport, gardening, etc. – competes for the time required to watch television

Figure 4 The effect of a change in demand on ratings

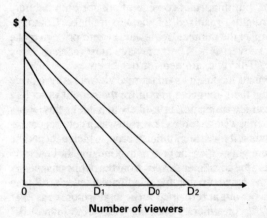

Number of viewers

Note: An increase shifts D_0 to D_2 – for example, show X becomes a cult. A decrease shifts D_0 to D_2 – for example, a good new show is set opposite show X at the same time slot

radio, as well as films, concerts, and theatres. These must all compete with other leisure-time opportunities such as walking, golfing, gardening, games, and socializing. Finally, leisure activities compete for time needed for working, family obligations, eating, and sleeping. All these activities require some input of time and most require some input of money. The key point is that for a particular television programme to attract the attention of a viewer for half an hour or more it has to compete success-fully for time spent doing other things. Even at zero price it faces tough competition, both from other free programmes and activities and from activities which, despite a money input, give expectations of high satisfac-tion. These concepts can be illustrated in terms of figure 3.

As with any demand curve, a change in the underlying conditions – say, the entry of a new television or non-television competitor – will shift the demand curve for a particular programme to the left. A change in underlying tastes – say, the show becomes a cult show amongst teenagers – will shift it to the right. These effects are shown in figure 4. If a competing channel puts on a poor programme in the same time slot, then the demand curve D_0 will shift to the right, to D_1. If some non-television alternative becomes more attractive – say, magazines become cheaper, or beautiful weather makes outdoor activities more attractive – then audiences will defect and the demand curve will shift to the left, from D_0 to D_2. Summer, unless it is extremely hot, as in Thailand, shifts television viewer demand to the left. Basically the demand for any programme, even at zero price, is determined by taste, the prices of other goods, income, and the demographics of the potential audience.

These are elementary but important considerations for both publicly organized and commercially organized television suppliers. Commer-cial systems must maximize the number of viewers at zero price to make the channel attractive to advertisers. Their message must reach as many consumers as possible. This is examined further below.

For publicly run channels the failure to maximize viewers at zero price may not be failure. Often their goal is to maximize the benefit to society from the channel. Viewer maximization is unlikely to achieve this. For a public station which does not wish to force viewers to watch culture, educa-tion, or propaganda against its will – in other words, which accepts the notion of consumer sovereignty – then the goal of maximizing the benefit to society means maximizing the consumer surplus from the public channel. A comparison of programme A and programme B in figure 5 reveals that pro-gramme A attracts fewer viewers at zero price but generates more consumer surplus. At a price of OP^1 consumers would buy more of A than of B.[2]

The case for a public channel to set a goal other than maximizing the number of viewers is shown in figure 5. Demand curve D_1 shows demand for one type of show – say, a popular game show which is one among many. Demand curve D_2 shows the demand curve for another type of show, say live opera. The opera has no close competitors and is highly desirable to a small section of the population. At zero price the number of viewers of the game show far exceeds the viewers of the opera. However, if one could ask the viewers how many would stick with each show as the price of viewing was increased, other things being equal, then the following would occur. The game-show viewers would

Figure 5 Consumer surplus for minority and popular programmes

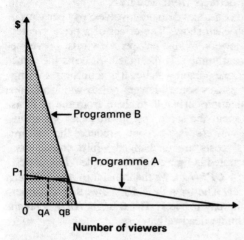

quickly defect to other game shows, still free, as the price to watch the game show represented in D^1 was raised. However, in this illustration, the opera viewers with no close substitute available stay with the opera in significant numbers even as the price to them of watching is increased.

This example shows that a strong case exists for channels, which may have to be publicly funded or publicly owned, to meet the intense desire of some minority groups for special programming. Such channels may also meet demands, say for education, that the government deems important. The implication is that a system which requires every channel to maximize the number of viewers at zero price is unlikely to maximize the welfare of society.

The demand curve analysis in figures 2, 4, and 5 assumes consumer sovereignty, the idea that each consumer knows what is best for himself. It also assumes there are no externalities. For example, in the case of educational television it assumes that those who watch are the only ones to benefit. Many would dispute this. A more educated society is usually thought to be a better society for everyone. Similarly if violent television makes people violent then the external effect of a violent show is to reduce welfare, however large the consumer surplus generated to those who watch and thrill to the show. It is possible that the negative externalities exceed the value of the consumer surplus.

These issues are discussed in chapter 11 but must be taken into account when discussing the welfare effect of alternative television industry structures. Public channels can usually more easily censor shows which are thought to have negative externalities. Many, however, would then argue that censorship itself detracts from welfare.[3]

A final point in relation to consumer demand involves 'pay per view', where viewers pay to watch each show. The effect of a price greater than zero is to deter some viewers. Whilst pay per view raises revenue for those who supply the programme it is inefficient. It costs the same to broadcast a show whether one person watches it or a million. Putting a positive price on a show causes some viewers not to watch it, and therefore the potential satisfaction derivable to them from the show is lost. Meanwhile producers incur the same cost to broadcast the show regardless of the number of viewers. Pay-per-view reduces the welfare of society, since producers' costs are unchanged whilst consumers' welfare is lower. This is illustrated in figure 2. The triangle *NED* reflects the lost welfare. The rectangle *OPEN* shows the transfer of money from the consumer to the producer. The triangle *PAE* shows the consumer surplus enjoyed by those who pay to view. The triangle *NED* is taken from consumers and is a simple deadweight loss.[4]

The nature of advertising demand

For forty years advertising has been the main driving force behind American television. In the 1970s it became a most important force in Italian television and in the 1980s it became the dominant force in much of Europe. Britain, Japan, and much of Latin America have experienced the influence of commercial television for three decades, and more recently Third World and Communist countries have adopted it.

Advertising on television is not just a matter of exposing viewers to a few commercial messages each hour. Advertising is the major worldwide source of television revenue, exceeding revenue from licences, public grants, subsidies, levies, and private grants and pledges. Television in the format familiar throughout most of the Western world in the 1980s would disappear without the revenue from advertising. This is remarkable. Forty years ago advertising was seen as too small a base upon which to build television as a mass media. Since 1948 advertising expenditure has grown at 9 per cent per year in Britain and the United States. In 1985 and 1986 it was growing even faster in countries as different as France and India. It is important, therefore, to discuss the economics of advertising, and of television advertising in particular.

Advertising in general has two basic functions. The first is to inform – about prices, quality, and terms of sale. The second is to persuade. For many sellers of consumer products advertising is a major market weapon, along with price competition and product differentiation. Advertising is a less risky tactic for producers of goods and services

Table 3 The world's largest advertisers, by rank, 1987 ($ billion)

Advertiser	Total spending
Procter & Gamble	2·1
Philip Morris	1·7
Unilever	1·3
General Motors	1·2
RJR/Nabisco	n.a.
Ford	0·9
Sears Roebuck	0·9
PepsiCo	0·8
Eastman Kodak	n.a.
Nestlé	0·8

Source: James Capel.

Table 4 Advertising as a percentage of gross national product, 1986

Country	% of GNP	$ per cap.
USA	2·4	240
Australia	1·6	
UK	1·5	160
Canada	1·4	
Spain	1·3	
Japan	0·9	82
West Germany	0·9	126
Brazil	0·7	
France	0·6	92
Italy	0·6	51

Source: Various.

than price competition, because price competition can lead to price wars. Advertising may affect consumer tastes and brand loyalty and create a barrier to potential new entrants to the industry. Advertisers seek to shift the demand curve for their product. They seek to shift it to the right and to make it more inelastic, permitting an increase in price. This is shown in figure 6 in the movement from D_0 to D_1.

Much advertising is self-cancelling. One car company may feel compelled to advertise against the others in order to maintain market share, not to increase it. A cursory examination of any magazine or a random viewing of television finds manufacturers advertising against motor manufacturers, soaps against soaps, and fast foods against fast foods. The net effect may be very small except for a massive subsidy to the media. This is what tobacco companies have claimed in their defence when accused of advertising to encourage people, especially young people, to start smoking. There may be some truth in the claim. Game theory refers to this situation as the prisoner's dilemma.[5] Advertisers can get into a situation where they are damned if they do advertise,

Figure 6 Demand for a product, with and without advertising

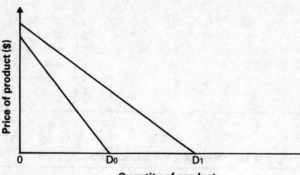

Quantity of product

because it will be self-cancelling, and damned if they don't, because their competitors will continue to advertise and so take sales from them.

Kaldor has argued, along different lines, that advertising in most countries is likely to be excessive.[6] Consumers certainly want some knowledge about the products they buy. However, it is unlikely they want the amount that advertisers wish them to have. Advertisers will continue to supply advertising up to the point where the marginal cost of advertising equals the marginal revenue from advertising for them. Kaldor argues that advertising and the product advertised are a joint product and the consumer has no option but to buy both or neither. If consumers could purchase information about products, rather than pay indirectly through advertising costs added on to the product price, they would likely buy less. For example, on soap and cereals, advertising represents over 10 per cent of the price.

There is considerable debate over both the desirability and the effectiveness of advertising. Complicated socio-economic issues are involved which have not been fully resolved. Some say that advertising persuades and manipulates, creating so-called bandwagon, snob, and Veblen effects. The first of these says that advertising makes people want things because everybody else has them. The second says that advertising makes people want things because other people don't have them, so that having them will make the consumer enjoy a snob effect. The third says that advertising encourages conspicuous consumption to keep up with the in group. Advertising is also accused of encouraging impulse buys and irrational expenditure and of creating a deprivation effect.

Many would see these effects as undesirable consequences of advertising, a form of externality. For example, an advertisement for a luxury automobile may sell more cars for the manufacturer and provide satisfaction for the new owner but still reduce social welfare. Some who did not buy the car may feel deprived and experience a fall in their level of welfare, outweighing the gains of both the automobile manufacturers and their customers. This example involves interpersonal comparisons which cannot be weighed.[7]

Advertising may also inform and entertain. Advertising is usually colourful and some find some of it enjoyable. Humorous television advertisements may be more entertaining than the programmes. In wartime when newspapers without advertisements were circulated readers asked to have the advertisements included.[8] In certain forms advertising provides much useful information, for example in the classified advertisements in newspapers, in the financial pages, and in many technical and professional publications. Relatively few television advertisements fall into the purely informative category, and most television advertising, but not all, is persuasive, to create an image. Television advertisements are also good at reminding the consumer about the product.

Persuasive advertising may still provide benefits to society. Products which are heavily advertised provide the consumer with a form of guarantee about the product. For advertisers goodwill is a valuable asset. It is in their interest to make sure that the product delivers, for if it does not the advertising is wasted. Names such as Kellogg's, Sony, Colgate, McDonald's and Johnson & Johnson guarantee the product and eliminate most of the risk of buying. Persuasive advertising may have the further benefit to consumers of lower prices if it allows producers to exploit economies of scale in production and produce at lower unit costs. In other words, it is not correct to assume that all advertising costs are passed on to consumers. Advertising may improve efficiency in production and purchasing by the consumer, allowing the consumer greater product satisfaction at lower prices.

To advertisers advertising is an investment, even though it is universally treated for tax purposes as a current expense. The goodwill from advertising may last for years – for example, a Coca-Cola jingle associated with a thirst-quenching image may remain in the consumer's mind for a lifetime. Pepsi even talk about the Pepsi generation. Studies have suggested that, for cigarettes, the advertising image lasts about six years.[9]

Treating advertising as a current expenditure for tax purposes makes it difficult to determine the effect of advertising on both current and long-term profits for the advertiser. For if advertising is in fact an investment, then in future years profits and the rate of return on non-advertising investment will be overstated. Treating advertising as a current expenditure understates reported profits in the current year and lowers taxes. Since all advertising expenditure is treated as a tax-deductible expense, there is an unintended

27

Table 5 Advertising follows the economy: changes in advertising expenditure and changes in gross national product, Japan and the USA, 1975–85 (%)

Year	Japan		USA	
	GNP	Advertising	GNP	Advertising
1975	6	10	8	5
1976	17	12	11	19
1977	13	11	11	12
1978	12	10	12	16
1979	14	8	12	13
1980	8	8	8	10
1981	9	7	12	13
1982	7	5	3	10
1983	6	4	7	14
1984	4	6	10	16
1985	3	6	7	10

Source: Various.

incentive to increase advertising expenditure above optimal levels. This is because few other investments are similarly immediately tax-deductible.

What determines the level of advertisers' investment and what advertisers get from their investment are hard to determine. There is a two-way line of causality. Research suggests that higher advertising leads to higher revenue, but that higher revenues also lead to more advertising.[10] While many firms spend a given percentage of sales revenues on advertising, advertising may be cut as a cost-trimming exercise if sales fall, or alternatively they may be increased as a means of generating revenue. Overall, total advertising expenditure moves with the economic cycle. Table 5 illustrates this for Japan and the United States.

It is sometimes argued that advertising encourages consumer expenditure and so generates economic growth and job creation. This is hard to test. The money firms spent on advertising would have had to be spent elsewhere, either in lower prices to consumers, who would then have bought more goods, or in other forms of sales promotion. The net benefits from the advertising industry are therefore very difficult to determine.

Related to this argument about advertising expenditure is one that says television advertising is a waste of resources and should be banned or curtailed on those grounds. While the growth in its share of GNP in most countries has grown with the introduction of television, banning television advertising would not necessarily mean a decline in that share. Rather, if denied access to television for advertising, advertisers are likely to find other means of sales promotion which may not be as efficient but which cost as much. There are always alternative advertising vehicles available. For example, the newspaper industry in northern Europe has every reason to be concerned as new television opportunities open up and offer new alternatives to traditional newspaper advertisements.

Figure 7 The link between viewer demand and advertising revenue: (a) viewer demand, (b) advertiser demand

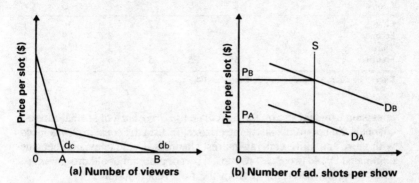

(a) **Number of viewers**

(b) **Number of ad. shots per show**

Advertising on television is not just a matter of exposing viewers to commercials and inconveniently interrupting programming for commercial breaks. Once advertising is introduced the whole nature of television changes. The adage 'He who pays the piper calls the tune' becomes applicable. What advertisers want is to reach potential consumers. They want maximum reach. That means that the stations who sell advertising slots can charge the advertiser more the more viewers they can guarantee will be watching their channel at the time of the advertisement. Advertising on television creates an incentive for television suppliers to set a goal of maximizing the number of viewers. This maximizes the suppliers' profits, other things being equal.

The link between the number of viewers and advertising revenue for the programme distributor are illustrated in figure 7. The first diagram, diagram 1, shows how programme B, although it generates less consumer surplus than programme A at zero price, attracts more viewers. Now *OA* viewers can be sold for a price of $x per thousand and *OB* likewise can be sold for $x per thousand. The price per thousand is determined by competition between all advertising vehicles, both other television and non-television. Consequently in diagram 2 the demand for an advertising slot in programme B is given by D_B and for programme A by D_A, assuming a fixed supply of advertising slots per programme and that advertisers regard viewers for each programme as of equal value. P_B will be *OA/OB* greater than P_A[11] Clearly, to the programme distributor, programme A is a better programme.

The preference option explains the fundamental weakness of a purely commercial system. A commercial system cannot take account of minority demands or intensity of preference. One of the biggest disappointments of the 1980s was that as the new means of distributing

Table 6 Preferences of eight representative households for ten different programmes, by rank

Choice	A	B	C	D	E	F	G	H
First	10	7	1	10	7	1	10	1
Second	9	6	2	9	5	2	9	2
Third	8	4	3	8	4	3	8	3
Fourth	5	5	5	5	5	5	5	5

Source: Based on *The Economist*, 20 December 1986.

television came on stream the anticipated *smörgasbord* of special-interest channels did not immediately materialize. Instead the consumer was faced with more and more general-interest channels. Cable television became dominated by old broadcast re-runs, a sort of museum of old programmes. This outcome materialized from the preference option.

Table 6 illustrates the preference option. It shows eight households who watch television during the prime-time hours. Each household has a unique set of tastes. When offered a choice of ten different shows they can rank them from highest preference to lowest preference. Their most preferred show is ranked first; the lowest ranked, least favoured is ranked tenth. In the illustration household A rank show No. 10 as their first preference and show No. 9 as their second. A household will watch a show only if it is in their top four rankings. If not they will turn to another channel or turn the set off.

A commercial television station faced with such preferences by viewers and intent on maximizing the number of viewers so as to maximize advertising revenue makes its selection of shows to offer as follows. It chooses No. 5. It then gets all eight households to watch the channel. If it selects either show No. 1 or show No. 10, then just three households watch in each case. There is a choice between three deeply satisfied or eight passably satisfied households. The profit motive forces it to choose the latter.

The ironic outcome of the preference option is that nobody feels particularly strongly about show No. 5, which is what the station offers. Meanwhile show No. 1 and show No. 10, which were elected first equal in the poll, never get shown. All too often in the real world show No. 5 is a game show or a situation comedy. Show No. 1 might be a concert or a documentary on poverty in Africa. Show No. 10 might be dragster car racing or kick boxing. All such minority-appeal shows, whether highbrow or lowbrow, have small but intensely interested followers whose demand will never be met.

Advertisers want mass audiences. The preference option shows the consequences of this on programming by commercial stations. Special interests will not be served. While this reduces social welfare when other means of satisfying demand for those special interests are not available, in the 1980s new alternative video delivery methods, particularly video-cassette recorders but also pay television in some markets, have helped reduce the welfare costs of this market failure.

To advertisers not all viewers are alike. Basically each household is valued according to the size of its income. The greater the spending power of viewers the greater their attractiveness to the advertisers and the more advertisers will pay to reach them. This creates an incentive for television stations to discriminate in favour of households with a high income and to offer programmes to which they can relate. Situation comedies about middle and upper-income households are favoured over ones about the poor, and sports such as golf and tennis are favoured over wrestling, whose viewers, statistics show, have household incomes below the average.

For this book there are several conclusions to be drawn about advertising. The first is that advertising is going to play an increasingly important role worldwide in the provision of the financial resources for television. It is a well entrenched phenomenon of late twentieth-century Western society, and television is the medium of choice for many advertisers of consumer products. Table 4 shows the proportion of gross national product spent by the major nations of the world on advertising. As can be seen, the United States spends a larger proportion of a larger GNP than almost any other country. Of total advertising expenditure in the world over half is spent in the United States. Much of this expenditure is used to finance the creation of programmes which are seen both in America and overseas. Huge advertising expenditures are the main reason why American television dominates world television.

Second, in the late 1980s many governments found advertisers' willingness to shoulder the total costs of television a welcome relief on the public purse. Worldwide, including the Communist countries, the attractiveness of commercials to finance television was increasingly appreciated in the '80s. Fewer and fewer systems remained totally commercial-free as countries like India, China, and the USSR accepted commercials.

Third, the benefits of financing television by advertising are significant for society. The demand for television advertising is strong and growing. Advertising revenue provides sufficient funds to finance programming at no direct cost to the public. It means apparently free television.

Fourth, with rare exceptions, advertisers do not interfere in the programmes offered.[12] Governments are prone to do so. The reason why commercial television leads to remarkably influence-free television is that advertisers are not concerned with the nature of the programmes surrounding their advertisements, with the obvious exception of pornographic and otherwise controversial shows. All they want is the maximum number of viewers of their message. This is so even in Latin America's two largest countries, Brazil and Mexico, where there is a virtual monopoly of commercial television and where, in both countries, political influence is rife. Certainly TV Globo in Brazil and Televista in Mexico can censor material which is unfavourable to favoured companies and there is little opportunity for alternative opinions to be expressed on television. However, even there, for advertiser control of programme content to be effective, it would be necessary for the advertisers' purchases of time to be very significant to the station and for the station to have no ability to replace those advertisements. In practice the only possible purchaser so powerful as to have such monopsony power is the government, and any government that wishes to censor programme content has better means than its leverage through purchases of advertising time.

Fifth, if viewers like the advertisements, either as entertainment or for short breaks to do other activities, which for some people is the case, then advertising may be superior from a social welfare point of view. Taxes, licence fees, and pay television by comparison impose real costs. And even if advertisements are seen as imposing neither welfare costs nor benefits, then if advertising creates improved efficiency for producers rather than higher prices advertising is still superior. However, if advertisements are seen as irritating and creating externalities, then advertising is inferior from a welfare standpoint. A law of increasing disutility operates for many people with regard to advertisements. A limited number of advertisements, well spaced, create little disutility whereas frequent interruptions are disruptive.

Finally, advertising as a method of financing television has repercussions on the wider society. It brings external benefits and costs. Whether the net benefits are greater as compared to total finance by the state, or by licences, pay-per-channel, pay-per-view, lottery, pledges, or sponsorship, or a mix of any of these, is at present impossible to determine. As an example of a lesser externality, children sing fewer nursery rhymes than they used to; instead they sing advertising jingles.

Advertisers must ensure that the audience they seek to reach actually sees their programme. To do this, estimates are made of audiences. Until 1987 advertisers in the United States relied upon a crude auditing process by the A.C. Neilsen company to audit their annual $20 billion expenditure.[13] In 1987 the big three American networks introduced so-called People Meters from a British firm, AGB research. The AGB meters required that viewers punch in identification numbers on specially programmed remote channel controllers as they watched television. Empty rooms no longer counted. The AGB figures suggested that the networks had been overestimating their audiences by some 10 per cent.

The nature of advertising demand, therefore, is such that the choice of programmes is left to the viewer. If they could pay the viewer with hard cash to watch a promotional short about their product, then advertisers would do so. In the United States in 1988 advertisers paid out about $100 for every man, woman, and child in television advertising, or $3 million every hour of every day to buy the attention of potential consumers. They would have been equally happy to pay directly for each viewer to watch their message for twenty-six minutes per day. However, that is impossible. Instead advertisers say to the viewers that they will provide fifty-three and a half minutes of free programming of any show that the viewers wish to see in exchange for six and a half minutes per hour of the viewers' time. In other words, there is no free television. The price is a time price.[14] It is six and a half minutes of advertising per fifty-three and a half minutes of programmes. It is a sort of honour system. The evidence is that many people do something else during the commercials but that the majority don't move. On a talk show the friendly host will admonish viewers, 'Stay tuned!' as a commercial break intervenes. Ultimately his livelihood depends on it.

The nature of government demand

Governments demand broadcasting time for a variety of reasons. In the public interest they wish to inform and educate. All governments wish to use the media, and especially television, for social purposes, however those may be defined. Lenin described the press as a collective propagandist, collective agitator, and collective organizer.[15] In their own political interest governments wish to propagate. Indeed, in the Communist world the primary function of television is to propagate, and Kruschev described the press as 'our chief ideological weapon'.[16]

There is a widespread government objective of educating the population and often a policy of using television for education. Yet educational television has not been the practical success to date that was once expected. Television appears to be an ideal way by which to reach audiences in much of the Third World and in remote areas of the Western world. In theory television, especially interactive television, could eliminate the jobs of most schoolteachers and college and university lecturers. In China in 1988 the government cut back the number of university places available to undergraduates from 750,000 to 680,000. Instead they planned to offer additional services on television. In British Columbia, a vast, little populated area of western Canada, the Open University has been a pioneer in the use of television as a means of taking university education to people hundreds or thousands of miles from a university campus. Students use the phone to ask questions and talk to tutors. In Britain university courses have been carried early in the day for years. Yet the number actually completing these higher-level courses has been disappointing.

Even more disappointing in the 1970s and '80s has been the lack of success of basic education for the vast number of illiterates in the Third World. In India and South America programmes funded by international organizations such as the World Bank and the United Nations have not worked well. By setting up community televisions in remote areas and feeding them educational material via satellite, broadcast, or video cassette it should be possible to bring basic education to the hundreds of millions of illiterates around the world. Many international organizations and governmental bodies have been willing to pay for such services. Most governments wish to see their people literate. Television could be a cheap way of providing low-cost education. State demand is there but demand by the population frequently is not, even at zero price. Mexico found more success in stimulating a desire to learn to read and write by using a soap opera to sell the benefits of traditional education than in using a soap opera itself as an educational vehicle. After watching the 1977 programme *Ven conmigo* thousands signed up for traditional courses in how to read. In *Ven conmigo* the hero achieves success once he has become literate.

Many governments also want their people to have access to the arts and culture. A commercial system will not meet this demand, because the profit motive leads to mass entertainment. A publicly run channel or a government-dominated system can be made to meet state demand for cultural programming, supposedly on behalf of the people. Consequently, even in the market-dominated United States, the federal government provides over $200 million each year for public broadcasting. In China and the USSR the state totally controls the television schedule. The absence of free exchange rates and the Communists' accounting systems make it impossible to determine what resources they allocate to this end. In countries like Britain and Australia there are quasi-official bodies appointed by the government which influence programming and place an emphasis on cultural programming. In Canada, for sixty years, the primary task of the public broadcasting system has been to support Canada's separate identity and protect her culture.

The quasi-official bodies that frequently run public stations are often made up of citizens selected by the government to ensure that the television system is run in the public interest. The difficulty with such a system is that those chosen to run the controlling bodies do not usually represent the tastes of the mass of the people. Responsible, committed, middle-class professional citizens with some sort of public success record are generally chosen to sit on the boards of these bodies. Whilst unlikely to be easily swayed by government influence and bullying, and so able to make sure the controlling bodies are free from government interference, such people are likely to be highly educated and to have interests different from those of the average citizen.

Although members of the boards of public corporations are unlikely to equate their own interests entirely with the public interest, a survey of the sort of material that the BBC offered in the 1950s, when the BBC monopolized television, compared to what the public revealed it wanted when it had the opportunity to vote with the channel control dial is telling. The BBC attempted to please the middle-class tastes of the board upon whom it was dependent.

No attempt is intended to judge the dilemma involved here between the public interest and freedom of choice. The point is that if the goals of society are of a utilitarian nature, to maximize the satisfaction of the greatest number and to maximize welfare, then the people should choose what programmes they watch. In a democratic society individuals vote to choose their leaders. Presumably they should be allowed to choose what television entertainment they want. When they have a choice between state cultural programmes and commercial entertainment programmes they choose the entertainment programmes, by a large margin. This may lead to negative externalities and so conflict with the government's goal of creating an educated, informed, and cultured society.

Finally, governments have a demand for television as a means to propagate. Control of the people in an authoritarian regime is critical. Governments will pay handsomely to maintain control.[17] Control of the media is basic to the control of society. Stalin called it 'the most powerful weapon of our Party'.[18] Few authoritarian regimes can be sanguine about the ability in the 1980s of satellites and video cassettes to undermine their control. *Glasnost* in the USSR is a reflection of the inevitable; the USSR could not be kept isolated from the outside world for ever. For the moment, in terms of broadcast programmes, the authoritarian state provides the mix of information, education, and entertainment that it deems appropriate. In the 1970s and most of the '80s viewers of much Eastern Bloc television were limited most of the time to dull, politicized programming. The one big exception was good sports coverage, because it did not threaten the regime but rather contributed to political goals by helping to build national identity.

The nature of other demands

Most television seeks to meet the demands of consumers, advertisers, and the state. Other groups have a demand for television time. Most notable are the religious groups which spend several hundreds of millions of dollars in the United States and in Latin America to buy time. They use that time to minister and to raise funds for their ministries.

Political groups also want time on television to put forward their positions and to seek public support. In some countries television stations are required to provide political parties with broadcasting time. In others the political parties and political candidates at all levels of government can buy time like any other advertiser.

Public interest groups too want to put forward their point of view and demand time. Usually they are able to get time under some sort of community service access requirement. In many countries such access is made available on the public system or else is a condition of a broadcasting station being granted a licence or a cable operator a franchise.

In conclusion, therefore, although advertising dominates the world's television industry, government demand and indirectly consumer demands are also major determinants of programming. The next section examines the means of supply available to meet the various demands discussed in this chapter.

The nature of television supply

Supplying television requires producing, distributing, and determining the means by which programme exchange takes place. The new technology has complicated the supply side of the television industry. New methods of distributing programmes have vastly increased the total supply of programmes to the viewer. With increased ability to supply television to the viewers, together with the growth in demand discussed in the last chapter, the derived demand for programmes, the raw materials of television, has also increased dramatically.

The new supply vehicles for delivering television are satellites, cable, and video-cassette recorders. The effects of the new vehicles in television history can be compared with the land transport industry over the last 200 years. Initially there were just wagons and horses. Canals were a major advance because they enabled the inland carriage of bulky items at much lower cost.[19] It was an improvement comparable to television over radio. Subsequently railways, buses, trucks, and cars provided more flexible and cheaper alternatives. Aircraft made things much faster and easier. However, just as canals carry goods, so broadcast television carries programmes. Cars, trains, and planes carry goods to their destination more efficiently. Similarly, new broadcasting techniques, satellites, cable, and VCRs carry programmes to the viewers more efficiently. Each method has its own advantages in different situations. The important point in both instances is that the product should arrive. By and large, how their video programmes are delivered is of no more consequence to the consumers than whether other goods are delivered by canal or jet plane. They just have to arrive at the right time and in good condition.

Satellites, cable, and VCRs mean a huge potential supply of programmes for consumers everywhere. Canadians with a dish could tune in to over 200 different channels in 1988. The satellite television guide consisted of 300 pages of listings for one month and was the size of a telephone directory for a medium-sized city. Europe in the late 1980s was in the process of increasing supply so that Europeans like North Americans, would have enormous choice. It was estimated that for

1990 Europe would require 1.5 million hours of programmes each year to feed the new supply vehicles.

From the government's standpoint the television public utility era, based on the fact that the usable broadcast wavelengths were limited and scarce, is ended. Satellite footprints ignore national boundaries. Although future satellites may be able to beam a footprint to approximate national boundaries, such technology is not available and it is not clear that it would be accepted in any case. In an age of satellite platforms and opto-electronics, in addition to current satellites and coaxial cable, government control will be even more difficult to enforce. National, regional, and social distinctions will continue to be eroded. So will the ability of sovereign states to exercise control over what their citizens watch, even though governments still continue to try to exercise control.

When broadcasting was the only means of delivering television programmes governments could control the supply of television. Since the broadcasting wavelengths are finite, governments argued, it was up to them to control the use of those wavelengths, a scarce resource, in the public interest. When they did not, as in the United States in the late 1940s or in Italy in the late 1970s, there was chaos. In the broad-casting monopoly era, therefore, the state not only could control supply but was obliged to do so. Television was then a public utility, but it is so no longer.

Suppliers' motives for supplying television have been modified by the introduction of the new supply vehicles. The profit motive has become more important. Pleasing the government has become less important. When the limited broadcasting wavelengths were either handed over to a monopoly state supplier or to a few oligopolistic commercial companies, pleasing those who had the power to give and to take away the right to the airwaves was vital. For commercial companies, when they were dependent on the state for a licence, the profit motive was constrained by the need to please the licence controllers. This was because when the government handed over the licence they usually gave it for a nominal fee. The economic rent that they handed over in the process was often considerable.[20] Increasingly free of government control, and operating in an increasingly competitive environment, the new television suppliers are no longer virtually guaranteed economic rents which they then can report as profits. Instead they must scramble just to cover costs.

Statements, sometimes made by programme suppliers, that they are motivated to serve the public interest and produce creative and cultural quality programmes do not necessarily reflect true motivation. Such statements can usually be made only at a time when the companies are making healthy profits. Lord Thomson said of the early franchises to run commercial television in Britain, the first commercial television in Europe, that they were a 'licence to print money'.[21] He was right, in speaking of a time when large economic rents were given away. The economic rents gave the suppliers both the luxury and the incentive to supply cultural programming.

In the new competitive environment any commercial organization that does not pursue profits quickly goes broke. It also betrays its responsibility to its shareholders. Quality programming, therefore, must take second place to profits anywhere in the world where market forces operate. There will be quality programming only if it is a means to profitable operation. If that means that programmes of a cultural and educational nature are not supplied in the quantities that the state would like, then the state must intervene with regulation, subsidies, or state ownership of at least one channel.

Cable television in the United States has demonstrated the consequences of the profit motive. In its early years pundits of the industry had suggested that coaxial cable would supply a great variety of new channels offering unlimited choice and diversity. The preference option and the need to maximize profits, especially in the early years of cable, created the incentive to provide just more of the same programmes. Increases in television supply in Europe in the late 1980s reflected the same pattern of mass-appeal content. As new commercial broadcasting channels were started in France and Italy the programmes carried were typically game shows, old movies, and American imports. New independent broadcasting stations in the United States likewise filled the airwaves by recycling old cast-off programmes from the networks.

Why distributors recycle old cast-off programmes reflects the interplay between programme supply costs and viewer demand. Supply is not independent of demand. Better programmes attract more viewers, who can be sold to advertisers. This is illustrated in figure 8. A more expensive programme, reflected in an upward shift of ATC_0 to ATC_1, causes viewer demand to shift from D_0 to D_1. Suppliers will continue to improve the quality of the shows they offer only so long as the marginal cost of improving the programme is exceeded by the marginal revenue from selling a bigger audience to suppliers. Many new suppliers found that if they reduced programme costs by recycling old programmes their costs fell more rapidly than their revenue from advertising.

Public corporations are motivated to please the public body for whom they work. How they please it depends upon the mandate of that body. A state television such as India's Doordashan might put a priority on propaganda for the ruling Congress Party and education. A public corporation such as Japan's NHK might have a mandate to work in the public interest. That public interest might be defined in different terms in different places and at different times. If the public interest is seen as education and culture, then the emphasis will be there. If it is to develop the latest technology, as in the case of NHK, then it will do so. If it is to develop the latest technology, as in the case of NHK, then it will do so. If it is to provide competition in entertainment with commercial stations, then the public corporation will end up playing the ratings game to maximize the number of viewers, for example Canada's CBC. It will then be subject to the workings of the preference option.

Figure 8 The interdependence between viewer demand and programme costs

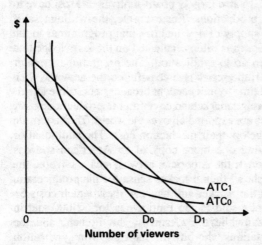

Note: The average total cost curve (ATC) is presumed to be a rectangular hyperbola. For distributors the total cost is the same whether one or a million watch the programme. For a pay channel a similar argument holds. In such a case the distributor maximizes the difference between total costs and total revenue. Better programmes allow him to sell more connections at the same price or a higher price

In the early days of television it was thought that, once shown, a television programme was obsolete. Repeats of shows, particularly on cable, have long dispelled such an idea. The profit motive has demonstrated that a television programme, once shown, is still a valuable raw material for the industry. Old movies, old situation comedies, and even old news programmes can be shown again and again. In the USA old British programmes from the BBC and London Weekend such as *Monty Python, The Two Ronnies,* and Benny Hill are shown on most evenings of the week. *Upstairs, Downstairs* is relentlessly repeated. Ted Turner paid $1.5 billion for a library of old MGM movies to feed to his channels. Rupert Murdoch wanted Fox partly for its old movies. The NBC television network converted the best of its 1987 newscasts into a video. To meet the derived demand of the new vehicles for delivering television programmes there will be a steady recycling of old programmes in the secondary or ancillary market. Still, programmes can only be repeated so many times, and the enormous derived demand for new programmes by the new delivery vehicles has consequences for all who provide programme material.

The supply of new and original programming will be inadequate to meet total demand in the 1980s and for the rest of the century. The commercial programme producers who supply both government and commercial distributors are also largely profit-motivated. Most have to borrow to finance their productions. For example, the willingness of the banks to finance the supply of new and original programmes to the networks in the United States is often predicated on the knowledge that the programmes can then go to syndication. The programme supplier relies upon the fact that if the series is successful on the network, then it can be resold a second time to independent broadcasters, cable television networks, and to foreign markets to cover all the production costs.

American programmes are exported all over the world. They are made available for a cost far below their production cost. The additional or marginal cost of supplying one more copy of an American show is negligible to the producer. If the American networks have covered the bulk of the costs of the show, then it makes sense for the producers to sell copies for whatever the market will bear. A show which costs $1 million to produce may be sold in the Philippines for $2,000 and in Thailand for $500. Meanwhile the Germans, the French, and the American independent stations who buy the same show in syndication pay tens or hundreds of thousands of dollars. Such price discrimination maximizes profits for programme suppliers.[22]

A consequence of American producers supplying export markets is that high-production-cost programmes from America are often much cheaper to buy than locally produced new programmes. With these conditions of supply, Third World television systems often find that the cheapest sources of material are American companies selling programmes at whatever they can afford to pay. The main reason for cultural imperialism is therefore economic. In many Third World countries the marginal cost of an American show is less than the average cost of even the most basic locally produced programme.

Nevertheless, since American purchasers of programmes, the US advertisers, spend $23 billion on programmes each year whilst export markets generate only $0.5 billion, American programmes are produced for the American market. Even though they are supplied to many more viewers outside America, it is the dollars that count, not the number of viewers.

In any industry supply increases when input costs fall. Technology has reduced the cost of producing programmes. New cameras are easier and cheaper to use. Masses of technicians are no longer necessary to support the production of a programme. In the United Kingdom, in 1988, Mrs Thatcher introduced legislation to remove restrictive practices by the trade unions in television partly because she was infuriated by the armies of technicians traipsing into her office following any reporter who interviewed her. As the broadcasting monopoly era ends, the ability of either commercial oligopolies or public systems to afford such inefficient methods, called X-inefficiency, will disappear under the pressure of competition.

Table 7 Proportion of imported television programmes, selected countries, 1983 (%)

America		Western Europe	
Canada/CBC	32	Austria	43
USA	2	Belgium/RTBF	29
Argentina/Canal 9	49	Finland	38
Brazil	30	France	17
Cuba	24	Iceland	66
Ecuador	66	Italy	18
Venezuela	38	Irish Republic	57
		Netherlands	25
Communist Bloc		Spain	33
Bulgaria	27	Sweden	35
Hungary	26	UK/BBC and ITV	15
Soviet Union	8	West Germany/ZDF	23
East Germany	30		
		Asia	
Middle East and Africa		Australia	44
Algeria	55	Brunei	60
Egypt	41	China	8
Kenya	37	India/Delhi	11
Nigeria	40	Japan	4
South Africa	29	Korea	16
Syria	33	Malaysia	54
Tunisia	55	New Zealand	75
Zimbabwe	61	Singapore/Channel 5	70

Note: These figures refer to imports or programming to national suppliers. They ignore direct imports to households and cable operators picking up signals from neighbouring countries. For example, Canadians do not watch 68 per cent Canadian programming.

Source: Tapio Varis, 'The international flow of television programmes', *Journal of Communications*, January 1984, p. 123.

New technology, therefore, has led to a lowering of costs in two ways. First, there are more efficient production methods available. Second, with more competition in the industry, X-inefficiency has been lowered. The ability of the old broadcasting trade unions in many countries to extract some of the economic rent from the monopolistic or oligopolistic suppliers in the industry in the form of high wages has been reduced.

In much of the world viewers are used to watching programmes produced and distributed by public or state television systems. They are used to vertically integrated suppliers who produce programmes as well as distribute them. However, it is not essential for the carrier or distributor of television programmes to be the provider of the content. A cable operator or independent broadcaster could operate like a telephone company, distributing programmes with advertising that programme suppliers had paid to have carried. Indeed, economic theory shows that in some circumstances vertical integration may not even be efficient.[23] Consequently IRI in Italy and Channel 4 in Britain rely on commercial suppliers for many of their programmes, and IRI's demands have helped support the Italian film industry. In the USA the access hours in prime time were supposed to have the same effect of creating new opportunity for creative talent.

The raw material for programmes consists of material of an informational, educational, or entertainment nature. Programmes may mix all three categories. Most news programmes in the West mix information and entertainment. Situation comedies in the United States in the late 1980s often included an informational and educational message about drugs, AIDS, and problems associated with modern living.

The impact of television on its own raw material has been considerable. Politicians and lawyers play to the camera, given half a chance. Television debates between the candidates in elections in some countries are the central event in the election process. This was the case in Canada in 1988. In 1987 in the USA the telegenic Lieutenant-Colonel Oliver North admitted to breaking the law yet won the hearts of many Americans during the televised Iranscam Senate hearings. Day by day the senators lost their aggressiveness as inquisitors as they perceived that viewer sympathy lay with the boyish-looking colonel. In the Lebanon and Israel demonstrators admit they demonstrate for the Western cameras.

Many sports, too, have been radically changed by television worldwide. Athletes earn salaries undreamed of forty years ago. Snooker, tennis, golf, motor racing, wrestling are amongst the sports which have become big business because of television. Many sports have even changed their rules to please television. Cricket went over to one-day matches when Kerry Packer in Australia showed that the faster-paced game was better for television. Golf changed from match play to lowest score because it made the game more interesting on television. Tennis went over to tie-breakers for television. Motor racing cars, whether televised from Monte Carlo or from Brazil, became speeding advertisements. Thirty years ago racing cars raced in their national colours but in the 1980s they adopted the colours of their numerous sponsors. Meanwhile more and more hoardings surrounded the tracks on which they raced before the television cameras.

Television has also redefined the market for the film industry. Table 8 shows the precipitous drop in movie audiences in the Western world since the introduction of television. In the 1980s the huge Indian film industry was decimated by video-cassette recorders and television. In India VCRs and VCR theatres showing video-cassette recordings, often pirated, to small audiences at low prices eliminated much of the world's largest film industry's box office.

Table 8 Decline in cinema attendance, selected countries, selected years (million)

Year	France	Japan	UK	USA
1967	216	319	292	968
1970	191	232	219	951
1975	187	172	116	1,028
1980	183	141	97	1,070
1983	201	159	65	1,219
1986	163	161	73	1,017

Source: Various.

The relationship between film and television is still changing. Although initially broadcast television took audiences from cinemas, films are also a raw material of television. By 1987 the film industry received more of its income from television and video than from the box office. As new suppliers to the television industry competed for programming the value of films increased. In addition the market for made-for-television movies expanded. Whilst these were often relatively low-budget movies in comparison with the $45 million costs of *Who Killed Roger Rabbit?* some were excellent. Movies such as *Letter to Brezhnev, A Room with a View*, and *My Beautiful Laundrette* made for Britain's Channel 4, won international awards. Finally, despite constant concern over pirating, the film industry enjoyed good sales of pre-recorded video-cassette copies of its movies.

VCRs and made-for-television films were not the total salvation of the film industry. Copyright laws in much of the world do not cover video, and their enforcement is rarely a top priority for the police. In Holland there is a thriving pirate video business because a law intended to protect the film industry by banning video sales and rentals of a movie for six months creates an incentive to pirate. Consequently film producers lose billions of dollars worldwide. Copying films is easy with modern technology. A copy of a newly released movie can be made in the time it takes to run the movie, and the technology to make simultaneous copies became available in the late 1980s. Consequently pirated copies of new movies are usually available within days of their release. Frequently pirated copies are available in export markets even before the film has opened in the local cinemas. All it takes is one dishonest film operator at a cinema in the producing country. Nevertheless pre-recorded audio tapes have sold in large quantities for many years despite the ease of copying them. On that basis there is every reason to believe that the majority of people will continue to pay for the movies they wish to watch on VCRs and television, either by subscribing to 'pay movie' channels on television, hiring videos, or else buying them pre-recorded.

Finally, supply is no longer constrained by geography. Satellites have made it easy and cheap to send programmes across a continent. The *Live Aid* concert in 1985 for the starving in Ethiopia showed how the world could be hooked up in a humanitarian venture. Chapter 4 and subsequent chapters examine how the changed nature of supply and demand has altered the structure, conduct, and performance of the television industry everywhere.

Notes

1 The approach used here has been used before for television and measures of the consumer surplus have been estimated. For example, in 1987 Booz Allen & Hamilton estimated that BBC 1 created a consumer surplus of about $2 billion.
2 The failure to recognize the nature of demand and the fact that the viewer is free to choose from a variety of other entertainment media can lead to sub-optimal use of scarce public resources. Both the Canadian Broadcasting Corporation and the British Broadcasting Corporation have been criticized for competing with the commercial networks for ratings. Public channels may well serve the public interest best by showing programmes which please a small minority of the public very much and letting the majority watch non-public television.
3 Discussing externalities as concepts is much easier than measuring them. Many are not measurable.
4 If programmes are shown again at a later date at a lower price, or zero price, then pay-television reduces to a form of price discrimination and the deadweight loss reduces to the rate of discount on the deadweight loss over the time until the programme is rerun.
5 An example of the prisoner's dilemma as applied to advertising where the firm is damned if it advertises and damned if it doesn't can be found in F.M. Scherer, *Industrial Market Structure and Economic Performance*, Chicago: Rand McNally, 1985, p. 145.
6 N. Kaldor, 'The economics of advertising', *Review of Economic Studies*, June 1950, p. 87.
7 Most neo-classical economics assumes independent utility functions and ignores the problems of interpersonal comparisons.
8 A number of surveys in the popular press suggest that in the United Kingdom many viewers prefer the commercials to the programmes.

9   F.M. Scherer, *Industrial Structure, Conduct and Performance*,
    Chicago: Rand McNally, p. 214.
10 A. Koutsoyiannis, *Non-price Decisions*, London: Macmillan, 1982, p. 137.
11 An increase in advertising slots will shift the supply curve to the right.
12 Controversial shows may be unacceptable to advertisers. When ABC
    Television in the United States put on a show called *Amerika* in 1987
    which had as its theme life in the United States following a successful
    take-over by Russia, Chrysler Corporation pulled out all its
    advertisements, worth over $6 million. The case of Chrysler and
    Amerika showed that although Chrysler could pull its own
    advertisements it could not stop the programme. Only in a situation
    where there were a few buyers of advertising time, so that each had
    some monopsony power, would advertisers be able to affect the
    programmes offered. Chrysler's advertisements were easily replaced.
    Furthermore Chrysler only refused to be associated with a single
    programme. When ABC put on a different show the Chrysler
    advertisements returned. Chrysler needed ABC as much as ABC
    needed Chrysler. In fact even though shows such as the CBS current
    affairs programme *Sixty Minutes* have attacked the products of the
    American auto manufacturers and they have refused to be interviewed
    on the CBS programme, they still spend millions of dollars on the
    network. The point is clear. The scope for advertiser censorship of
    programme content is very limited, not only in the United States but in
    any commercially based television system.
13 A.C. Neilsen used to solicit 2,600 households to fill in diaries for a
    week. These represented one out of every 30,000 households. They
    created figures that were statistically significant. However, the diaries
    were open to many criticisms. Viewers had to record in fifteen-minute
    blocks which programmes they watched. Somebody switching on for
    the six o'clock news at five minutes to six was deemed to have watched
    the preceding situation comedy. Human error was a constant problem.
    In an additional 1,700 homes electronic meters picked up when a
    television set was turned on and turned off. This meant that if the
    room was empty or if the viewer was not paying any attention to the
    programme the household was still counted as watching the show.
14 The consumer may also pay for commercials in the form of higher
    prices. The hundreds of millions that car makers spend on advertising
    may be passed on to the consumer. However, advertising may enable a
    company to exploit economies of scale so that by producing larger
    volumes unit costs fall. See A. Koutsyannis, *Non-price Decisions*,
    London: Macmillan.
15 Marshall McLuhan, *Understanding Media*, New York: Mentor, 1964,
    p. 191.
16 ibid.
17 Peter J.S. Dunnett, *The World Newspaper Industry*, London: Croom
    Helm, 1988, p. 217.
18 Marshall McLuhan, *Understanding Media*, New York: Mentor, 1964,
    p. 191.

45

19   Robert Fogel, *Railroads and American Economic Growth*, Baltimore, Md: Johns Hopkins University Press, 1970, p. 9.
20   The economic rents earned by the ITV companies in the United Kingdom have been estimated as between £1 billion and £2 billion a year in the 1980s.
21   Anthony Sampson, *The Changing Anatomy of Britain*, London: Hodder & Stoughton, p. 406.
22   The literature of price discrimination shows that in many situations price discrimination allows a greater quantity to be sold than if there is a single market. Given the public-good nature of television programmes, price discrimination from a purely economic standpoint is likely to increase welfare. This conclusion is dependent on there being no net external costs from selling programmes at their very low marginal cost in many markets, particularly in the Third World.
23   Douglas Needham, *The Economics of Industrial Structure: Conduct and Performance*, London: Holt Rinehart & Winston, 1978, p. 192.

Chapter four

Structure and conduct

The basic conditions of demand and supply largely determine the structure and conduct of the industry. Demand and supply conditions determine such characteristics of any industry as the ease of entry, the nature of costs, the role of conglomerates, the degree of vertical integration, the extent of price competition, and other aspects of behaviour. The following sections examine these topics from a general perspective as regards the television industry before turning to the specifics of different countries in the remaining chapters.

Barriers to entry

The erosion of barriers to entry made possible by technological progress has been critically important for the change in the structure of this industry which has taken place during the last quarter of the twentieth century. Revised approaches to public policy dealing with television in many countries also facilitated entry. In the broadcasting era government could and did control entry strictly. However, in the late 1970s and early '80s a number of governments were elected which were pro-free market, most notably those led by Margaret Thatcher in Britain and Ronald Reagan in the United States. Even some left-wing governments reduced the emphasis on planning and adopted a more pro-market stance, for example countries such as France and Australia. The public policy stance switch from control towards quasi-deregulation in many Western countries encouraged private investors to undertake most of the costs of implementing the new media technology.

The repercussions were widespread. Commercial broadcasting was started in France and Italy. Britain decided that all cable and all satellites should be privately funded. With a more benevolent eye from the government regarding commercial television, and with the incentive of huge potential revenues and later profits, newcomers rushed to enter the industry. This happened not only in Europe and the United States but also in countries like China and India.[1] Many failed but some had staggering success in a world where government television monopolies and tight, government-regulated oligopolies were increasingly giving way to national and international competition.

The number of buyers and sellers

The major change in structure has been the increase in the number of suppliers. Satellites permitted a multifold increase in their number. Costs and demand conditions will determine how many will survive. The potential number of suppliers increased from at most five for any given transmission area, often a country, to several hundred. For example, there is room for enough satellites over the United States to carry about 900 channels to the United States, Canada, and Central America.

The United States has led the way in encouraging new entrants, for several reasons. First, its experience with a commercial system made it more predisposed to allowing the market rather than the state to determine the number of suppliers. Second, its space technology spin-offs gave it a technical advantage. Third, a larger advertising market created a greater source of income from advertising for new suppliers. Finally their high incomes made the consumers themselves a potential source of revenue for pay television. The change in the US television industry was dramatic and the United States is a likely harbinger of developments in the rest of the developed world. In 1974 the United States had three large networks and a handful of independent broadcasters. Fifteen years later there were over 6,000 cable systems, over 300 independent broadcasters, and some fifty satellites delivering television. The three networks had been joined by a fourth.

Meanwhile on a worldwide basis the demand for advertising has been on the rise. The 1980s were a decade of yuppies and increasing materialism in many parts of the world. Growth in incomes, population, and incentives to spend, such as easy credit and credit cards, combined with rising nominal wealth in the form of rising share prices and property values, was accompanied by advertising revenues rising faster than inflation. In India advertising grew by 50 per cent in 1986, while in France it will more than double between 1985 and 1990. The growth in advertising created the stimulus for new suppliers to enter the television industry.

The consequence has been that the structure of the industry currently consists of four major categories of programme distributor. Sometimes, but not necessarily, distributors are vertically integrated and produce their own programmes. The four distribution sectors are broadcasting, cable, satellite, and video cassettes.

These categories are not independent of each other. (1) Traditional broadcasters use satellites to deliver programmes. (2) The modern multiplex cable television is possible only because the cable-system operators can collect programmes from satellites. Satellite television involves both low and medium-powered satellites whose purpose is mainly to deliver to distributors such as cable and local broadcasting stations for rebroadcasting, and high-powered satellites. High-powered satellites are the basis of direct broadcast satellite television. With high-powered satellites technology inversion allows small low-cost household dishes to pick up the signals. As the price of receiving dishes falls towards $500 or £250 and dishes become more sensitive DBS television from both medium and high-powered satellites becomes a viable competitor to cable. The cable or broadcast redistributor is then by-passed. The household picks up the signal direct from the television supplier, with no middleman. (3) Broadcasting, satellite, and cable all use video cassettes in the process of originating programmes, although video cassettes are also widely used by consumers independently of the other three means of distribution.

In the late 1980s these four basic groups of suppliers were competing with each other for advertising revenue and consumers' time. Pay television and video cassettes also competed for the consumer's entertainment spending. Each group was in a state of transition. Even in broadcasting new technology, including new terrestrial microwave transmission techniques and low-powered transmitters, made broadcasting more competitive. It was not clear that any system had an overwhelming advantage. There was growth and expansion in all sectors. Major participants in the media such as Rupert Murdoch had a stake in all categories. The fight was not over outright winners and losers but over market shares and the rate of growth of each group's share.

However, the pattern of development was clear. The days of monopoly suppliers were over. In place of a single supplier or a handful of state-owned or controlled suppliers there were a large number of competing suppliers. Barriers to entry had been eroded. Even where governments wished to maintain a monopoly of supply it was very difficult. Video cassettes and satellite footprints entered the market with programmes over which governments had little control. In attempting to maintain some control the authorities in Bulgaria in 1988 required that all VCRs be registered.

Nevertheless some entry barriers remained. First, the broadcasting airwaves were still a finite quantity even if low-power transmitters and the more efficient use of the airwaves increased the number of possible broadcasters. To broadcast television required a licence in all countries. Second, there were significant starting up costs. Although a low-powered transmitter is not very expensive, to staff, programme, and market the operations of a broadcasting station is a significant undertaking. Third, there are economies of scale and scope.[2]

The cable sector involves considerable entry barriers. Cable has the characteristics of a natural monopoly. It is inefficient to have two sets of cables serving the same area, just as it is inefficient to have two sets of telephone wires. To install cable either under the ground or on posts above the ground requires the approval of government. Generally governments award the right to install cable as a franchise to a single firm. Alternatively they can install it themselves, as they have in West Germany, where the Bundespost has the responsibility of cabling the country. Installing cable can be exceedingly costly. Companies which dug up downtown Detroit lost millions of dollars when few signed up, while in Britain a number of the early franchisees backed out in the late 1980s in the face of rising costs.

Satellite television also involves high entry costs. The most expensive are the high-powered DBS satellites such as France's TDF 1, which cost about a quarter of a billion dollars. Vertical integration occurs when the television distributor owns the satellite or the transponders on the satellite. However, satellite television companies do not have to send up the satellite and usually they lease a transponder from a satellite company. The leasing costs are high. Typically they run at about a million dollars per year on a medium-powered satellite. In addition the satellite television company must buy programmes and sell advertising. It may take years before there is a large enough audience to sell to advertisers at prices high enough to cover costs. In the meantime the satellite television companies need deep pockets as they wait for audiences to build up.

The video cassette recorder was the joker in the pack as regards television developments in the 1980s. VCRs have had a profound effect on the rate of growth and the profitability of the other three groups' respective markets. Entry barriers into supplying video-cassette programming are low. Video cassettes are cheap to produce. New cameras allow high-quality programmes to be created, using inexpensive equipment. Movies can be bought, pirated, or hired. Television programmes can be copied. They can then be distributed by mail-order or through retail outlets and advertised through any of the advertising media. Whether the content is old comedies from the 1950s or videos about keeping fit, mending the car, or cooking, video cassettes compete for the time of the viewing public. They can offer the programmes that minority interest groups demand. To the extent that they reduce market size for the other groups they reduce the number of suppliers in the other three categories that can be sustained.

VCRs can also serve as a complement to the other distribution methods. As recently as the late 1980s Britain was still toying with the idea of beaming out television programmes at night to be recorded for later use. The real question for the other distributors is the extent to which VCRs increase their market as a complement – for example, recording programmes for later use – and the extent to which a hired film simply takes viewers away and so decreases demand. However, if commercials on recorded shows are 'zapped', that is, eliminated with the fast-forward button on the VCR, then there is no complementarity for the advertiser whose message is fast-forwarded.

For all categories of television distributors there is competition. They compete with suppliers in the same sector of the industry and with suppliers in other sectors. Cable operators may have a local monopoly but cable programme suppliers compete with other cable channels. Broadcasters compete with broadcasters. Both sectors must also compete with each other and with omnipresent VCRs. Contestability theory also emphasizes the importance of potential new entrants to the market for the conduct of established firms. For example, the private phone companies would like to own the vehicles which carry television to viewers. Governments may let them supply television in the future, particularly if other suppliers act contrary to the public interest.[3]

The relationship between costs and demand

Cost in any industry can be broken down into fixed costs and variable costs. For cable operators and satellite distributors the fixed costs are high. The fixed costs include such costs as those of negotiating a franchise for cable, the cost of installing the cable or buying an existing operator, the lease of a satellite transponder, as well as other overheads. For a broadcasting station fixed costs include the cost of the station and the cost of purchasing or leasing a transmitter as well as all other overheads. For a local broadcasting station fixed costs may be quite moderate.

Variable costs are those which the supplier can influence in the short run, unlike fixed costs. Besides staff and marketing the major short-run cost to a television distributor is the cost of programmes. Programmes can be bought in or produced in-house. Whether there is vertical integration or not, costs vary enormously. Local television can show a programme interviewing the curator at the local museum or a council meeting at very low cost. A local broadcasting station can buy-in repeats of old shows at low cost too. Even local news programmes need not be expensive. Much light entertainment is fairly inexpensive to produce, which often means lower costs to stations buying the programmes to broadcast. Game shows can be produced for several thousand dollars per episode. For example, in the United States the highly successful *Wheel of Fortune* cost about $7,000 per episode to produce, and in Italy game shows cost much less than that. Soap operas in Brazil are produced for as little as $3,000 per episode.

On the other hand, slick programmes for the American networks or period-piece productions for public systems like the BBC, CBC, and

NHK, in Britain, Canada and Japan respectively, cost much more. The Canadian Broadcasting Corporation spent $11 million to produce *Fools' Gold* in HDTV format. A half-hour situation comedy for an American network typically costs a million dollars and ABC's series *War and Remembrance* cost $110 million. Japan's more extravagant game shows involve sending participants and the whole game production team to exotic places around the globe. The Japanese even financed an ascent of Mount Everest so that they could film the conquest. Whether produced internally by the distributor or bought from independent producers, such shows are very expensive.

The relation between programme costs and viewer demand in a commercial system was discussed in the last chapter and illustrated in figure 8. As the distributor improves product quality the average total-cost curve shifts upwards. As the ATC curve moves up the better product attracts more viewers. Consequently the television distributor can sell more viewers in each commercial slot. The goal of the distributor is to maximize profits, and that requires selecting the correct mix of product quality, as determined by the preference option, to maximize the difference between total revenue and total costs.[4]

As new suppliers enter the industry they will take viewers away from established distributors. That will be reflected in figure 8 in a leftward shift of the established distributor's demand curve. As the market fragments costs remain the same while demand shifts to the left for all firms. Fragmentation therefore creates an incentive for all distributors to lower programme costs with inferior programmes if they are profit maximizers. However, fragmentation can only go so far. With too many new entrants few will be able to cover costs at any output, a situation found in Italy in the mid-1970s. An industry rationalization then follows.

The US broadcasting networks still serve huge audiences, although not as large as in the past. These networks, which unintentionally programme for much of the rest of the world, have little option but to spend heavily on programmes. The size of US advertising demand justifies it. Small percentage decreases in audiences, reflected in the ratings, mean a huge decline in advertising revenue. It is a straightforward example of marginal costs and marginal revenues. Since marginal revenues are so high – a 1 per cent rise in the ratings is worth millions of dollars – the networks, as profit maximizers, are compelled to incur high marginal costs. A network that tries to cut costs is likely to find that advertising revenue falls even faster than costs as ratings slip. Unless all the networks can agree together to cut costs and the slickness of their programmes – in other words, to form some sort of cartel – rivalry impels them to spend heavily.

US programmes are then made available to the rest of the world television industry at low cost. The theory of price discrimination and marginal pricing explains why. For the networks it makes sense to sell the shows for whatever the market will bear, since the cost of running off another copy of the programme and distributing it is negligible, and any additional revenue from secondary markets is a contribution to profits. These shows are made available to all other television markets both in the United States and abroad. In all these markets there is a strong incentive to show low-cost network cast-offs purchased at a small proportion of their original total cost. In terms of reach per dollar they are often much more attractive than buying-in locally made programmes or producing one's own. Consequently the US networks' shows influence industry structure worldwide where they compete with local producers and help keep programme costs down. Local producers of programmes argue, with justification, that the competition is unfair and that they are victims of discriminatory pricing.

Conglomerates and horizontal integration

Monopoly is usually assumed to be undesirable and not in the public interest unless it can be proved otherwise. Monopoly of the press has always been regarded with special concern because of the public-interest implications for freedom of expression. This was so in the days of newspapers and radio, before television. Some governments, such as that of the USSR, have argued that the means of communication are so powerful that they must be held by the government as a state monopoly. However, as regards private firms in a market economy, horizontal integration of the media and control by conglomerates are a cause of continuing concern.

At the same time many of the new media require huge investment and involve high risk – for example, cable operations and direct broadcast satellites. In such cases only large organizations with access to a large amount of finance are able to enter. In Europe the entrants to cable and satellite television include some of the richest men, such as Rupert Murdoch, Robert Maxwell, and Silvio Berlusconi, who all have large interests in the traditional media. In the United States the three networks have all been involved in cable and satellite television and in the supply of programmes to them. They can often enjoy economies of scale and scope by spreading overhead costs, applying common managerial techniques, spreading risks, and enjoying pecuniary advantages such as discounts from programme suppliers.

The following chapters on the individual countries will discuss the role of conglomerates in those countries. The trend is to the involvement of media conglomerates in several sectors of the media. There is also a trend to international involvement. American media companies are involved with European satellites, European firms are buying into the

53

US media markets and into each other's markets. Japan likewise is buying into the US market. Unless governments impose restrictions on ownership, new entrants to the new media frequently have worldwide interests and connections throughout the media. This is both a cause and a consequence of the lowering of national boundaries between the media markets worldwide. A globalization of manufacturing, advertising, and most sectors of the media means that national markets are frequently too small for companies such as Bertelsmann, News International, Thomson, Pearson, and Hachette. They have grown beyond national boundaries, as have many of the advertising agencies with which they must work and the firms whose advertising they carry. At the same time they have sometimes also grown beyond the ability of national governments to regulate.

Vertical integration

Vertical integration refers to the extent to which any one firm in an industry carries on internally several stages of production. Vertical integration can be forwards, as when a programme distributor buys a station, or backwards, for example when a programme distributor starts to produce programmes. In Britain the BBC is vertically integrated backwards and forwards and produces nearly all its own programmes. Most public systems, such as NHK in Japan, are similarly vertically integrated, producing many of their own programmes. In Third World countries, however, vertical integration is sometimes a luxury they cannot afford and they have to rely heavily on cheap imports.

The advantages of vertical integration for the firm in terms of market power are generally far fewer than those of horizontal integration. The economic literature even argues that vertical integration can lead to an improvement in social welfare by increasing efficiency and so lowering prices.[5] For that reason governments have placed strict controls on horizontal integration whilst placing limited restrictions on vertical integration. The chief justification for restricting television distributors from being producers is that they may limit access by independent producers with creative ability. For example, when the major US networks were forced in the 1970s to buy-in most of their prime-time shows, opportunities for new talent to develop and gain access to the market were increased, it was argued. Where a broadcasting network or a cable operator has a monopoly of distribution it can use its gatekeeper position to squeeze suppliers with whom it competes at the production stage. Clearly, vertical integration is not without dangers and each case requires judging on its merits.[6]

Conduct and the varieties of competition

Firm's conduct refers to any firm's choosing its goals and strategies and then implementing them. This involves selecting the products to be produced and pricing, distributing, and marketing them. Commercial television involves two groups of customers, the advertisers and the viewers. The advertiser is one source of revenue, so is the primary customer. The television programme is sold to the viewers, who are simultaneously resold to the advertiser. The television product is both the show itself and the audiences it attracts, who are then sold to advertisers. Conduct involves both price competition and non-price competition.

In terms of a time price to viewers, commercial channels charge consumers the same price if they send advertising messages for the same amount of time per hour. Typically the consumer gives up about six and a half minutes per hour in the United States on all network channels. However, some European and Latin American channels carry more messages, up to fourteen minutes per hour. In India there may be twenty minutes. Finally, shopping networks, which are continuous advertising and sales promotions, offer information and possible financial gain in return for viewers' attention.

Advertisers usually pay a given price per advertising spot dependent upon the reach of the programme and the demographics of the audience. Prices are competitive, since there are many other advertising vehicles available. Usually there is a fixed time available each day for commercials at most stations or networks. Excess demand for time tells the station that its prices are too low; inadequate demand tells it that prices are too high relative to other advertising vehicles. Prices are determined as a given amount per thousand reached so as to clear the market for advertising, be it local or national, unless the government regulates prices. Should a show fail to reach the anticipated number of viewers the station will provide the advertiser with free advertising hours in compensation. In the United States in 1988 the cost per thousand in prime time was about $20 per thousand viewers of a thirty-second advertisement.

As regards cable and pay channels, the price of an additional show is usually zero. Basic fees for cable are a flat rate, regardless of shows viewed, and are paid to the local cable monopoly. Pay channels, as opposed to pay-per-view, also charge a fixed rate per month per additional channel or tier of channels. In the United States these rates are now deregulated, and the cable companies can charge what the market will bear. In countries such as Canada a regulatory board determines when prices may be increased.

In public systems advertising is usually limited either partially or totally. Licence fees for public television are set by the government.

They are determined by the lobbying process, the wealth of the country, and the aspirations of the government. Once again there is a flat rate, be it monthly, as in South Korea, or bi-monthly, as in Japan, or annually, as in Britain. Instead the television supplier as part of the lobbying process must satisfy the requirements of the government or whatever quasi-government body is the regulator. Displeasing that body may result in lower licence fees or stipends from the broadcast authority.

Other relevant prices include input prices. When distributors buy-in programmes from independent producers, budgets and prices are important, although the product's potential to attract and hold audiences is the primary concern. Prices between affiliates and networks or between cable networks and cable operators can be in the form of barter. Programmes may be supplied to distributors in return for a share of the advertising time. Most competition, however, is non-price competition. Stations adopt programmes they think will attract viewers. Product differentiation in the television industry is the main means of competing between different distributors. More attractive shows lead to higher advertising revenue.

Product differentiation can take the form of differentiating whole channels. In the case of pay television, where a monthly fee is paid for channels additional to a basic package, there are channels such as movie channels, sports channels, and children's channels. More usually the competition and product differentiation are in terms of programmes rather than whole channels. The preference option encourages competing commercial channels to line up similar shows against similar shows. Soap operas run against soap operas, game shows against game shows, and sport against sport. Such a copycat approach to timetabling enables a station to prevent a competing station from gaining an advantage in the market. The preference option encourages the commercial networks to imitate a rival channel's success. It also encourages them to make spin-offs from their own successes to maintain the loyalty of viewers.

Viewer loyalty is usually to programmes, and that loyalty is frequently fragile. Small changes in programmes can cause major defections, especially if competing channels offer similar programmes at the same time. A news programme, for example, may gain many additional viewers if the anchor man creates the right image and lose them if he does not. Soaps likewise can gain viewers if a character hits the right note. In *Dallas* for that reason Bobby Ewing returned from the dead. Consequently, since many viewers associate shows with leading personalities, most successful shows are very dependent upon their stars. For this reason when privatized television began in Europe the new stations immediately poached from the state channels, offering huge salaries to established personalities.

Television suppliers cannot appeal to a diversity of tastes at the same time. In this respect a television channel is unlike a newspaper or a magazine. Newspapers and magazines can succeed if they make only part of their product appeal with some intensity to their readers. Readers may not want the chess column, the crossword, the agony column, the church column, or even the local or national news. So long as they want one part with some intensity, even if it is just the classified advertisements or the television programme schedule, they buy the whole paper. When it became possible to have dozens of television suppliers it was thought there might be considerable 'narrowcasting'. There would be a channel to serve each interest, the equivalent of an agony channel, a chess channel, a local news channel and so on. By and large this has not occurred. Instead there are numerous channels but each offers mass entertainment.

Figure 9 The law of central tendency and its effect on programming

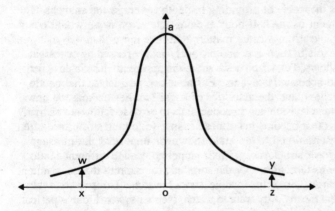

Note: Television preferences centre on light entertainment. The major networks cluster round the centre (rather as most business offices cluster round a town centre, where the customers are likely to be). The diagram is two-dimensional but in fact all networks can cluster at the centre, exploiting a third dimension of product differentiation around the central preferences. Consequently a large number of popular channels can meet demand at the centre before it is worth exploiting the extremities (be they mud wrestling or ballet)

Failure to narrowcast can also be explained by the law of central tendency. Figure 9 illustrates this. If the tastes of viewers are examined it is found that although a few like mud wrestling and a few like opera most prefer middle-of-the-road entertainment. A new entrant focusing on one of the extremes could anticipate *wx* or *yz* viewers. A new entrant to the centre can anticipate sharing *oa* viewers. The centre, represented by game shows and situation comedies, can support many suppliers before it is worth a supplier targeting the fringe.[7]

Failure to narrowcast can be explained too by the ability of substitutes such as books, magazines, video cassettes, live theatre and concert performances, films, and computers to act as delivery vehicles for specific services. Minority interests can be met by these non-television methods. Demand for them via television is limited. Product strategies to deliver culture and the arts have failed commercially in every instance to date. Television has proved itself to be a superb entertainment medium but a poor cultural and educational tool. Consumers who want culture and the arts tend to want them live. As a second best a recording on video is a close substitute for a live broadcast.

One consequence of the fickle nature of entertainment demand and the ability of the viewer to switch off has been that all products are reduced to entertainment, even the news, as suppliers in a commercial system attempt to hold viewers and maximize reach. For the majority of people television is the chief means by which they get the news. Yet television is incapable of providing in-depth coverage and analysis. The spoken element of the half-hour evening television news would cover one typed page. Complicated matters that take more than two or three minutes to explain, such as economic analysis, get passed by or relegated to specific shows. Television news serves an apparently insatiable appetite for new and spectacular events. Earthquakes, accidents, the meetings of world leaders, and the activities of royal families make good news. However, the television news product fails to provide follow-up on many of the events that become headlines because follow-up stories are often dull and unsensational, even stale, however important the message.

The two basic structures, private and public, lead to different conduct. Public systems tend to supply the sorts of programmes the government body in charge thinks the people should watch. The private system provides what the majority want to watch. Neither system alone is perfect, as was argued in chapter 3. There is much to be said for a mix of the two if welfare is to be maximized. Unless one is totally opposed to advertising, a subjective judgement, commercial television is a good means of producing light entertainment to meet the demands of the centre in figure 9. However, it requires supplementing with a public system if the demands of the fringe in figure 9 – the upper fringe, of course – are to be met. The size of the public service required to meet the fringe will decline if new entrants work towards the fringe and if other substitutes for minority programmes are available. There is also a case for public television if the government feels it is necessary in the public interest, for example for education or to preserve a national culture.

The chapters that follow examine the basic conditions, structure, conduct, and performance of countries that make up over four-fifths of the world's population and an even greater proportion of world income and output.

1   In China and India the new entrants were programme suppliers. In both countries the government continued to hold the means of distribution as a monopoly.

2   One unusual low-cost broadcasting station was that started in 1987 to broadcast to the 800 citizens of the former gold rush town Dawson City in Canada's northern Yukon. The mayor installed a 6W transmitter and subscribed to a variety of US pay satellite channels in the name of the long deceased George Dawson, founder of the city. He then retransmitted the channels as a means of supplementing the dull Canadian public television service. In Canada there was no law against picking up the signals from the United States, so his system was not illegal.

3   In the United States in 1988 there were two instances in which local phone companies were allowed to diversify into television. When the phone companies install optical fibre lines it will make even more sense to let them carry television signals on them.

4   It should be noted that in figure 8 total revenues are given by quantity times price and total costs by quantity times ATC. This means that a small profit per unit (price – ATC) may be justified by a higher quantity.

5   Douglas Needham, *The Economics of Industrial Structure: Conduct and Performance*, London: Holt Rinehart & Winston, 1978, p. 193.

6   Chapters 5 and 6 discuss the cases of the cable company TCI in the US and the ITV companies in the UK. Both cases show the potential for inefficiency in vertically integrated firms.

7   Peter O'Steiner, 'Programmes and preferences and the workability of competition in radio broadcasting', *American Economic Review 43*, 1953, p. 191.

Chapter five

North America: world provider

The United States

The United States' television industry is by far the largest anywhere in the world, dominating television worldwide. This dominance creates worries and concern wherever American programmes are shown, and that means almost everywhere, from Egypt to the South Pacific. Later chapters discuss this. However, as this chapter shows, the forces that determine what is produced in the United States with its population of 240 million are mostly domestic. The two or three billion people in export markets who are also exposed to American television have a small influence on the conduct of the US television industry. Quite simply, US television responds to the $23 billion of advertising expenditure it receives inside the United States, not the half billion it receives from export markets. For American television dollars, not minds, count.

Consumer demand and the advertisers

In the late 1980s consumers in the United States continued to watch increasing hours of television. More people watched television for longer than ever before. In 1987 the average American with a *per capita* annual income of $18,000 watched four hours and ten minutes of television each day. That was an increase of 15 per cent over a decade earlier. Then 93 per cent of households watched one of the three major networks, ABC, NBC, or CBS.[1] In 1988 the figure was 70 per cent and less than 44 per cent of all households in prime time. A senior executive at one of the networks, NBC, thought that the networks' share could fall to 60 per cent. However, Laurence Tisch, the head of CBS, had thought as late as 1987 that it would stabilize at over 70 per cent. One thing was clear: a more heterogeneous population was watching television from a greater variety of sources, and network television was in what Robert C. Wright, president of NBC described as the 'eye of a hurricane'.[2]

Table 9 US households' allocation of viewing time per week, 1985 (hours)

Networks	32·2
Independent broadcasting	12·8
Pay channels	10·2
Cable-originated*a*	8·4
Public service	1·7
Total weekly viewing	61·1

Note: a Channels carried only on cable but supported totally by advertisements.
Source: Nielsen Media Research.

During the 1980s the composition of US society changed, in many ways modifying the nature of consumer demand for television. Society aged. The baby bulge entered its forties. People lived longer. Income inequality increased. There were many more retired and semi-retired citizens. The proportion of non-caucasians increased. The number of hispanics exceeded 20 million, about the total number of blacks. The hispanics, mostly Mexicans, also had the fastest rate of population growth in the country. A significant Asian population, particularly Filipinos, Koreans, and Chinese, was established in parts of the country, in total over 5 million. Asians had the highest education levels and highest incomes in the country in 1988. More women entered the labour force, meaning that fewer stayed at home as television viewers during the day. Household incomes rose in real terms, largely because a greater proportion of the population was working.

Finally in the 1980s American households showed themselves to be big spenders, particularly on imported goods. Failure to save meant that America was unable to finance the government's deficit. On the other hand it was consumer spending that kept the economic boom rolling in the last years of the Reagan presidency. This was good news to the advertisers, who advertise both imported and domestic products and for whom television was still the medium of choice.

Americans watch television shows. It is important to stress the fact that Americans watch shows. They watch neither particular stations nor particular technologies. In fact 70 per cent of viewers use remote controls to switch repeatedly backwards and forwards around the dial. In the process they switch from broadcasting to cable to satellite, increasingly with the option of switching to VCR if the other supplies fail to satisfy. Few viewers know and probably even fewer care who supplies the shows they watch or what technology is used to deliver them.

Most of the shows viewers watched in 1988 were still free to the viewer. Even where cable channels were pay channels virtually all were packages bought monthly. In other words, on a daily or hourly basis all shows came free. An extra hour of a paid channel cost nothing more.

Pay-per-view television, where the consumer is billed for each show that is watched, was still largely a promise in 1988 and a novelty for events like big boxing matches.

Table 10 Average US television viewing time, November 1987 (hours per week)

Gender and age group		Total	Mon.–Fri.	Mon.–Fri.
Time slot			10.00–16.30	16.30–19.30
Average all persons		29·40	4·23	4·25
Women:	over 18	33·42	6·05	4·59
	18–54	24·35	4·49	3·16
	55+	41·17	7·48	7·07
Men:	Over 18	28·58	3·17	3·52
	18–54	23·45	3·29	2·51
	55+	37·07	5·06	6·08
Teen:	female (12–17)	23·13	2·30	4·12
	male (12–17)	24·16	2·22	3·54
Children:	2–5	25·26	5·26	4·19
	6–11	22·46	2·22	4·25

Gender and age group		Mon.–Sun.	Sat.	Mon.–Fri.
Time slot		20.00–23.00	07.00–13.00	23.30–01.00
Average all persons		8·46	0·47	1·07
Women:	Over 18	9·56	0·36	1·19
	18–54	6·58	0·37	1·06
	55+	12·06	0·32	1·24
Men:	Over 18	9·02	0·35	1·19
	18–54	6·26	0·35	1·15
	55+	11·19	0·34	1·17
Teen:	female (12–17)	7·16	1·00	0·38
	male (12–17)	7·40	0·59	0·41
Children:	2–5	5·05	1·43	0·19
	6–11	6·06	1·43	0·23

Source: Nielsen Media Research.

Demand for television delivered by cable increased rapidly in the '80s. In 1988 52 per cent of households spent an average $13.27 per month to watch basic cable.[3] Despite hefty rate increases more and more households signed up for cable. From 1984 to 1988 demand for cable television grew dramatically, and largely at the expense of the broadcasting networks. The exact rate of increase in demand is hard to assess, because not only did cable rates increase but the packages of basic cable were improved. Table 11 shows the rise in the number of cable subscribers.

Table 11 The growth of cable television in the United States

Year	Homes passed by cable (million)	Subscribers (%)	Total No. hooked to cable (million)
1975	4·2	46	1·9
1976	9·2	47	4·3
1977	13·4	48	6·4
1978	18·3	51	9·3
1979	25·7	54	13·9
1980	32·8	56	18·3
1981	41·2	55	22·7
1982	49·5	56	27·7
1983	55·9	57	31·9
1984	60·5	57	34·5
1985	65·6	57	37·5
1986	67·2	58	39·2
1987	71·8	58	42·3

Source: CSP International Inc.; *Business Week.*

The following observations about the nature of American viewing are important for an understanding of the television companies' conduct. First, many viewers watch television rather than a specific channel. Second, viewers are fickle. They quickly jump from one show to another. Third, many viewers watch just a few stations. Households which buy access to many channels have been observed to watch just a few of them.[4] Fourth, viewers' attention span is short. Television must cater to this in both advertisements and shows. Bored viewers quickly flip the dial. Fifth, a list of the top shows for various years (see table 12) shows what US consumers want to watch at zero price. They want entertainment.

American advertisers pay for the bulk of US television entertainment, which then becomes the world's entertainment. Yet American advertisers do not really want to entertain. What they want is reach. They buy television time so that American viewers will watch their commercials. Despite the fact that the link between watching a television commercial and sales is unclear, advertisers spent $23 billion in 1987 for commercial air time. Of this nearly $6 billion was spent by the motor manufacturers and their dealers alone to push automobiles on a public that owns more car seats than there are people to sit in them.[5]

The key point is that advertisers want to reach those who may buy or continue to buy their products. That means affluent households are more attractive than poor families. American television shows are slanted towards the affluent. America is a dollar democracy in which each viewer gets to vote for shows approximately in proportion to his household income.[6] The deprivation effects on the American poor and the millions

around the world who are ultimately exposed to the shows do not enter
into the demand decision when advertisers decide which shows to support.

Table 12 The top network programmes, USA, selected years

	1977–8	1982–3	1987–8
1	Laverne and Shirley	Sixty Minutes	Bill Cosby
2	Happy Days	Dallas	A Different World
3	Three's Company	Magnum, P.I.	Cheers
4	Sixty Minutes	M*A*S*H	Growing Pains
5	Charlie's Angels	Dynasty	Night Court
6	All in the Family	Three's Company	The Golden Girls
7	Little House on the Prairie	Simon and Simon	Who's the Boss?
8	Alice	Falcon Crest	Sixty Minutes
9	M*A*S*H	Love Boat	Murder, She Wrote
10	One Day at a Time	NFL Monday Night Football	Wonder Years

Note: The Top Ten shows of all time were *M*A*S*H Special* (28 February 1983), *Dallas* (21
November 1980), *Roots, Part VIII* (30 January 1977), *SuperBowl 1982, SuperBowl 1983,
SuperBowl 1986, Gone with the Wind* (7/8 November 1976), *SuperBowl 1978,* and *SuperBowl
1979.*
Source: A.C. Nielsen Company.

Table 13 Top advertisers by expenditure, USA, 1987 ($million)

Philip Morris	1,558
Procter & Gamble	1,387
General Motors	1,025
Sears Roebuck	887
RJR-Nabisco	840
PepsiCo	704
Eastman Kodak	658
McDonald's	650
Ford Motor	640
Anheuser-Busch	635
K-mart	632
Unilever	581

Source: Advertising Age.

American advertising expenditure is shown in table 14. For advertisers
television is only one means of reaching consumers. The table shows
that television advertising is a favoured means of national advertising
and of image advertising. For local advertising other media are the
favoured methods. Network television has to compete with other
television suppliers as well as the other media. When in 1987 the major
networks raised prices at the same time as the numbers they reached
declined advertisers were able to shift to cable television, to independent,
television stations, or to other advertising vehicles, to reach consumers.

Table 14 US advertising expenditure by classification, 1985 ($ million)

Medium	1985	Change over 1984(%)
Television	20,533	5·3
Newspapers	25,170	7·0
Magazines	5,155	4·5
Radio	6,490	11·6
Outdoor	945	8·3
Business papers	2,375	4·6
All other	34,082	10·3
Total	94,750	7·9

Source: McCann-Erikson.

New and improved advertising vehicles continually attempt to attract television advertising dollars. Traditionally there are billboards, newspapers, magazines, flyers, and radio. In the late 1980s new options included television screens on shopping carts, advertisements on video cassettes for resale and hire, and advertisements on split screens for supplying data services. Even advertisements at the movies made a return.

New competition put downward pressure on advertising rates. For the networks, whose prime-time ratings dropped by 9 per cent in 1988 over 1987 after falling 10 per cent in the previous three years, the new suppliers were a source of deep concern. In 1988 the independent broadcasters Tribune Company and Turner Broadcasting put together their own networks to offer broad reach to advertisers, previously a virtual monopoly of the networks, adding yet more to the networks' problems.

The big three broadcasting networks also came under attack as improved People Meter ratings services, introduced in 1987, were better able to tell advertisers how many and what sort of viewers got to see their advertisements. The new People Meters suggested that for years the networks had been overestimating their reach. Just as advertisers are uninterested in programme content so long as it reaches the potential consumer, so advertisers are uninterested in the vehicle used to reach them. Although traditionally the big three networks have attracted most of the dollars spent on television advertising, this is no longer guaranteed. Like viewers, advertisers have little loyalty to any particular network.

The growth of advertising approximately follows the business cycle. There is in addition a phenomenon that affects television advertising every four years in the United States to create the quadrennial effect. This is caused by the presidential election and the Olympic Games. These events attract viewers and so advertisers spend more. In 1988 expenditure, which had been flat at the networks for three years, increased by 11 per cent.

For cable operators it meant that in 1988 advertising revenue for the first time exceeded $1 billion.

Advertising agencies in the United States play an important intermediary role between the producers of goods and services and television. The agencies create the messages that, it is hoped, will attract viewers and potential customers. The messages must keep viewers from switching channels or zipping and zapping on their VCRs on recorded programmes. To be successful a commercial must get people to watch the message and then remember it in a positive manner. This is a formidable task. Table 15 lists the biggest advertising agencies in the USA and the world.

Table 15 The world's largest advertising agencies, with billings, 1987

	Company	Billings ($ million)	Nationality
1	Saatchi & Saatchi	11,360	UK
2	Dentsu	6,780	Japan
3	Interpublic Group	6,620	US
4	Omnicom Group	6,270	US
5	WPP Group	5,950	UK
6	Ogilvy Group	5,040	US
7	Young & Rubicam	4,910	US
8	Hakuhodo International	2,900	Japan
9	Eurocom	2,760	France
10	D'Arcy Masius B&B	2,490	US

Source: James Capel; *Advertising Age.*

The advertisers must avoid many pitfalls to get the message across. They want to avoid wasting the expenditure of up to a million dollars a minute at a SuperBowl, or, even worse, alienating potential customers. Since the late 1970s many advertisers have used celebrities to sell the product. The association of the celebrity and the product appears to bring results. PepsiCo paid Michael Jackson $5 million to promote Pepsi. Pepsi won a Clio advertising award in 1988 for a short adventure advertising story featuring Michael J. Fox. (A beautiful neighbour asks Fox for a Pepsi. He fights storms and motor-cycle gangs to get her one). Foreigners such as the Australian Paul Hogan, of *Crocodile Dundee* fame, selling Foster's beer and Robert Morley selling British Airways had great success in associating the foreign culture with the product.

Advertisers have also relied heavily on humour, since most consumers respond to it. Isuzu made people laugh with outrageous claims for their cars. They told customers the sports cars would go over 990 m.p.h. and that their wagons would hold more people than the Astrodome. These too won Clios.

Advertisers also hire some of the best film makers to produce slick and sophisticated advertisements. Adrian Lyne, who directed *Fatal Attraction*, has made advertisements for Kellogg's Special K cereal, for Ford, and for Revlon perfume. Advertisers can also link themselves with a popular movie. McDonald's paid $12 million to use characters from *Who Framed Roger Rabbit?* for their super-size fries and drinks. Quaker Oats paid $25 million for joint commercials and give-aways related to *Willow*. Not all succeed in selecting popular movies. Glad Bags spent $4 million to promote *Million Dollar Mystery*, a movie that ran for one week.

Advertisers may use novelty. For example, an Apple computer advertisement during the 1984 SuperBowl was shown just once, although it cost $500,000 to produce. Waiting to see the famous advertisement was nearly as big an event as the game itself. In 1988 PepsiCo offered $10,000 to the first person to call in at a specified time in the last quarter of the SuperBowl. This encouraged viewers to watch the game, and so the advertisements, to the end. It was a good strategy, since the game was won by half-time. In 1989 Coca-Cola gave away 20 million 3-D glasses for a $7 million half-time spectacular.

At all costs advertisers wish to avoid advertisements that turn the consumer away. A local advertisement is more likely to irritate the viewer and be repeated too often, but sometimes national advertisements backfire. A notable example was the Herb advertisement for the fast-food chain Burger King. The advertisements featured the awkward Herb, created for the advertisements, and prizes were given to consumers who identified the real live Herb as he travelled the Burger King chain of restaurants. However, Herb turned the viewers off and created an impression that dull, awkward, middle-aged losers ate at Burger King. Burger King fired the agency but the damage to the chain, which was competing with the always slick McDonald's, was enormous, leading to widespread franchisee disaffection. To avoid insulting and irritating advertisements that annoyed the consumer the motor manufacturers in 1988 initiated a policy under which they controlled much local car advertising. Local car dealers who sometimes acted like eleven-year-olds before the camera were not perceived as image builders for the manufacturers.

To encourage the advertising agencies in an increasingly shrill, cluttered, and competitive advertising world some agencies were paid bonuses based on market shares. Traditionally the agencies received 15 per cent of billings, which for major accounts can involve tens of millions of dollars. In the late 1980s as competition intensified and agency ownership changed they sometimes worked for less.

Although the effectiveness of advertising is hard to assess, making payment by results questionable, some advertisers began to pay by results in 1988, reflecting the increased competitiveness between agencies and also the advertiser's need to use the advertising budget effectively. The cigarette company R.J. Reynolds's vice-president for marketing said, 'We look at how well consumers recall an ad and whether the advertising generates strong emotional responses from consumers.'[7] On that basis bonuses and decisions about a $160 million per year advertising budget were made. Nissan, Campbell's Soups, and General Foods all introduced some sort of advertising price system based on measured results.

The Reynolds case reflected how difficult it is to measure the effects of advertising on sales, since the time lags involved are known. An agency may be paid a bonus or forfeit one because of the success or failure of earlier advertising or other factors. Late in 1988 the Supreme Court found that cigarette smoking was indeed addictive and awarded damages against a cigarette company based on its advertisements of thirty years before.[8] In other words the Supreme Court found not only that cigarette smoking is dangerous but that advertising is effective and was able to persuade people to smoke. Furthermore the Supreme Court's findings ratify the notion that advertisements could still be effective several years later in persuading consumers to buy a product.[9] That suggests that advertisements should be treated by accountants as an investment and not as an expense, which would make advertising more expensive to firms and decrease all advertising demand.

For a long time the hispanic market in the US was largely neglected as too poor and too small. In the late 1980s, in response to rapid income and population growth, advertisers re-evaluated the market.[10] For the first time advertisements were specifically written to meet hispanic demands. Together Philip Morris, Procter & Gamble, Coors, Anheuser-Busch, and McDonald's spent over $50 million in 1988.[11] The commercials were shown on both the Spanish-language networks, the dominant Univision and the smaller Telemundo.[12] These two companies dominated the hispanic market in the United States in 1988.

Children exert a powerful influence on how household income is spent. Children's television advertisements have created a lot of controversy because they are seen as encouraging materialism and consumerism amongst children. The US toy industry is a multi-billion dollar a year business where Hasbro and Mattel are two of the largest manufacturers. Both had 1988 revenues of over a billion dollars. Fashion dolls alone are worth nearly half a billion dollars in sales. Barbie is the most famous of all the dolls and has been around for thirty years. To protect the product Mattel spends over $20 million on television advertisements each year to plug the 200 Barbie products.[13] Hasbro and Mattel respectively also produce Transformers and Masters of the Universe, which together earned nearly half a billion dollars in 1987. Not that heavy television advertising guarantees sales and success. Coleco's Cabbage Patch dolls, unlike Barbie, lasted only a few years and in 1988 Coleco was in bankruptcy.

The desire of advertisers to reach consumers is therefore the driving force behind the US television industry. However, it is not the only way producers of goods and services can reach consumers, nor are advertisers the only groups interested in supporting television.

Direct selling, religious and political demand

If they could, advertisers would pay people outright to watch their message. They cannot, but since 1987 they have been able to sell direct to the consumer, using television without any programme breaks. With the growth of new supply sources such as cable, and as part of the Reagan policy of deregulation, government limits on the number of minutes per hour of advertisements by the networks were removed. This policy opened the way for all-advertising shows. Although common sense suggests that demand for an all-sales-pitch show in competition with a wide variety of expensive and slick entertainment shows would be limited, they have in fact had some success.

The most successful all-sales shows have been the shopping networks on cable television. These channels simply show items for sale and a phone number. By phoning in to one of the hundreds of operators who are available twenty-four hours a day the consumer can buy the item. It is a form of interactive television in that the viewer responds to the message. A common format involves a television host who intercepts some calls and treats the successful purchaser on television to a flattering congratulatory interview about the purchase. Nearly $2 billion worth of goods were sold in this way in 1988. The most successful of these networks were Home Shopping Network (HSN) reaching 45 million households in 1988, followed by Cable Value Network (CVN) reaching 19 million, and Quality Value Network (QVN) 12 million. By 1988 all the big retailers such as Sears and J.C. Penney had some sort of television sales venture planned.[14]

Another new sort of show since deregulation is shows which promote would-be personalities. Many people are flattered to appear on talk shows at no cost. However, shows such as *What's New?* on cable television charge people as much as $5,000 to appear on the show. Remarkably, given the rich choice of programmes available, some viewers choose to watch vanity television.

Religious television has played a small role since the beginning of broadcast television in most countries. However, in the 1970s and '80s religious television became big business in the United States. Then in 1987 and 1988 scandals set back ten years of phenomenal growth.

Table 16 Satellites over North America, with location 1987

C band			Ku band		
Name		Location	Name		Location
Spacenet	S2	69W	Spacenet	S2	69W
Satcom	F2	72W	Satcom	K2	81W
Galaxy	G2	74W	Satcom	K1	85W
Comstar	D4	76W	SBS	4	91W
Westar	W2	79W	SBS	3	95W
Satcom	F4	83W	SBS	2	97W
Telstar	T2	86W	SBS	1	99W
Westar	W3	91W	GStar	GS1	103W
Galaxy	G3	93W	GStar	GS2	105W
Telstar	T1	96W	Anik	C1	107W
Westar	W4	99W	Anik	C2	110W
Anik	AD1	104W	Morelos	M1	113W
Anik	D2	110W	Morelos	M2	116W
Morelos	M1	113W	Anik	C3	117W
Morelos	M2	116W	Spacenet	S1	120W
Spacenet	S1	120W	ASC	1	128W
Westar	W5	122W			
Telstar	T3	125W			
ASC	1	128W			
Satcom	F3	131W			
Galaxy	G1	134W			
Satcom	F1	139W			
Aurora	F5	143W			

Source: Satellite Entertainment Guide

Table 17 US religious television audiences per week, 1986 (million)

Swaggart	2·3
Schuller	1·7
Roberts	1·2
Falwell	0·6
700 Club	0·4
PTL	0·3

Source: Time.

Cable television created a new opportunity in the 1970s for a different brand of television religion. Fundamentalism replaced the traditional mainstream-denomination television services. Between 1982 and 1987 the number of religious television stations increased from sixty-two to 221. Over 30 million people could receive the daily *700 Club* on Christian Broadcast Network (CBN), the largest religious network. The next two largest networks were PTL and Trinity.

Fundamentalists offered two sorts of programming. One was that represented by PTL, run by Jimmy and Tammy Bakker. PTL's message was that God loves you. (The initials PTL stood for Praise the Lord, although some said they stood for Pass the Loot.) Their message was simple: God loves you, we all love you. Viewers were asked to subscribe to the show so that it could continue to broadcast. Those who subscribed would be repaid many times over and, it was suggested, repaid in this life as much as in the next. Before its fall PTL was reaching an audience of 13 million.

PTL fell when the highly charismatic Jimmy Bakker admitted to past sexual indiscretions and to paying a former church worker over $250,000 to remain silent about their affair. It was also disclosed that the Bakkers maintained an expensive life style, including an air-conditioned kennel for the dog, and had received over $4 million in the previous two years from PTL. In 1988 Bakker was under investigation for tax evasion and fraud on the grounds that he had misappropriated funds belonging to the tax-exempt religious group he led.[15]

The second type of religious broadcasting was the 'Hell and Damnation' brand. The message in this instance was that all are sinners and that the programme being shown is the way to avoid eternal damnation. In 1988 Jimmy Swaggart, a chief exponent of this sort of ministry, was disgraced by another sexual scandal, this time involving a prostitute. Bad publicity also surrounded a claim by another leading preacher, Oral Roberts, that if his viewers did not come up with another $8 million he would be called back to God.

The PTL and the Jimmy Swaggart sex scandals were setbacks for the religious television industry. Subsequently all the television ministries experienced a sharp decline in donations. It is likely that they will survive. Within two months Jimmy Swaggart had returned to television, having refused to submit to a one-year preaching ban imposed by his mother Church. He simply left the Church. As in so much of television the loyalty was to the star, not to the institution he worked for. The Bakkers returned in 1989.

Despite the scandals there is a strong demand for religion on television. Americans are a religious people. Ninety-four per cent believe in God and 40 per cent attend church each week. For many of the old, the poor, and the housebound religious television meets an unsatisfied demand. Huge numbers of Americans, up to 60 million a week, watch these programmes, which are slick and compelling. Studies show that those who actually contribute are frequently low-income earners. They also show that religious television complements rather than substitutes for church attendance, so increasing churchgoing.[16]

Religious programming relies almost entirely on contributors to cover the cost of buying air time from the local stations and cable operators as well as for producing the shows.[17] Contributions exceeded $1 billion in 1988, or four times what Congress allocated for public television. PTL alone received more in offerings than all the 40,000 churches in the powerful Southern Baptist Convention combined.

One consequence of these revenues is that Christian Broadcast Network is one of the largest cable companies in the United States. The host and head of CBN, Pat Robertson, was a candidate for the 1988 Republican nomination. The fact that he was a very real contender early on in the race who was taken seriously by all the other candidates and the press reflects the power of religious television in the United States. Before relinquishing his presidential ambitions for 1988 Robertson had spent over $20 million on promoting his campaign. The political importance of the new television religion was further reflected in the presence of President Reagan at the National Religious Broadcasters' Conference (NRBC) in 1988. The number of NRBC members had increased despite the sexual scandals surrounding some of the members and it was a lobby whose members he could not afford to ignore. In 1989 Vice-president Quayle addressed them to thank them for their support.

Political demand both for advertising time and for time on any news programmes during the long presidential race is unmatched outside the United States. In the six weeks before the presidential elections in November the parties spend two-thirds of their advertising budgets, some $60 million. Even then the parties have to be careful about how they advertise. With hindsight the Democratic Party concluded that the gloom-and-doom images of Jimmy Carter in 1980 and George Mondale in 1984 had failed to attract voters.[18] They put forward a more positive message for the 1988 candidate, Michael Dukakis. Nevertheless Dukakis was unable to throw off the image of being soft on criminals portrayed in a highly controversial but very successful advertisement supporting then Vice-president George Bush. Successful if 'dirty' television advertisements were given much of the credit for turning voters against the once leading Dukakis and producing the Bush victory in 1988.[19]

The hundred million or so dollars spent on the presidential candidates does not include the many tens of millions spent to buy television time by other candidates. Candidates at the federal, state, and municipal level all rely on television to ask for votes in a system where judges and school administrators as well as members of the different legislatures are elected.

Finally there is a demand for educational and public television, the sort of programming that dominated much of European television until the 1990s. But whereas government demand has traditionally dominated television programming in most countries such demand has always played a minor role in the United States. For 1988 the Congress voted $214 million for public television, less than what any of the networks budgeted just for their news divisions. Trusts, sponsors, and pledges provided the bulk of the revenue of public television, which in 1987 spent over $1 billion on programmes for minority interests. This was still less in total than half the revenue of the public systems of either Japan or Britain. Consequently the Public Broadcasting System (PBS) only partly met US demand for minority programming. A new tax on the sale of commercial broadcasting stations should provide future additional revenue of between $200 million and $300 million a year for PBS.

The changing nature of supply

Industrial organization literature on firm motivation is lengthy but inconclusive. Firms clearly do more than maximize profits, as assumed in most of the static world of economic theory. Show and flamboyance dominate television, and show-business motives are often complicated. When the networks dominated television there was sufficient monopoly profit to allow them and their programme suppliers some leeway to ignore the day-to-day discipline of profit and indulge in X-inefficiency. In the new competitive era profits play a bigger role. Shareholders and investors demand that those who run the television companies achieve financial success and those who don't go bankrupt.

However, entrepreneurs such as Ted Turner and Rupert Murdoch are prepared to take enormous risks. Exactly why is unclear; in part, it would appear, for the risk itself and the pleasure of seeing their empire grow.[20] Power, influence, and excitement also seem to play a part. Describing one project, Turner said, 'I'm like Indiana Jones. I went on an adventure.'[21] However, without profits none of those goals would be achieved, and it is the pursuit of profit which largely determines the supply of television in the United States.

The year 1976 is an appropriate point from which to date the beginning of the new media age in the United States and the rapid increase in television supply. In 1976 Home Box Office (HBO) was first offered on cable television as a pay service by Time Inc. Although the use of relay cable can be traced back to 1936 in the United States, of pay television to the 1950s, and of satellite distribution to the early 1960s, it was not until 1976 with HBO that the three technologies were merged into a commercially successful pay-cable operation.

Developments since 1976 are a harbinger for the rest of the world. Cable in the United States was already operated on a commercial basis, and this facilitated the introduction of the new delivery methods. Subsequently many other countries have concluded that the commercial model rather than the publicly financed model is the way to implement the new technologies. The way in which events have unfolded in the United States provides a lesson in the way events are likely to unfold in the rest of the Western world and possibly in other countries.

Until 1976 the dominant technology was broadcasting. The new methods of supply have dramatically changed the methods of programme delivery, and the age of television scarcity has been replaced by an age of abundance. The constraint on supply of limited broadcasting wavelengths has been overcome, and the four major supply vehicles – terrestrial broadcasting, satellite, cable, and VCRs – compete together. Yet although the delivery vehicles have changed the basic products have not. The raw materials of television are the shows. These can be broadly categorized as light entertainment, sports, educational and cultural, and news and documentaries. Light entertainment includes situation comedies, game shows, melodramas, and a variety of talk shows, entertainment gossip, films, and cartoons. New delivery methods mean more choice for the consumer, but up to 1989 in the US they mostly meant just more of the same sort of programming.

The key decision-makers in the industry who largely determine what programmes will be shown include a number of television executives who move easily between the three networks and the eight major programme suppliers. It has been said the industry is run by 200 people.[22] Under a 1970 consent decree with the FCC the networks gave up control of much programming and allowed independent programme producers a market in which to sell their productions. In fact programmes are supplied to the networks and the other television systems by a relatively small number of studios. The dominant studios are Columbia, Disney, MGM/UA, Orion, Paramount, Twentieth Century–Fox, Universal, and Warner.

One key decision-maker is Grant Tinker, who deserves a place in television history because he led NBC between 1983 and 1986 from being the perennial last-place network to being the leader in ratings and profits. He had earlier success in the industry when he and his wife, Mary Tyler Moore, set up Mary Tyler Moore Entertainment in the 1970s and produced such well received programmes as *The Mary Tyler Moore Show* and the innovative and highly acclaimed *Hill Street Blues*. Having led NBC to top place, Tinker wanted a new challenge. He chose as partner Gannett Corporation, the newspaper publisher which also owns ten television stations.

Gannett publish 124 newspapers in the United States but carved a place in the annals of the newspaper industry with their successful launch of America's first general-interest national daily. *USA Today* defied the critics, who said a general-interest national daily would not find a large enough market in regional USA to generate sufficient advertising revenue. The critics argued that national advertisers preferred television. Nevertheless by 1988 the paper enjoyed the second largest circulation in the United States and profitability.

Under Tinker Gannett spun off a television version of the newspaper with the same name, *USA Today*, and filled, like the newspaper, with consumer polls and information and frequent show-business interviews. In this way, with product diversification, Gannett entered the industry. Even before the programme was first aired in 1988 thirty-second spots on the show were selling for $125,000, second only to the popular game show *Wheel of Fortune* among the non-network programmes.[23]

Wheel of Fortune, along with *Jeopardy* and *The Oprah Winfrey Show*, are the products of the independent programme supplier to the independents called King World Productions Inc. King hit upon the winning *Wheel of Fortune* in 1983 and followed it with the other two shows. In 1988 the firm enjoyed profits of $100 million on revenues of $285 million but was unable to find another winning formula as the three shows began to age.[24] King reflected the problem of small producers who have to find successful formulas in quick succession if they are to survive.

The successful programme suppliers tend to be diversified companies who can use the other divisions to support them when the going is rough in the highly speculative process of predicting the fickle tastes of the viewer. Paramount provides only 12 per cent of Gulf & Western's revenues. For many studios debt is a way of life as they channel huge sums of money into shows which the odds show have only a one-in-ten chance of success. It is a high-risk business and even if a show is successful it may take years to make a profit. The sale price to a network at one time would cover the cost of production. By the late 1980s cost-conscious networks would pay about 80 per cent of the cost. The rest of the revenue from a show had to come from syndication. For shows like *M*A*S*H* syndicated revenues can be considerable, but shows usually have to run for three years to be worth syndicating. The independents who run syndicated material show it nightly, not weekly, so need a full supply. Failed producers in 1988 who two years earlier seemed to have the magic touch included Cannon Group and New World Entertainment, whilst De Laurentiis's stock had fallen to a thirtieth of its all-time high.

Waiting to enter the industry so that they can distribute and supply shows to the television viewer are the phone companies and other public utilities interested in diversifying out of slow-growth industries. It bears recalling that the first US radio network was operated by AT&T. In 1988 Houston Lighting & Power Company bought all the interests of Rogers Cable, Canada's leading cable supplier, in the United States for $1·4 billion. Houston was the first public utility to be allowed to enter the television industry. Both BellSouth, created out of AT&T when AT&T was dismembered in 1983, and Picturetel have developed sophisticated systems for interactive television, using optical fibre. Although the FCC has said it will urge Congress to allow the phone companies to provide cable, a Federal Court ruling still barred them from entry in 1988.[25]

Government and industry structure

Although the US television industry is a private-enterprise system the influence of government regulations on its structure is pervasive. The 1934 Communications Act legislated that the Federal Communications Commission should be responsible for allocating the finite and therefore scarce broadcast airwaves. In the 1950s the FCC concluded that it also had a responsibility for controlling cable television. Consequently in the United States the major vehicle by which federal government policy regarding television is carried out is the FCC.

Other federal institutions and legislation have important implications for the industry's structure and conduct. The Federal Trade Commission and the Supreme Court are both influential. For example, the FTC has examined 'advertorials' and in 1984 the Supreme Court concluded in the Sony Betamax case that it was legal for consumers to record programmes in their own home on a VCR. Free-trade legislation, the 1917 Espionage Act and the Sherman and Clayton Acts dealing with anti-combines legislation are all relevant. Table 18 summarizes the major pieces of relevant legislation.

Table 18 A selection of federal government legislation and regulations affecting the US television industry

1970	Federal Consent Decree limits networks' prime-time programming to create access period for independents
1979	Decision to increase number of independent broadcasters
1982	Removes anti-trafficking three-year rule
1983	Removes regulations on children's advertising
1984	Removes regulations on length of advertisements
1984	Replaces 7–7–7 rule with 12–12–12 rule (TV-AM-FM)
1984	Removes cable rate regulations in Cable Policy Act
1984	Betamax decision allows citizens to tape from TV
1984	Libel victory for CBS over General Westmoreland
1984	Federal Appeal Court strikes down 'must carry' laws
1985	Citizens permitted to own satellite dishes
1987	FCC junks the fairness doctrine
1987	Seven words maintained under indecency regulation
1987	Federal Court requires FCC guidelines on children's TV
1988	Congress imposes 2 per cent transfer fee on sale of television stations. Tax ($300 million p.a.) to PBS
1988	Congress threatens to re-regulate
1988	FCC reimposes syndicated exclusitivity rule

Source: Various.

State and local governments also pass legislation which affects the television industry. Most importantly local governments have the right to grant franchises to cable companies. As a consequence municipalities can impose the conditions under which cable companies operate. State laws, on the other hand, determine such things as the right to work. This affects whether suppliers have to use union labour and therefore where many programmes are produced.

Since 1980 the United States has followed a policy of deregulation in much of its economy, including the deregulation of much of the television industry. The two pro-free market chairmen of the FCC in the Reagan administration were Mark Fowler until 1987, followed by Dennis Patrick. Both men were dedicated to removing government involvement in television. Contrary to views held in other countries regarding the public interest, the FCC's approach has been that television is just another service. Mark Fowler called television a toaster with pictures and said that the public interest would determine the public interest.[26] The decision to maintain even some regulations for broadcasting was a compromise. Patrick wanted them all removed.

In contrast to broadcasting, the cable industry until the 1980s was still small and struggling. It was not regulated in its formative years, so as to encourage growth, and in the Reagan era, as it became more powerful in the market, remained unregulated.

One crucial policy change was the announcement for 1984 that the 7–7–7 ownership rule wold be replaced by a 12–12–12 rule. Firms could now hold twelve television, twelve AM radio, and twelve FM radio stations. However, no firm was allowed to reach more than 25 per cent of the market. That meant that small and intermediate-sized firms could buy more stations but that the networks, who already reached 25 per cent of the market with their large stations in the metropolitan centres, were still constrained in terms of growth.

The outcome of the relaxation on cross-ownership was a merger boom from 1985 to 1987, fuelled by the rise in the stock market. Take-over bids were levelled at all three networks, there was a concentration of power in the cable industry, and media conglomerates and firms in related industry vied to gain an advantage in the growing and fast-changing fields making up the new media.

The effect of deregulation in the 1980s has been considerable. Removing price controls on the cable industry in 1984, the FCC encouraged additional change in the structure and conduct of that sector. Granting licences for low-power television enabled more independent stations to enter the industry. Lower barriers to entry and fewer regulations have further helped in the decline of the three networks as new entrants have challenged their former monopoly.

Looking back, government policy was largely responsible for the US lead in television satellites in the 1980s. The lead can be traced back to the federal government and its response to the USSR Sputnik launch in the 1960s. Sputnik encouraged the US government to invest heavily in space technology so that even in 1988 the United States still dominated satellite launches, despite the 1986 setback of the Challenger shuttle disaster. In 1988 the United States had some fifty satellites in terrestrial orbit for communications purposes.

The broadcasting sector was dominated until 1975 by the three networks, ABC, CBS, and NBC. There were a small number of independent broadcasting stations and a few cable systems. The cable systems were used largely to redistribute broadcast programmes to areas out of range of the broadcasting transmitters. The independent broadcasters took second place in their markets to the affiliated stations. The recent economic history of the US television industry therefore is basically the story of new entrants and challengers to the established networks, previously a tight oligopoly.

The networks never actually owned most of the television systems. In 1952 the FCC limited the number of television stations they could own to seven. However, through affiliates, to whom they gave programmes in return for a share in their advertising time slots, the networks controlled the distribution and exchange of television programmes. Until the late 1970s an unaffiliated station had no means of acquiring the quality of programming that the networks could supply. For an unaffiliated station affiliation meant additional viewers and hence additional profits. Furthermore, since the networks owned the biggest stations in the largest urban areas, the barriers to the entry of new would-be networks were very high and in fact insurmountable.

Satellites and cable led to a restructuring of the industry, a restructuring that was still going on as the 1980s drew to a close. Satellites and cable lowered barriers to entry, allowing a dramatic increase in the number of sellers in the industry. In the '80s VCRs finally became popular and further modified the television industry context.

Cable

The cable sector was transformed by satellites. Before 1975 cable had been mainly a broadcasting appendage facilitating the distribution of television to hard-to-reach places. In 1975 Time Inc.'s Home Box Office transmitted the Ali–Foreman 'Thriller in Manilla' world heavyweight boxing match via satellite to its subscribers on cable television in New Jersey. The success of this experiment encouraged HBO to go to a nationwide facility to distribute movies by satellite to cable systems all over the United States. Local cable companies could offer HBO for an extra charge to those already using cable to reach network television.

Soon after the HBO launch the then unknown Ted Turner had the brilliant idea of sending the signal from his UHF station, WTBS, in Atlanta, Georgia, via the same satellite as HBO to cable operators nationwide. His insight was to realize that by charging local cable companies just a dime for each subscriber to his station both he and they could make money. He persuaded cable companies already offering HBO to add his station to their HBO package at no extra cost. This would make their cable package more attractive to potential subscribers and increase cable demand. The cable company would sign up more subscribers to HBO and as a result increase revenues by more than the dime a subscriber that it paid for WGTN.[27]

By 1977 HBO was making a profit. Cable was offering something more than the same network fare. Imitating HBO, new entrants began to package more programmes for cable. As cable began to offer more choice subscribers with good broadcast reception also began to sign up in increasing numbers. When this happened it was apparent that the potential cable market was enormous. The cable era was under way. There was a rush to build cable systems and to supply programming to them. Newspaper publishers, oil companies, financial services, retailers, broadcasters, and film producers all entered the industry. By 1980 there were fifty national programme services, such as the Movie Channel, Cable News Network, Black Entertainment Television, and ESPN, available.

Table 19 Leading US satellite-delivered advertiser-supported basic cable services, 1987

Service	Reach (million)	Description
ESPN	39	Twenty-four hour sports
WTBS-TV	38	Turner 'super-station'
Cable News Network (CNN)	36	Turner's News, Weather, Sports
SIN Television Network	34	Spanish-language
CNN	33	Second Turner CNN
USA Network	33	Family programming
Music Television (MTV)	31	All-stereo music video
Headline News	30	Turner's 24 hour news
Nickelodeon	29	Children and teens

Source: CSP International Ltd.

A most important decision by the FCC was that the power to grant a franchise for a cable operation lay with the local government, usually the municipality. Municipalities gave the franchise to those who offered the best service, supposedly in the public interest. Sometimes they also received 5 per cent of gross revenue. However, since the maximum payment was 5 per cent the competition between aspiring cable franchisees was in terms of the extra services they would supply. Given the belief that future profits could be considerable, the bidding often led to promises of elaborate and unnecessary services. For example channels for public schools and for private schools on systems with 108 channels. Since contenders were unable to bid with dollars, the allocation procedure inefficiently auctioned off cable franchises to those who promised most services.[28]

The resulting situation on any particular cable system was one of intense competition beforehand to the right to the franchise and then a monopoly afterwards by whoever won for the duration of the franchise, usually fifteen years. Cable systems are natural monopolies in the sense that slinging two sets of wires along the telephone poles or digging two sets of ditches to lay cable underground is an obvious waste of resources. Holding a cable monopoly appeared very attractive, hence there was high bidding to get a franchise.

By the early 1980s it was apparent that there had been overbidding. In many big cities the municipalities held out for too much and nobody met the requirements. Although, once it has been built, the costs of running a cable system are moderate, the capital costs are very high. For many franchisee start-ups cash-flow problems in the early years meant the systems were not completed. For others, once the system was built the local municipalities regulated subscriber prices, so the anticipated high profits did not materialize. Consequently as late as 1985 there was no cable in New York city. In Chicago the original plan had been scaled down. In Pittsburgh the franchisee had pulled out. Washington D.C.'s system was embroiled in legal battles and Philadelphia had made five awards, the first four backing out. Cities such as Pittsburgh, Chicago, Washington, and St Louis eventually settled for bare-bone systems, far inferior to the first proposals.

Cable operators found that, once in place, they could not usually hold the local authorities to ransom. In one case in 1973 the then fledgling TeleCommunications Inc. (TCI) turned the programmes off in Vail, Colorado, and transmitted a picture of the local mayor with a caption blaming him for the shut-down. The mayor permitted the rate increase, but that was not the way things usually went. For if a local community felt really badly treated and closed the cable down, then it left both parties in a losing situation. The local community would have no cable television, but the cable operator would have no cash flow. The cable operator could not take the system away.

Deregulation in the mid-1980s ushered in merger mania in the cable television industry. In 1984 Congress removed the power of local authorities to regulate prices. Subscriptions were totally deregulated by 1987. Consequently the prices of independent broadcasting stations and cable operator systems began to escalate, reflecting the rise in their potential profitability. With most of the capital costs of cabling the nation undertaken, the cash-flow prospects for cable were excellent following deregulation. A period of concentration and rationalization began.

TCI had bought 750,000 subscribers from UA Communications in 1985 for $1,000 each. In 1986 456 cable companies changed hands for a total value of $8·9 billion. That represented a price of about $1,750 per subscriber. In 1987 the price per subscriber rose to nearly $2,000, or nine times the average annual basic cable service fee in 1987. The stock market has been a good forecaster of industry success and failure in the past, so clearly many investors were optimistic about cable's future. By 1988 the price per subscriber had risen to $3,000, reflecting the rapid rise in cable charges.

Prices for basic cable services rose by 30 per cent in 1986 and 50 per cent in 1987, albeit for more channels. In 1987 cable ratings grew by 24 per cent and subscriptions to pay channels by 14 per cent. By 1988 over 80 per cent of households had access to cable and 52 per cent were signed up. This represented 45 million households paying over $13 a month, in total some $7 billion. The rule of thumb was that as viewers defected from the networks half went over to cable and half went to VCRs.

By 1988 TCI had come to a commanding lead in the industry, with twice as many subscribers as Time Inc.'s ATC. In 1988 TCI enjoyed revenues of $2 billion, four times the 1985 figure, and had a cash flow greater than the three networks combined. The value of its assets exceeded $15 billion, making it the 174th largest company in America. Although the name is less familiar to most television viewers than the names of the networks, by the end of the decade TCI was more powerful and influential than any of the networks in the USA. Not only was TCI the largest cable operator in the country, it had interests in four of the top six cable companies and in over thirty other cable systems. Since 1985 TCI has owned United Artists, the largest cinema chain in the country. TCI has further interests in two of the top three home-shopping channels, movie channels, entertainment channels such as Discovery and the Entertainment Channel, video stores, and, since 1988, Ted Turner's TBS.

TCI's rise was dramatic. It avoided the overbidding of the late 1970s and early '80s and picked up cable companies in difficulties or frustrated by the doldrums of the early 1980s. TCI then negotiated bare-bone systems and cut costs ruthlessly. For example, in Pittsburgh, the losing Warner-Amex system was bought out for $93 million, the number of channels cut from sixty to forty-nine, the payroll was nearly halved, and losses were transformed into profits. TCI has a reputation for being equally ruthless with cable programmers. NBC abandoned plans for an all-news service in 1985 when TCI offered low rates. Both ESPN and MTV (a channel showing non-stop music videos from the top forty) came off second best to the monopsony power of TCI. Without TCI's 8 million subscribers they would have been undermined in the market, whereas

TCI could survive without them. TCI could use alternative similar programmes if any were available or else encourage their start by guaranteeing a market. TCI used its gatekeeper power to extract discounts of up to 30 per cent from cable programme suppliers.

If these monopsony practices led to lower prices and better service to the consumer TCI would have used its gatekeeper position in the public interest. There were stories of consumer complaints which suggested that such was not always the case. In Springfield, Oregon, 500 citizens stormed the TCI offices when rates were doubled in a period of two years and the PBS channel was cancelled and replaced by home shopping in 1987.[29] In 1988 TCI was fined $44 million following an incident in Jefferson City in 1981. The city council, unhappy with the TCI service, tried to get TCI to leave when its licence expired the next year. TCI threatened to sue the city, undermine any new franchisee, let the cables rot rather than sell them, and said it would sell satellite dishes at low prices.[30]

Concentration in the cable industry was increased yet further in 1988 when a consortium of TCI, ATC, and Taft Cable bought out SCI, the fourth largest cable system in the United States, with 1·45 million subscribers. Also in 1988 United Communications and United Cable merged, to become the third largest cable company in the United States, with 2·2 million subscribers. TCI owned a major share of the former and a large share of the latter, so that TCI ended up with 52 per cent of the new company. TCI's size was of concern to critics in the press and the government. Fearful of restrictions in the event of a Democratic victory in 1988, TCI acquired as many companies as it could before the election. It was also restructured into six separate divisions so that a forced break-up, such as that imposed on AT&T, would not be a disaster.[31]

Meanwhile potential new entrants were waiting to challenge TCI and the cable operators. The telephone companies and the networks both hoped that they might be allowed by the FCC to own cable operators. These aspirations fuelled the rise in the price paid per subscriber in take-overs. The entry of the networks and the phone companies promised a new round of take-overs at yet higher prices.

There are economies of scale and scope in cable, and TCI exploited them to the full. Economies of scale and scope are derived from the ability to package programmes and from marketing. TCI played a 'godfather' role for channels such as CBN, Arts and Entertainment Channel, and Black Entertainment Channel, guaranteeing them huge audiences. In return TCI received discounts.

Between 1985 and 1988, following several years of stagnation in the early and mid-1980s, cable therefore established itself as a major distribution vehicle of television programming. Advertising revenue grew from $380 million in 1983 to $1·4 billion in 1988. Media conglomerates with an interest in the industry included most of the major newspaper companies. Time Inc., New York Times, Knight Ridder, Hearst, Tribune, and Times-Mirror all had cable systems.

Time Inc. had been the major cable system operator in 1978 when it bought ATC. However, a number of failures, such as its cable magazine *TV-Cable* in 1984 and a loss of confidence in cable at about the same time, exemplified by the sale of USA Network, allowed TCI to overtake ATC. By 1988 TCI was more than twice the size of ATC, with over 8 million subscribers. Reflecting the importance of timing, TCI diversified and produced a cable magazine, *Cable Week*, distributed to over eight million subscribers to support its cable operations. Time Inc, had acted too early.

Cable is capable of delivering many services as well as television. Not all its potential uses, many of which are highly imaginative and technically sohisticated, have had success, and many suppliers have lost money. Interactive television, or videotext, attracted the newspaper companies as well as finance companies and retail stores in the 1970s and 1980s. Unlike one-way cable, interactive cable met with a lukewarm response despite its apparent attractiveness in terms of the variety of services it could offer. Knight Ridder, for example, lost $30 million on a system that offered home banking yet attracted just 4,000 users. Videotext failed because the cost to the consumer of using the services was simply too high. This was the case everywhere in the world with videotext, except in France, where government subsidies made using videotext a national pastime.

Satellites and programme supplies

Satellites were the *sine qua non* of the multi-band cable industry, releasing cable from its dependence on broadcasting. Medium-power satellites were originally intended for the transmission of long-distance telephone signals, including videosignals only as an afterthought. The video signals were intended not for private households but to send programmes from distributors to exhibitors, for example from a network to its affiliates. Until 1984 it was illegal for private citizens to use dishes to pluck signals from the air and enjoy a free ride on the programmes they carried. Nevertheless by then half a million US households had dishes, which they used to enjoy abundant television. The dishes were most popular in remote areas with poor broadcast signals.

The first commercial satellite was Telstar and the first satellite company was COMSAT, a private company set up by Congress in 1962 with stock held by the general public and by Western Union and RCA. In due course other corporations launched satellites for the transmission of data. By 1988 there were over fifty US satellites in orbit on the C band and KU band. Each C-band satellite can carry up to twenty-two channels on its transponders, whilst each K band can carry three high-power channels. All in all, with two degrees separating each satellite, about 900 miles, there is room for some 900 channels, with 1988 technology, over America. It is estimated that the three networks need thirty channels each and the public system needs four channels, leaving plenty of space for other distributors of television. The satellite companies supply the transponders to the television distributors on leases at prices that range between $1 million and $3 million per year.[32]

Initially the programme distributors intended their satellite signals only for rebroadcasting. In 1975 a receiving dish from a C-band satellite might cost $150,000. As technology improved the cost of dishes fell. Ku-band satellites involve technology inversion, meaning that as the satellite gets more powerful the dishes can be smaller and cheaper. In the late 1970s people in isolated areas unable to get a good broadcast signal began to buy dishes at a cost of $10,000 or more. So did apartments, hotels, and bars as a means of attracting customers. They could pull in the dozens of signals being transmitted to television exhibitors. By the early 1980s, as dish prices continued to fall, the number of people using dishes to pluck free television out of the air was sufficient to encourage some of the distributors to scramble their signals, for example HBO.[33] By 1988 out of 132 channels over sixty were scrambled and dish owners were paying monthly fees for descramblers, similar to the monthly fees paid to subscribe to cable. The effect of scrambling was to cut dish sales by two-thirds, to a quarter of a million annually.

It is possible for direct broadcast satellites to deliver television direct from the satellite to the home, using high-powered satellites. CBS television planned to begin DBS in the United States in 1985. However, progress was delayed after many satellite launches had been postponed following the 1986 Challenger disaster. Then as CBS fortunes declined the DBS plans were shelved. Thus whereas the United States led the way in both broadcast television after the war and in cable in the late 1980s, progress in DBS has been slow to develop in the United States. Japan began DBS in 1987, and for 1989 and 1990 Europe had plans to go ahead with DBS. Meanwhile in the United States DBS was on hold.

The increased derived demand for television programmes by the new distributors affected all sectors of the media. For the film industry television and VCRs became the major market, replacing the box office. In New York rentals of movies for VCRs rose by fifty-two times between 1982 and 1987. By 1986 over 50 per cent of American homes owned a VCR and rented over four movies each month on average. Consequently box office revenues in the United States for films were $1·6 billion whilst sales and rentals for home consumption exceeded $2 billion. However, VCRs were a two-edged sword for Hollywood. They also had the effect of making the television networks reluctant to show movies already shown on pay cable or available on video cassette.

For one programme supplier, the Disney Corporation, television proved to be its salvation. Disney productions were once a mainstay of television but by the early 1980s Disney were rarely seen and seemed to have been by-passed. Then, following speculation about take-overs and decline, Disney were revitalized. They started the Disney channel in 1984 and within four years over 3 million households were subscribing to their wholesome fare. Started at the same time as the Playboy channel, Disney by 1987 had attracted four times as many subscribers as the struggling Playboy. Meanwhile Playboy's rival Penthouse channel had folded after a brief entry into the market. Once the curiosity of television pornography has been experienced, long-term viewer interest wanes. Video cassettes serve that market better for occasional use. Demand for quality light entertainment on television endures, and this has been the source of Disney's success. Based on their stock of old Disney material, and meeting a demand for family and children's fare, Disney attracted subscribers. Families less than satisfied with network children's television, or wanting alternative babysitting, made the rival Nickelodeon channel a success also.

Disney also concentrated on providing programmes such as *The Golden Girls* and *Disney Sunday Movie* for the networks. To the independents Disney distributed the popular *Siskel and Ebert at the Movies*. Their own production of movies increased from ten in 1986 to sixteen in 1987. To cover all the bases in the entertainment pipeline Disney also bought cinemas, aggressively exported Disney video cassettes, exploited their library of old cartoons and films, and built theme parks in Europe and Asia. There were even rumours in 1989 that Disney might integrate downstream and take over the once mighty CBS.

Table 20 Revenues and profits at the major US networks, 1982–7, ($ billion and $ million respectively)

	ABC		CBS		NBC	
Year	Revenue ($b)	Profit ($m)	Revenue ($b)	Profit ($m)	Revenue ($b)	Profit ($m)
1982	2·3	305	2·2	280	1·8	105
1983	2·6	371	2·4	301	2·1	152
1984	3·3	408	2·7	412	2·4	210
1985	3·1	418	3·8	375	2·7	318
1986	3·1	510	2·8	245	3·0	434
1987[a]	3·5	600	2·9	208	3·2	480

Note:
a Estimate.
Source: Company reports.

Less well known producers such as King also benefited from the growth of the non-network market. In 1988 the secondary market was worth over $3·5 billion. In contrast each network spent about $1 billion each to purchase prime-time material. Although the secondary market included reselling network syndicated programmes, the importance of the networks as a purchaser of programmes was declining markedly.

The repercussions on broadcasting

Broadcast television went through a brutal mid-life crisis during the 1980s. It was a mature industry at the beginning of the decade whose structure had remained little changed for four decades. It had grown fat after years of operating as a tight oligopoly. In the 1980s the industry had to deal with the new media of satellites, cable, and VCRs, and also new forms of low-power broadcasting and merger mania. As a result all three networks came under new management.

At ABC and NBC new owners, Capital Cities and General Electric respectively, brought a reputation for cost-consciousness. Between 1981 and 1987 the chairman of GE, John Welch, sold off more than 230 GE businesses. After buying RCA he quickly sold the television production unit to Thomson of France. At CBS in 1987 cost-cutting included axing over 200 staff from the news division and an agreement to pay the former chairman, Thomas Wyman, $400,000 per year for life as well as a lump sum of nearly $3 million. Laurence A. Tisch, a financier and major shareholder, replaced Wyman in 1986.

One of the first groups to be affected by the cost-cutting was labour. In 1988 the most publicized strike was the twenty-two-week-long strike by the Writers' Guild of America, but the desire to replace labour with capital – for example, one-man cameras – and to use temporary technicians created other strikes. Another group to be affected were the studios which produced most of the prime-time shows for the networks. They too felt the pressure to cut costs reflected in fewer car chases, location shootings, and similar expensive trimmings. Still, such measures alone were inadequate to stop the fall in network profits and market share.

The networks responded to the new environment in different ways. ABC and NBC continued to attempt to move into the new media. As the FCC slackened regulation both these networks acquired additional broadcasting stations. They also attempted to use their production facilities to produce programmes for the independent stations and for cable, although they could not own the cable operators.

NBC offered Ted Turner $300 million for his Cable Network News (CNN) in 1985. When CNN rejected the bid NBC planned their own all-news channel but abandoned it because of a price squeeze from TCI. In 1988 NBC announced that they were starting a new business news channel, even though business news has not had great success on television. Television serves the tired, the old, and the bored, not businessmen. The new channel, Consumer News and Business Channel (CNBC), announced that it would run consumer-oriented features about money matters. This time TCI announced that they would carry the new channel to over 4 million homes.

The scale of the operation suggested that NBC had other plans for CNBC. First-year costs were $79 million to cover programming, marketing, administration, and the hire of a transponder. The anticipated strategy was that the emphasis on business news would decline and that CNBC would then become a challenger to CNN. In this way NBC could enter the market without a direct challenge to CNN.

Meanwhile pint-sized Capital Cities, valued at about one-fifth of ABC, acquired ABC in a friendly reverse take-over in 1985. The new management began to cut costs, to encourage ABC's emphases on sport, and to expand into cable. ABC had done well with ESPN, which it had bought from Texaco for $202 million after Texaco had bought out Getty Oil, which owned ESPN. ESPN earned $65 million in profits in 1987 and was estimated to be worth $1 billion. Nevertheless new entrants to the supply of cable sport such as the regional networks threatened ESPN in 1988. Also to cut costs in the entertainment division ABC used only some of the stars of the series *Dynasty* in each episode in order to cut costs of $1·6 million per episode.

CBS, the only network not to have been taken over in the previous three years, adopted a policy of staying with broadcasting. Like ABC, CBS had invested in cable programming in the early 1980s and lost money. Under Laurence Tisch, CBS's record division was sold to Sony for $2 billion, whilst the magazine division was sold to an independent group for $1·6 billion, both in 1987.

CBS had for years been the top station in the United States. It had a reputation for quality, particularly in news, where standards had been set by the legendary Ed Murrow and later by Walter Cronkite.[34] In the early 1980s, under the influence of Fred Silverman, first ABC and then NBC revamped their programme format and tipped CBS from its pedestal. Then in 1985 a right-wing group called Fairness in Media, headed by Jesse Helms and including Ted Turner and the inside trader Ivan Boesky, made a bid for CBS valued at $5·4 billion. Ninety-seven groups opposed the Fairness in Media take-over. Still, CBS had to spend over a billion dollars to repel the take-over and buy back 25 per cent of its own shares. The buy-back required borrowings whose service charges ate heavily into the cash flow. There was a rapid deline in the corporation's profitability. For 1987 CBS profits fell by 87 per cent, and in 1988 CBS made its first quarterly loss for fifty years.

After the Fairness in Media bid CBS appointed Laurence Tisch, and under him CBS sold off non-broadcasting divisions and created a

The world television industry

Table 21 The largest television suppliers and distributors in the United States, 1987

Group composite	Top 1000 rank	1988 market value ($ million)
1 Capital Cities/ABC	73	5,962
2 Tele-communications	121	4,273
3 CBS	137	3,924
4 LIN Broadcasting	184	2,930
5 American TV & Communications	198	2,723
6 Viacom	392	1,347
7 United Cable Television	421	1,262
8 Comcast	447	1,174
9 Scripps Howard Broadcasting	596	780
10 Multimedia	615	732
11 Cablevision Systems	642	683
12 Turner Broadcasting System	714	577

Note: General Electric, owner of NBC, ranked third (Gannett ranked sixty-sixth, Tribune ranked 172nd).
Source: *Business Week*.

cash hoard of over $3 billion. The down-sized CBS had adopted a strategy despite the turmoil in the industry of concentrating on its basic product.

The flamboyant Ted Turner, founder of CNN, has added colour to the industry ever since 1977. A week after his failure to acquire CBS he made the error of paying $1·5 billion for the MGM/UA library of old films. This vertical integration gave him programming for his Turner Broadcasting Systems. However, he overpaid by nearly a billion dollars, according to some analysts, and by 1987 was having difficulty meeting interest payments.[35] As a result he let Time Inc. buy a 10 per cent interest in TBS. Although in 1988 when NBC approached TBS to buy CNN their approach was rebuffed, later in the year as his debts mounted he had to give in to a consortium of cable companies, headed by TCI. The consortium acquired a controlling interest in TBS. Late in the year TBS launched another new cable network called the Turner Network (TNT).

Increased competition and the fragmentation of the market have changed the industry's structure and put pressure on the networks. Amidst the turmoil of change the best hope for the broadcasting networks is a change in the regulations that prohibit them from owning cable systems and syndicating their own old shows. The policy stance of the FCC towards regulation in the 1980s would not rule this out. Currently the networks may produce programmes for cable systems. However, the programmes they buy and produce for broadcasting cannot be resold by them to cable and the independents. Rather, they must let syndicators sell them, thus transferring considerable profits to the syndicators such as Viacom International. Viacom made profits of $200 million just on reselling the first collection of *The Cosby Show*. If the government let the networks syndicate their own old shows and own cable systems, then the networks would have better prospects. Instead the current regulations work towards lowering the concentration of the television industry by restricting the established broadcasting networks.

There were many new entrants into the broadcast sector when the FCC in 1979 authorized low-power broadcast television. Low-power broadcast television has a range of only a few miles, which as broadcasters gave stations a small market area. The new independent television stations found a new larger market thanks to cable, which under 'must carry' provisions had to carry all local stations. Consequently the number of independent stations grew from ninety-five in 1978 to 250 in 1987. Distributed by cable and using first syndicated shows and programmes from independent suppliers, the new independents could be viable without depending on network programming. Indeed, independent broadcasting was so attractive that some cable operators, for example Tribune Company, sold off their cable systems so that they could buy into broadcasting. Tribune sold nine cable systems so that the FCC would let it buy the KTLA station in Los Angeles.

A fourth national network has been contemplated in the past but never realized. The increase in the number of independent stations and the capacity of cable encouraged several firms to put together a number of stations into embryo networks. Tribune was one such contender to create a fourth network. Tribune is primarily a newspaper company, which publishes the *Chicago Tribune* and owns the Chicago Cubs baseball team as well as an assortment of newspapers and television stations. By 1987 Tribune television stations could reach 20 per cent of the population. As well as KTLA Tribune purchased stations in Chicago, New Orleans, New York, and Atlanta. Tribune also produced shows, including the widely shown *At the Movies* and *Dempsey and Makepeace*.

However, the most notable attempt to start a new network was that made by Rupert Murdoch with Fox in 1987. Fox Broadcasting traces its roots back to the purchase of Twentieth Century–Fox, the film company, film library, and television programme producer, in 1984. The purchase was a joint venture between Marvin Davis of Metromedia and Rupert Murdoch. Both put up $250 million. When Marvin Davis changed his plans Murdoch bought him out. Murdoch then paid $1·6 billion for Metromedia. The purchase gave Murdoch television stations in six major US markets: New York, Los Angeles, Chicago, Washington, Houston, and Dallas.

Murdoch has always been an innovator and a risk-taker. The Metromedia stations were not the biggest in those markets but they gave him an entry to them. He had run a satellite television channel called Sky for several years in Europe and perceived that with the change in technology in the 1980s there was a chance that a new broadcasting network could be created. He needed access to the major markets. With the Metromedia purchase he had access, even if his stations were not currently the market leaders. Murdoch appreciated that consumers and advertisers are not loyal to stations. Having bought the library of old Twentieth Century–Fox movies he had a plentiful supply of programming. Twentieth Century–Fox also produced such popular shows as *People's Court* and *Entertainment Tonight*. With a strategy that he called counter-programming – that is, programmes supposedly different from the networks' – it would be possible to cream off viewers from all the networks.

Nevertheless the notion of a truly powerful fourth network, like CBS was in the 1970s, is an idea whose time has passed. With fragmentation of the viewer market the networks as a tight oligopoly have had their day. By 1988 80 per cent of American homes were passed by cable and over 50 per cent of homes had signed up, so that the big cable companies such as TCI had become the new gatekeepers of what the viewer sees.

By 1988 the fastest-growing area of the United States television market was hispanic television. This market is obviously separated by language, since for entertainment even multilingual people prefer their own language. In 1988 130 stations, mostly in Texas, Arizona, and California were broadcasting either part-time or full-time in Spanish. Furthermore hispanics watch 32 per cent more television than the rest of the population.[36] The most popular show on hispanic television in the late 1980s was *Sabado Gigante*, a three-and-a-half hour live show along the lines of the famous *Ed Sullivan Show* of the '60s. The show offered a mix of stars, dancing, and comedy and was an attractive vehicle for advertisers.

The hispanic advertising market doubled between 1983 and 1988 to nearly half a billion dollars. As the incomes of hispanics increased even the networks focused more attention on the hispanic market. One estimate forecast a $2·5 billion advertising market by 1992.[37] To gain an entry CBS planned a fourteen-hour mini-series called *El Pueblo/LA* which paralleled the recognition of blacks in the *Roots* mini-series in the 1970s. Other shows such as *Bravo* began to broadcast with sound tracks in both languages.[35]

Integration and costs

The 1980s saw both vertical and horizontal integration in the television industry. Deregulation permitted the broadcasting networks to integrate vertically backwards into production and produce more of their own prime-time shows. Murdoch and Turner bought up supplies of old movies at high prices so as to feed their new television networks. With deregulation and a technology-induced fragmentation of the industry most media conglomerates developed interests in a number of industry sectors – including video production, broadcasting, cable, satellite, or video cassette – and in other sectors of the media: films, newspapers, magazines, recordings, radio, and publishing. Diversification was a strategy for spreading risks amid the turmoil and uncertainty.

Costs in the industry involve capital costs, overhead costs, and input costs. Costs vary enormously from the fairly low costs of starting up a UHF broadcasting station to the huge costs involved in acquiring a major stake in the industry. GE paid $6·4 billion to acquire RCA and the NBC network in 1986, and Capital Cities bought ABC for $3·6 billion. In the restructuring of the industry that took place in the 1980s, internal growth was too slow a path to a significant share of the market. To acquire industry share, mergers were necessary. As a result of mergers, in 1988, in terms of reach by broadcasting, Metromedia (Fox) ranked fourth and Tribune ranked fifth. Ahead of them were the three networks, two of which had recently been bought out. In cable TCI paid out over $3 billion from 1984 to 1987 to acquire 150 cable operators.

Operating costs in television also vary widely. At the networks, where the labour unions have a greater presence, where personality people receive enormous retainers, and where fat has accumulated for years, costs tend to be higher than at local stations. At NBC 2,800 technicians and workers belonged to the National Association of Broadcast Employees and Technicians. Another 11,000 workers at the networks belonged to twenty-one other unions, including the International Brotherhood of Electrical Workers and the Writers' Guild.

Labour accounts for 75 per cent of the budget of a network news division. Each of the major networks news divisions employs about eighty full-time reporters. Regularly $100,000 news features are made yet never shown. When a half-hour news segment costs on average half a million dollars such apparent waste can be economic. They are fillers, to be replaced if a major news story breaks. Features make up 60 per cent of a news budget, which at CBS for 1987 was $300 million. All the major networks laid off staff in the mid-1980s, attempting to reduce costs. At NBC the news staff fell by 300 from 1986 to 1988 after the news division lost $200 million in 1986. At CBS after the hostile take-over bid by Fairness in Media and Ted Turner some 230 staff out of 1,230 and $30 million from the budget were cut. Meanwhile, reflecting what a low-cost operation can achieve, Fox Broadcasting employed only seventy full-time staff in 1987.

The costs of the programmes, whether produced internally or bought from a supplier, vary very widely. One episode of *Moonlighting* in

1987 cost $3·1 million.[39] The average prime-time show cost about $1 million per hour. News programmes cost about half a million per hour. Game shows are very cheap to produce but they are risky and only a few achieve the popularity of *Jeopardy* or *Wheel of Fortune*. However, *Wheel of Fortune* earned revenues of $125 million on costs for a full season of $7 million in 1987. It will be recollected that in 1985 Ted Turner paid $1.5 billion for part of the MGM/UA film library, even though some of the movies had been shown on network television already. The 2,000-odd movies were good reusable fodder for his television systems. On the other hand, local community programmes need be little more than home movies made with a camcorder. By the end of the 1980s there were over 10 million video cameras in American households, and increasingly their footage was sold as news, even to the networks, when unexpected disasters struck.

The networks try to get the maximum return from their news departments. This means producing current affairs shows as well as the morning and nightly news programmes. Shows such as the highly rated *Sixty Minutes* by CBS allow the news department to spread joint costs. In an attempt to keep costs down CBS continued to show two low-rated news shows *Forty-eight Hours* and *West 57th*. This made economic sense because news shows are cheaper to produce than entertainment shows and the lower advertising revenue received during those shows was more than offset by the lower costs of producing them.[40] Such shows also enhanced the public image of CBS, but not its ratings nor its Wall Street image.

In any event low-cost strategies are not always a winner. Revenue can fall faster than costs. In 1987 one independent network was created by TVX Broadcasting Group in Virginia by buying up stations. The chief executive officer of TVX defined his strategy: 'You find the cheapest stuff you can find – movies, old re-runs, Fox programs – and you fill 'er up . . . Hell, there are a lot of people out there that are going to watch static, so it's foolish to pay for anything better than that.'[41] TVX lost $48 million in its first year.

One example of a successful ultra-low-cost network was that put together by presidential candidate Michael Dukakis in 1988 during the Iowa primary. Rather than buy advertising time he bought programming time on a number of local television stations and set up his own temporary network. The total cost of reaching 1.5 million homes from his Des Moines headquarters was $15,000. Another low-cost operation is the smallest CBS affiliate, which operates in Glendire, Montana. With a staff of eight full and part-time employees and a highest salary of $14,000, total costs were kept below a quarter of a million dollars for 1987.

Beneficiaries of increased demand for programmes are the stars, who get stellar salaries. Charismatic actors attract viewers. TV's top-paid star in 1987 was reportedly Bill Cosby, with earnings approaching the $100 million mark. Sylvester Stallone got $20 million for the movie *Rambo III* in anticipation of high video returns. Dan Rather of the CBS Evening News made $2.5 million in 1988 for reading the news. Tom Brokaw, anchor man on the news at NBC, made nearly $2 million, whilst Peter Jennings of ABC made less than $1 million. Andy Rooney, who adds a few words of wisdom on such topics as the variety of bathroom taps at the end of the CBS programme *Sixty Minutes*, received $400,000 in 1988, whilst another reporter on the show, Diane Sawyer, received $1·2 million. Religious television too depends on the personal charisma of its star preachers to attract donations.

Often the stars are worth such sums to those who pay them. In the high-risk business of producing television shows the stars often make or break the show. They are a form of insurance in a high-risk, high-potential-profit industry where most shows do not succeed. Of 300 scripts that get to the networks for consideration each year only a handful will be aired in the new schedule in the autumn and perhaps only one or two will last long enough to be worth syndicating. When each rating point is worth $75 million per year a star who can add a couple of ratings, as Bill Cosby could in the late 1980s, is clearly worth tens of millions to the producers. These stars represent a positional good, a good in perfectly inelastic supply which in response to a rise in price can supply no more of the item. There is no substitute for the real thing.

The same logic of programme producers applies to national commercials. By 1987 television advertising spots could cost the buyer over $1 million a minute. It was therefore worth while for the advertisers to make sure that the advertisements they were offering were very attractive to the viewer. They wanted the best. Many of the world's top film producers and actors were hired, and television advertising involved some of the most creative artistic and production talents available. For example, Buick hired the same people at Apogee productions who did the special effects for the *Star Wars* movie to make a commercial showing the new 1988 two-seater Buick Reatta coupé rising out of the desert dawn. The latest technology allowed them to put fifteen tracks together at the same time in a treatment described as more like painting than filming to create beautiful imagery. The advertisement cost half a million dollars. On average a thirty-minute commercial for network television costs $90,000 to make but many like this cost much more.

Advertisers must beware of unintended negative messages. The drug scandal involving the Canadian runner Ben Johnson made advertisers wary of using any athlete in case their use of drugs became public. Johnson lost $5 million worth of endorsements and was threatened with legal action by advertisers such as Toshiba who had already used him.

Finally, television sometimes gives not just financial but real political power to its stars. Sam Donaldson, top reporter for ABC News, makes it his business to get a question to the President every day. He has become a phenomenon in the US media, one not always appreciated. After losing office in 1979 President Carter said that he wished two people on to his successor. They were Menachem Begin, who had caused Carter much heartache over the Camp David agreement, and Sam Donaldson.[42] Television has allowed Donaldson to become a powerful news agenda setter and public opinion maker.

The varieties of US conduct

Both price and non-price conduct changed in response to the restructuring of the, industry. Pricing involves the prices of programmes and programme inputs, the prices of advertisements and the prices of pay channels. Non-price conduct, on the other hand, is reflected mostly in the sorts of programming supplied to the viewer.

As the structure of the industry changed in the 1980s, so did relative prices. Deregulation removed many price controls, with the following consequences. (1) The networks increased the time price of commercials charged to viewers. In 1984 the number of minutes per hour was raised from six to six and a half. In 1987 it was raised to seven minutes, whilst at Fox it was raised to eight. (2) The terms of exchange between affiliates and broadcasters changed. Cable operators that used to be paid to carry services such as ESPN began being charged for them in the late 1980s. (3) The cable networks increased the money price to viewers of basic cable services at rates of between 20 and 40 per cent per annum between 1984 and 1988. (4) The price of satellite receiving dishes dropped dramatically, as did the prices of VCRs and video cassettes. (6) The prices of independent stations and cable systems increased. Stock market prices and mergers all reflected this. (5) Advertising agencies came under pressure to lower their commission on television advertisements and programme producers to lower their prices.

In 1988 network television was still the most powerful mass medium for reaching large audiences. Despite all the new competitors it was still the national advertisers' first choice. The networks were able to hold down the price of a thirty-second slot because they added an additional minute of advertising per hour to their programming. Some typical prices are given in table 22.

In the 1980s the networks also came under increasing pressure from their affiliates. The affiliates swap advertising slots for programming with the networks. In the mid-'80s increasing numbers defected from the networks, refusing to accept some shows on this barter basis. When a new night-time show with the comedian Dick Cavett as host was

Table 22 A selection of US programmes with associated prices of thirty seconds' advertising, various years ($)

Fox Joan Rivers Show, 1987	17,000
CBS Evening News, 1987	40,000
Hispanic TV show El Gin, 1988	20,000
Amerika, 1987	176,000
Miami Vice, 1987	158,000
Family Ties, 1987	258,000
The Cosby Show, 1987	352,000
SuperBowl, 1983	400,000
1984	475,000
1985	525,000
1986	600,000

Source: Various.

started by ABC in 1986 over 100 of ABC's 214 affiliates declined to run the show. As a result ABC had to scrap it. This reflected how severely the dependence of the affiliates on the networks had been weakened.

The change in the relationship between affiliates and the networks first appeared in 1984. Until then all the networks and their affiliates showed network daytime soap operas from 10.30 a.m. to 4.30 p.m. The low-cost-production daytime soaps were highly profitable for the networks. In 1984 some affiliates found that talk shows such as the *Phil Donahue Show*, originally an independent Chicago station's daily talk show, distributed by satellite, brought them higher ratings. Moreover affiliates could keep all the advertising revenue.

Likewise at six o'clock or seven o'clock many affiliates found it advantageous to run cheap syndicated game shows like *Jeopardy* or *Wheel of Fortune* rather than the news. Others in later time zones would run the network news feed early, say at 5.30 p.m. to steal a march on the rival affiliates, then show the syndicated game shows whilst the rival was showing news from another network. The new programmes from each network, for all the hoopla and costs, are very similar.

The affiliates who showed no network news gave up the free news feed in return for shouldering the additional costs of the syndicated game show or situation comedy and the ability to sell all the commercial breaks for themselves. Trial-and-error cost-benefit analysis in many cases showed this to be a good strategy. The affiliates had the networks at a disadvantage. The networks could rarely find an independent station with as large a market share as the affiliate. The affiliates based on network programmes had become the most powerful local stations, so de-affiliation was rarely an option for the networks. At the same time the affiliates were free to turn down feeds of some network programming if it suited them.

In pricing cable to subscribers all the cable operators use a system of tiering, with the first tier being basic cable. From 1984, when price controls were removed, to 1987 the average cable charge rose from $9 to $23. The cable companies argued that the basic cable packages were improved, so justifying hefty increases in the price of basic packages. Higher tiers always included attractive additional channels such as HBO, which would be advertised on the basic channels.

Just as the affiliates found the terms of trade turning in their favour as regards the networks, so the cable operators found them improving as regards cable suppliers. With new competition to supply programmes, cable channels such as ESPN found that instead of receiving payment from the cable operators they sometimes had to pay the cable operators to carry their channels. Their revenue then came from advertising. In the case of ESPN the new sport suppliers were regional sports networks.

Re-regulation or a dramatic fall in the price of satellite aerials were the major threats to future prospects in the cable sector in 1989. From 1985 to 1988 the price of a satellite dish system fell by 300 per cent whilst the average cost of cable rose. On the other hand some fifty-seven stations – nearly half the total – which had been free to satellite dish owners were encrypted between 1986 and 1988 following the decision by HBO to encrypt. Furthermore the capital cost of a dish was also still considerable, about $4,000 for a full system, although quotes as low as $400 were available. In addition there was always the possibility that the law would treat material on the airwaves as copyright and not something to be plucked as a public good. Consequently in 1988 the threat to cable was still more potential than real.

However, as dish technology improves and dish prices fall further, as dish owners get used to the idea of paying for encrypters, and as Europeans in the 1990s depend more on satellite and set an example, satellite may yet have its day in America. Forty-eight per cent of US households are not yet hooked up to cable, and nearly half of them will never have access to cable. Even those hooked up to cable can switch and no doubt would switch if the present value of the cost of cable subscriptions ever exceeded the present value of the cost of a satellite dish and the cost of encrypters.

As the price of VCRs and video-cassette rentals fell both cable, particularly pay-movie channels, and the movie industry felt threatened. VCRs give the viewers control over what programmes they view and when. As the cost of video cassettes and rentals fell and increasing numbers of US households acquired VCRs in the mid-1980s cable experienced new competition. At the same time VCRs complemented cable by being a time-switching device. Cable also had the advantage of being on tap, eliminating trips to rental stores. In 1988 video cassettes could be hired for under $1 in most of the United States and VCRs were available for under $300. Cable had shown it could survive the VCR threat.

The change in the price of cable operator systems and independent broadcasters has already been discussed, as has the reduction in the commission to the advertising agencies who prepare and place advertising. These issues were discussed under industry structure and the downward pressure on programme costs and prices.

The scope of product differentiation

Technological change and deregulation have affected both price strategy and non-price conduct in the 1980s. Non-price strategies in the television industry refer mostly to the quantity and quality of the programmes available to the viewers. In all areas these have increased dramatically in quantity and changed in terms of quality.

Mark Fowler, who headed the FCC in the early years of the Reagan administration, was a former radio disc jockey and his moniker then was 'Madman Mark'. His goal at the FCC was to eliminate 'pervasive government control over the lives and commerce of American people'.[43] Under Fowler and his equally pro-deregulation successor, Dennis Patrick, many restrictions were removed. One of the most controversial was the elimination of restrictions on children's television in 1983, allowing children's shows which were virtually non-stop advertisements.

General entertainment. The preference option dictates much network product strategy. Show hosts tell the viewers, 'Don't touch that dial', but what is important is to make sure a large number do not want to. Broad-appeal programmes such as dramas, situation comedies, and game shows, as well as sport and news, are essential to maximize advertising revenue. The high risks associated with fickle viewers means that the networks tend to play safe with prime-time shows. Although there have been changes in the products over the years, from comedies such as *Archie Bunker* to more relevant shows such as *Hooperman* in the 1980s, the requirement that shows must have mass appeal limits quality. Comedy and adventure dominate.

Really successful shows such as *Dallas* encourage imitations from other networks, such as *Dynasty*. Ageing but successful shows like *The Cosby Show* in 1988 encourage spin-offs like *A Different World*. There are a number of product strategies for launching new products. Brandon Tartikoff, president of NBC Entertainment under Grant Tinker, said that all hits are flukes but advised producers to view sceptically any show whose concept took longer than ten seconds to explain, to pick shows with women in mind, never to schedule weighty shows on Fridays and Saturdays, and never to schedule a show just because the producer liked it.[44]

97

These general entertainment prime-time shows from the networks are the main source of exports. They are sold abroad for whatever the market will bear, since the marginal cost of another tape is negligible. Certainly the dramas do not represent the real USA. Sets for shows like *Family Ties* suggest housing and life styles beyond the means of most North Americans. Sixty-five per cent of real workers but only 10 per cent of television characters do manual jobs. Those under eighteen and over sixty-five are underrepresented by a factor of three. Crime and criminals are vastly overrepresented. Of any 300 characters thirty will be police officers, while judges and lawyers together outnumber scientists and engineers by ten to one. The deprivation effect which overseas viewers are sometimes thought to experience from watching Western television and the perception of the United States as a lawless, violent society takes place in the United States too.[45]

When Fox Broadcasting announced its first prime-time shows in 1987 it adopted a counter-programming technique. Fox announced the new shows in the spring so as to avoid competition with the networks' new shows, traditionally offered in the autumn. The shows themselves, however, were not very different from what the other three offered. The nature of television precluded such product differentiation.

One problem for Fox was that the strategy used by Murdoch in his newspaper markets to increase market share was inapplicable in television. With his newspapers Murdoch added sensation and trivia and moved the newspapers down market to appeal to the broadest number of readers. Some critics said he just lowered quality in the process. With a television network there was nowhere down-market to go. A television network cannot appeal to market niches or serve different interests simultaneously as a newspaper can.[46] The networks already geared their products to the lowest common denominator market at which Murdoch was aiming. The equivalent of tabloid journalism is seen in shows such as Quantum Media's *Morton Downey Junior*, not in a complete network.

Although Fox's 123 affiliates reported themselves satisfied with the new network, Fox Broadcasting lost $80 million in 1988. One programme, *21 Jump Street*, proved popular and attracted 6 per cent of the audience in 1988, but the format was traditional network television. The Fox strategy of moving down market with a late-night show hosted by Joan Rivers, a highly strung comedienne, was a disaster from October 1986 to April 1987.[47] It was cancelled. Fox thought that Joan Rivers was a big enough name to attract a six-point rating, the break-even point, and gave her a $10 million contract. In fact the show was little different from other late-night shows, only more vulgar and crueller. Viewers preferred the established offerings such as *The Tonight Show*, with Johnny Carson, still at the top after twenty-five years, or sleep.

In 1988 in a further effort to consolidate his media empire Rupert

Murdoch purchased *TV Guide* magazine for over $3 billion. The magazine enjoys the highest circulation of any US magazine and it allows Murdoch to promote Fox Broadcasting.[48]

News as entertainment and information The ratings game and the preference option determine the formula for network news. With advertising time selling at very high prices an extra rating point in the daily news half-hour was worth $21 million per year in 1987. Advertising demand dictated the news formula at the networks. As a result the network news has become 'profoundly condescending'.[49] It is essential for news programmes to maximize audiences. Economic marginal analysis explains the rationale of the fabulous network news budgets. If in 1987 a $20 million increase in budget had translated into one more rating point, then network profits would have risen by $1 million. Anything, therefore, including a dilution of news content, which increases ratings is justifiable.[50] The news must entertain. What hard news there is is there because it is good business: the viewers want it.

Not all the news people understand this. When CBS cut the staff at CBS News in 1986 the chief anchor man, Dan Rather, claimed that the public interest was being sacrificed. Rather had been a superb television journalist who first made his name by reporting President Kennedy's death twenty minutes before the other networks. However, he obviously did not understand why he was being paid $2.5 million to read the news. It was not for the sake of the public interest. The public interest had taken second place years before. Rather, like all the anchors, is good-looking. The show he presented interested the public. It was not too demanding, it was not too analytical, it was not boring. It was what the viewers, particularly affluent viewers, wanted. It was good entertainment at half the cost of a drama to produce.[51]

Sometimes the news is dominated by the entertainment dimension. At the 1988 Moscow summit CBS taped the news early so as to catch the noonday sunshine. On some news reports all the news was news of the summit that week; the rest of the world was excluded. This allowed the networks to show such newsworthy pictures as Reagan snoozing during a speech and snippets of catty exchanges between the leaders' wives.

Other cases of entertainment as news are worth recording as a reflection of product strategy for the news programmes. In 1987 in Texas a little girl, Jessica McClure, fell down a well and was trapped. After more than a day of wonderful effort she was rescued with relatively minor injuries. The story dominated the news for days, even though dozens of American children are killed every day in tragic accidents, and worldwide thousands die of hunger. The need to emotionalize and personalize, to appeal to Americans' sense of compassion, reduces the

99

news on such occasions to drama. Even more ridiculous as major news was the effort to save three trapped grey whales in 1988, a story which was on the evening news for three days. Grey whales are not an endangered species, but helicopters, hovercraft, special harnesses, tractors, and even two Russian icebreakers were used. Eventually two of the whales were freed whilst one, named Bone, died. They were freed by squads of Inuits working with chain saws. The Inuits later remarked that without the television cameras they would simply have killed the whales and eaten them.

It is stressed that this dilution of the news is not necessarily a condemnation of US television news. It reflects the fact that commercial television in the United States is an entertainment vehicle and that by and large it serves the US public well as such. It meets the public's interest. Television presents the news as entertainment and so encourages the majority of Americans to get some hard news. Analytical detail for the deeply interested minority is widely available elsewhere, on radio and in print.

An analogy can be drawn with Latin America, where propaganda to encourage literacy did not work.[52] Yet a soap opera with a story line about new literates who then enjoyed career success had a great effect on enrolment for literacy classes. The indirect approach of network news as entertainment and as an appetizer may be in the public interest as well as the public's interest. It means that many people acquire at least a little news about current events in the United States and the world.

New television delivery vehicles have meant more news and more news documentaries. In 1980 Ted Turner started Cable Network News to provide news twenty-four hours a day over cable. In 1988 CNN earned nearly $200 million, about half from advertising revenue and half from subscriptions, and was profitable. Since 1980 there have been other new entrants to the television news supply. Not all succeeded. Satellite Broadcast News, a joint venture of Comsat, IBM, and Aetna Life, lost $100 million before being abandoned.

In 1984 CONUS, a news-feed service co-operative was started, in which local stations fed their news stories to a central location in the Mid-west. By 1987 many local stations were equipped with Newstart vans fitted with 90 in. satellite aerials and facilities for editing stories in the vans. CONUS had a staff of eight covering the Geneva summit talks and provided a competent news service, comparable to the networks', for independent stations. The network world news monopoly was over, and a network without a news division was clearly a possibility.

One response of the networks has been to feature special-interest stories to compete with the improved national coverage by independent stations. At CBS they increased the budget for news, CBS's traditional *forte*, by 27 per cent to $348 million in 1987. All the networks have made a push to sell their news overseas. For example, ABC supplies British commercial television with most of its US news coverage. NBC took a different tack, cutting the broadcast news budget and creating CNBC. Understandably, many NBC affiliates were upset by the NBC strategy of entering cable news, but it made sense. In news programming as elsewhere each network had become just one supplier among many.

Sport for all tastes United States television has radically modified the economics of sport, making it big business. In 1988 firms paid out $1·35 billion for advertisements during sports programmes and a further $3·5 billion to sponsor them. The biggest sponsors were Philip Morris, RJR Nabisco, Anheuser-Busch, Coors, and Coca-Cola. Motor racing received $276 million, golf $126 million, tennis $49 million, and marathon running $31 million. Boris Becker from tennis, Michael Jordan from basketball, and Greg Norman from golf all received over $4 million each in endorsements in 1988.[53]

The two biggest sports advertisers and therefore underwriters are Chevrolet and Anheuser-Busch, who each spend over a quarter of a billion dollars a year on sport-related advertisements and sponsorship. The importance of such support is reflected in the names of some of the biggest sporting events. In motor racing there is the Player's Challenge. Although cigarettes are banned from television the event was named in the days of cigarette television advertising and gets plenty of television coverage. So do the Marlboro skiing events. In horse racing the Kentucky Derby is now the Budweiser Kentucky Derby and in boat racing the best known boat is also named after Budweiser. Likewise most of the major golf tournaments such as the Kempener Open are named after their sponsors. Virtually no sport has been unaffected; even lacrosse and rodeo have benefited.

The strategy of the networks has been to focus on sports which are of interest to higher-income groups. Tennis, golf, football, and baseball have wide appeal to high-income groups. All these sports also have the advantage of natural breaks during which there can be messages from the sponsors. Formerly amateur sports have become professional as a result of the money available from television – for example, marathon running. The 1988 New York Marathon was covered by ABC for the whole two and a half hours it took to complete. Sponsored by Mercedes-Benz, although not yet called the Mercedes-Benz New York Marathon, a Mercedes-Benz sports car could be seen following the leader for the duration of the event.

Sports programmes are no guarantee of audiences and profits, and the networks have overbid for the right to show big events. In 1988 ABC lost $80 million on the Winter Olympics, whilst NBC lost about the same amount on the Summer Olympics. In both cases ratings showed that viewing was 20 per cent below the levels promised to advertisers. In addition to the cost of the right to televise the games, the costs of actually televising the Olympic events were enormous. To cover the 179 hours of the Games in Seoul NBC sent a staff of 2,000, 120 computers, and 20,000 video tapes. They bid $300 million for the rights, their production costs were $110 million, and they lost $80 million. The audience shortfall in promised ratings was made up by no-cost advertising later in the year.

US television virtually underwrites the Olympics. This is because the American networks traditionally bid competitively for the right to show major sporting events, including the Olympics. Table 23 shows what they have paid since 1960 as they observed how the Olympics held viewers to their sets and so to the commercial messages beamed with the events. Meanwhile other nations with a single television supplier bidding for the right to cover the Olympics, such as Britain or Japan, exercised countervailing power and paid much less.[54] The total paid to the Seoul Olympic Committee for rights by all countries, including the USA, was just over $400 million.

Table 23 The effect of television on the Olympics: US rights fees, 1960–88

Year and Olympic site	Network	Prime-time hours	Rights fee ($)
1960 Rome	CBS	5	394,000
1964 Tokyo	NBC	4	1,500,000
1968 Mexico City	ABC	10	4,500,000
1972 Munich	ABC	41	7,500,000
1976 Montreal	ABC	49·5	25,000,000
1980 Moscow	NBC	–	–
1984 Los Angeles	ABC	81·5	225,000,000
1988 Seoul	NBC	80·5	300,000,000

Source: Runners' World.

Competition between the networks for sport means that much of the profits to be had from selling sport accrues to the sports and not to the networks. To date they have not agreed to create a cartel to bid together against the sport suppliers such as the NFL and the Olympic Committee. With the increase in demand for sports programming from new suppliers such as ESPN and the regional sport networks the sport businesses can anticipate an even greater share of sports television's revenues.[55]

In response to the demands of US television new sports, new variations of sports, and new leagues have been created. For example, the

United States Football League sought to fill the summer months with football when the National Football League was not operating. When it failed in 1987 a new inside version of football was started, called Arena, to meet the same perceived demand for summer football.

Golf too has changed. Golf appeals to the wealthy and televises well, with many natural breaks. To meet the demand of television the Seniors' PGA was introduced so that the elderly wealthy could nostalgically watch former heroes. The Women's PGA was started so that their wives could join in. Golf even changed its format from match play to lowest gross score for the benefit of television. Golf then introduced yet another twist to please the viewers when it started the skins games. In this variation of the old skins game played by amateur golfers the sponsor, not the player, puts in a given amount for each player on each hole. The money accumulates until one player wins a hole outright. Consequently it is possible for the viewer to enjoy the excitement of watching players putting for tens and hundreds of thousands of dollars on each hole.

Football is the one form of television that a large number of middle-aged, affluent professional US males watch. Both the networks and the advertisers are therefore very keen to hold on to that audience. From 1982 to 1987 the NFL received $2·1 billion from television. Despite losing $150 million on football in 1985 and 1986, the networks signed a new $1·4 billion deal for the next three years. Of the 1982 contract over 55 per cent went to the 1,600 players in the league. Under the contract each of the twenty-eight teams gets an equal share of the television revenue, although some teams are shown more and attract more viewers.[56] The NFL also made another deal in 1987 with ESPN so that the cable channel, 80 per cent owned by ABC, covered some of the games on Sunday evenings. This was good diversification for ABC into cable but caused indignation amongst their network affiliates, one of whose top-rated shows was ABC's *Monday Night Football*.

Cable such as ESPN with its demand for sport twenty-fours a day has benefited those sports with narrower appeal than the networks can exploit. Consequently advertising on cable has helped minor sports financially and allowed their participants to enjoy the same sort of benefits as in those covered by the networks. Wrestling has become the seventh biggest sport in the United States because of cable. As the cable industry has evolved regional sports networks have been established.

The limited regulation of cable gives it an advantage in bidding for sports programmes against local and even network broadcasters. With unregulated prices cable is able to pass the higher costs on to the subscriber in the form of higher subscriptions. For example, in the southern United States support for hockey is limited and the NHL has never been able to get a network television contract. However, it has sold rights to ESPN. In 1988 Cablevision Systems bid $51 million for the right to the league over the next three years, outbidding even ESPN. Cablevision's innovative plan is to beam the NHL games to those areas where support is greatest, covering several games each night and slotting each game to its best market.

Limited variety from the new media

The networks have not developed a successful strategy for beating off the new suppliers of news, sport, and entertainment. There is probably no such strategy. The new suppliers have chiselled away at the network audience while seeking to attract new viewers. The product strategy of the new suppliers has involved imitation, repetition, and the development of new products. Critics in 1988 were still expressing dismay at how few new programme products the new suppliers had introduced. Cable television's supposed ability to narrowcast, to demassify, as forecast by Alvin Toffler, had not been fully exploited.

Table 24 The top shows on US cable television, June 1987

Bass Masters
Prime Time Wrestling
Championship Sports
Truck and Tractor Pull
Wildlife Chronicles
Partners in Crime
Wagon Train
Larry King Live
Short Stories

Source: Paul Kagan.

Table 24 shows the top cable shows in 1987. Much cable programming consists of old network re-runs. This led to criticisms that United States cable is a museum for old programmes and a dumping ground. Certainly whilst the cable companies were building the systems and capital expenditure was high, as well as during the years from 1985 to 1987 when the industry was being rationalized, product strategy was to minimize programme costs. Nevertheless new products have been introduced. MTV has attracted younger viewers and allowed television to become more like background music on radio.

Until 1984 daytime television was dominated by the network daytime dramas, the 'soaps'. These daytime dramas, first sponsored on radio by soap firms like Procter & Gamble, attracted audiences of around 50 million daily, 80 per cent women. In 1988 they still drew sizable audiences for shows such as *General Hospital* (8 million households), *The Young and the Restless* (7·4 million), and *Days of our Lives* (6·8 million) but their virtual monopoly, together with the game shows, of daytime programming was over.

In 1984 when *The Phil Donahue Show* was first shown on a number of cable systems it quickly became very popular. With the host acting as moderator or leader audiences could question, discuss, and respond to guests. New shows such as *The Oprah Winfrey Show* soon followed. The format was cheap and popular. Soon the temptation to increase audiences by appealing to audience fascination with the bizarre and macabre became irresistible. Interviews with prostitutes, transsexuals, and mud wrestlers, hate groups, teenage lesbians, and similar tabloid curiosities followed. Phil Donahue, who continued to deal with saner topics on most days, wore a dress on one show and said, 'Survival is the name of the game.'[57] By 1988 the worst of these talk shows was probably that of Morton Downey Junior. His show from WWOR in New Jersey on occasion ended in violence, with the host physically assaulting a guest. He described himself by saying, 'I'm rude, I'm overbearing. . .'[58]

Running Downey a close second as tabloid television were the shows of Geraldo Rivera. Rivera came to fame with a two-hour special put out by Tribune in which the sealed vaults of Al Capone, discovered in the basement of a former Chicago hotel, were opened. After two hours of suspense they revealed very little. However, the ratings were spectacular and *Geraldo* had a following. Other Rivera event shows followed, such as a mock trial of President Kennedy's assassin Harvey Oswald, with viewers phoning in as jury. Then a daytime show was introduced. Rivera's daytime show has also been known to end in violence. On one occasion provoked and angered civil rights activists threw chairs and broke Rivera's nose when he had a white supremacist as guest. For Tribune it marked further successful vertical integration into production, and the *Geraldo* show earned $20 million, more than any other Tribune production.[59] Another success for Tribune was to sell a two-hour documentary with Geraldo to NBC called *Devil's Worship: Exposing Satan's Underground*. This showed that the networks too would move down market to get ratings during the November sweeps when audiences are measured.[60]

New delivery vehicles created new options for the programme suppliers. So-called first-run syndication became possible in the 1980s. In 1988 *Star Trek* achieved another media breakthrough. Having begun on network television, then had success at the movies, *Star Trek* finally premiered on independent television. For the 1988 season Gulf & Western's Paramount subsidiary agreed to let a syndicate of over 200 independent stations show a new series, *Star Trek: the New Generation*. This provided the independents with a strong show to run against the networks and guaranteed the supplier, Paramount, that the show would not be cut by the networks after a few episodes. As the networks' share decreases and the independents become more powerful first-run syndication of major dramas will increase. The new *USA Today* show adopted the same approach.

Unable to beat them, NBC joined its independent rivals. Limited by the government to the amount it can produce for its own network, NBC in 1988 began to produce shows for first-run syndication. This product strategy is yet another way by which a network can diversify to protect its interests in the industry.

Disappointments and uncertainties

There are product failures in all industries. In the US television industry pay television as a vehicle for narrowcasting stands out. A general lack of interest in cultural programmes over cable led to losses and failures on cultural channels. ABC, wishing to be a part of the new television, lost over $100 million on an assortment of pay-television misadventures. A cultural show called *ARTS* in co-operation with the Hearst Corporation, the legendary newspaper company, showed ballet and symphonies to tiny audiences. A programme for mothers, many of whom by the 1980s had gone out to work during the day, called *Daytime* also flopped, as did *Satellite News Channel* in co-operation with the Westinghouse company.

The most successful pay television has been Time's HBO, but even its future is problematical. In 1987 the number of subscribers continued to grow, but many subscribers were also cancelling. The problem with the tier system for pay channels is that the free broadcasting services and basic cable provide so much choice. Deregulation has also created an incentive for cable operators to improve the basic channel, effectively buying programmes in bulk at a discount for all their subscribers and then raising basic rates. The benefits to the consumer of an additional pay channel on an on-going basis are therefore often small. On those occasions when a movie is desired, over 60 per cent of households can use their VCR and a hired video cassette of a new movie release.

Pay-per-view television in 1988 was still in its infancy. The Tyson–Spinks fight in June 1988 was available over pay-per-view and attracted many viewers. When the fight lasted less than two minutes it was said that the biggest loser was pay-per-view television, followed closely by viewers who had paid heavily – as much as $50 to see the fight. The big winners were the two boxers, thanks to television. Tyson received $14 million and Spinks half that.

Pay-per-view is one form of interactive television. It may be operated by telephone or by other means but it requires some sort of interaction with the supplier. New easy-to-use technologies could give it a boost at any time, but so far interactive television products, with the possible exception of some home shopping and video games like Nintendo, have had little success.[61]

Early interactive videotext services flopped throughout America. Teleconferencing via satellite was still not widely used in 1988, to the relief of the hotel and airline industry. Home shopping enjoyed a boom in 1987 but slowed again in 1988. All applications have enormous potential. Investments in interactive television products have been made by major corporations, including IBM, CBS, J.C. Penney, Sears, Honeywell, Citicorp, RCA, GTE, Bank of America, AT&T, Times-Mirror, Time Inc., and Knight Ridder.

At the same time cable's flexibility has allowed experimentation. Rather than show the same products to all viewers J.C. Penney introduced a system called Telaction where consumers used their phones to call up products on their television screens. J.C. Penney paid the phone charges. Once connected to J.C. Penney, consumers could use the phone dial to walk through the store's departments. As they pressed different numbers new selections of goods were shown. Other companies such as Comp-U-Card used similar techniques but substituted personal computers for television as monitors. Comp-U-Card argued that marketing is king and that technology is but a server. They concluded that personal computers and a free phone number were the simplest technology for home shopping. This says that as personal computers become common household products they may be substituted for television in some interactive applications. By 1988 there were 40 million personal computers in the USA waiting for new applications.

Few interactive products so far have passed the market test and earned profits. Basically consumers have demonstrated a preference for more traditional substitutes. They go to the bank rather than bank from home; likewise they prefer to go out shopping. Businessmen prefer personal contact even if it costs more and involves long flights and stays in hotels. However, tastes change, and new technology will make the new television methods more friendly. Large investments by many large and successful companies continue. For example, in 1988 a consortium of BellSouth, Northern Telecom, and Heathrow built homes of the future in Orlando, Florida, where fibre-optic cable carries phone, cable TV, movie rentals, security and computer data into the home. The probability of videotext success in the future is still high.

Other new television products in the late 1980s included 'advertorial' programmes, full-length programmes devoted wholly to selling the product. The removal of regulations on the networks' children's programmes in 1983 allowed toy manufacturers to create programmes such as *Masters of the Universe* and *The Transformers*. These are based on toys of the same name and their object is to persuade children to want the toys. Hasbro Bradley's Transformers were the first toys ever to earn $1 billion in the first year of production. Whilst such programmes may be socially undesirable, and groups such as Action for Children (AFC)

107

lobby to have them banned, it does not mean that they are an assured success for the toy makers. Children are as fickle as their parents. Reflecting public concern about this product strategy, Congress in 1988 ordered the FCC to revise its regulations concerning children's advertising.

In terms of conduct PBS gets a mixed review. PBS relied on pledges for much of its finance but was not nearly so successful in its pledge efforts as the religious channels. Pledges to support PBS amounted to 22 per cent of revenue or a little over $300 million. To remain on the air PBS relied mostly on foundations such as the Ford Foundation for over half its revenue and the government for 15 per cent. In 1988 Congress imposed a 2 per cent tax on the sale of radio and television stations which should provide several hundred millions for PBS in the 1990s.

To many viewers of PBS the endless periods of boring pledge drives and the lengthy interruptions of the best programmes are more irritating than standard commercials. Yet PBS does fill a market niche for minority programming. The best television news analysis in 1988 was in the hour-long news programme the *McNeil/Lehrer NewsHour*, winner of a number of awards. PBS imported the best of British television, so that in prime time fully half of programming consists of British imports.

Much of PBS product strategy, however, was disappointing. Even without the constraint of ratings maximization PBS quality was patchy. Endless nature programmes were shown. In the late 1980s, faced with financial constraints, PBS allowed sponsors' announcements to become longer and more like advertisements. Some of the programming, such as *Leave it to Beaver* and *Lassie*, was simply not quality nor educational programmes. Nevertheless PBS attempted to meet the minority demands unmet by commercial systems, and without it US television would be much inferior.

Politics and television conduct

Political demand was discussed above in terms of political parties buying time. The Fairness Doctrine, which required that both sides of an issue be presented, was junked in 1987 in the courts. This had a 'chilling effect on free speech', according to Dennis Patrick of the FCC.[62] In its place television conduct came under the First Amendment. The critical and disappointing point is that television exerts enormous influence over voters, and often the short clips on television lack substance and distort the truth.

Telegenic political candidates have an advantage. Kennedy and Reagan are perhaps the extreme examples. Television debates clinched the presidential race for both of them. Reagan showed his leadership qualities when he interrupted a moderator named Breen in the 1980 election.

Quoting Spencer Tracy playing the Republican candidate in the movie
The State of the Union, Reagan said, 'I'm paying for this microphone,
Mr Green'.[63] The fact that he was quoting a B movie and misnaming
the moderator did not matter. Appearances were everything.

Another example of the role of telegenics and politics occurred in
the summer of 1987. At the Iranscam hearings a second Watergate was
anticipated, a televised hearing by Congress which would show Congress
in a good light. However, the lieutenant-colonel who seemed marked to
take the blame put up a superb television performance before the Tower
Commission. Oliver North might have done wrong but he appeared stead-
fast, loyal and patriotic. Within a week he was a hero. He was later
awarded honorary degrees and mentioned as a suitable vice-presidential
candidate.

The lesson of telegenics was not lost. The non-charismatic Republican
candidate George Bush chose as his running mate Senator Daniel Quayle.
Quayle's chief virtues were good looks and wealth, and he added glamour
to the lacklustre Bush campaign. With presidential campaigns running
for months, candidates were bound to get a lot of television coverage,
which could determine the outcome of an election. Richard Nixon first
had shown this nearly thirty years earlier when he had refused to wear
make-up for the first television debate with Kennedy. Nixon appeared
to have five o'clock shadow, which was credited with tipping the balance
in the closely fought campaign towards Kennedy. Clearly, television can
determine who will be the most powerful person, politically and
economically, in the world.

Many product strategies have not worked. Ted Turner lost $26 million
when he organized the Goodwill Games in Moscow after the Soviet
withdrawal from the 1984 Olympics in Los Angeles. CBS introduced
the *Morning Program* in 1986, which was so light and breezy that it
suggested it is possible to underrate an audience and undermined CBS's
reputation for news quality. The USFL, created for television, lasted
a bare two seasons. Joan Rivers's episode at Fox lasted six months. Every
year many new game shows, situation comedies, and dramas are started
in September and dropped within weeks if the ratings are poor. Two
of twenty-two new network shows in 1987 survived into the 1988
season.[64] Failure, in other words, is measured in one way: does it
reach? High ratings are the criterion used to judge success. For every
success there are dozens of product failures.

Performance in the USA

In terms of the performance criteria laid out in figure 1 the networks
continued to decline in both reach and profitability. CBS lost a further
14 per cent of its audience in 1987 and, having seen profits drop by a

quarter of a billion dollars in 1986, made its first quarterly loss in 1988. Network shares were falling to the 60 per cent level overall and 40 per cent in prime time. The network oligopoly was over, and in its place were powerful new suppliers. If this implied more competition and more choice for advertisers and consumers it was to be welcomed.

Amidst the turmoil of change the best hope for the broadcasting networks is a change in the regulations that prohibit them from owning cable systems and syndicating their own old shows. The policy stance of the FCC towards regulation in the 1980s would not rule this out. Currently the networks may produce programmes for cable systems. However, the programmes that they buy and produce for broadcasting cannot be resold by them to cable and the independents. Rather they must let syndicators sell them, thus transferring considerable profits from them to the syndicators such as Viacom International. If the government let the networks syndicate their own old shows and own cable systems, then the networks would have better prospects. Instead the current regulations work towards lowering the concentration of the television industry by penalizing established firms.

The biggest of the new suppliers were the leading cable operators. In the space of a few years TCI had become so powerful that it already had a defence strategy in the event of its being broken up under anti-trust regulations. TCI's powerful gatekeeper role, its ability to create barriers to the entry of programme suppliers, was of concern.

In terms of performance in 1988 supply on cable was disappointing as regards product quality and variety. Alvin Toffler's forecasts of great variety had not been met.[65] Cable television had become a dumping ground for old television shows, old movies, and cheap talk shows. However, it was too early to conclude that cable will not fulfil Toffler's expectations of demassification. The cable industry is still in the process of maturation and claimed that $2 billion were budgeted for new programmes in 1989.

The expensive process of building cable systems had taken most of the 1980s. The year 1988 was a turning point. It was only in the last few years of the decade that the companies had the cash flow necessary to improve programming following a period of building and rationalization. It was argued that TCI, fearful of a break-up by the FCC, would improve the quality of its programmes as a defence against such an event. However, as of 1987 cable had not distinguished itself. Of twenty-three channels examined by *Consumers' Report* only CNN, Nickelodeon, MTV, Arts and Entertainment and Lifetime were noticeably distinctive. Voters also liked some of the pay channels such as the Disney channel.

All broadcast stations must operate within the guidelines set by the FCC. Consequently the FCC standards set a lower level on performance as regards programme quality. Stations that fail to meet FCC standards can have their licence taken away. Although this is rare it does happen and in 1986 the FCC defranchized station RKO in Los Angeles. Likewise the FCC has clearly taken note of years of complaints about the behaviour of TCI. The mere threat of FCC action in the future acts as an incentive to supply quality programming. The public, however, has judged cable television. It buys it, whatever it says to *Consumers' Report*.

In terms of the traditional performance goals American television is satisfactory. It does create jobs. Increased competition has eliminated much of the X-inefficiency that characterized the industry. There is technical progress, although the move to HDTV had been frustrated by the desire to attain compatibility with the 160 million 525 line sets that US households own now. American concern about the fall in the educational standards of the young are related, some suspect, to the amount of television watched. This is an important externality of television. Likewise there is concern over violence on television and its possible social consequences. These issues are discussed in the final chapter.

Exports of programmes bring over half a billion dollars to US producers. Many of the shows exported are general entertainment and are sold for whatever the market will bear. Since the marginal cost of the exported programmes is virtually nothing, the programmes can be sold at very low prices to very poor audiences and still contribute to the producer's profits.

The failure of the related consumer electronics industry must be included with performance. The original networks were set up so that television sets could be sold. In 1980 Zenith and RCA still accounted for nearly half the US market for television sets. In 1988 Zenith was the only major firm left and sold imported sets. It seemed ironic, therefore, that the US government should choose to discourage the move to the use of the Japanese standard of HDTV, thus denying the US viewer access to this much superior product.

For advertisers television provides competitive prices and a plentiful supply. Following Kaldor one can argue that there is too much advertising and that much of it is self-cancelling. This is a criticism of advertising, not of the media that carry it.

In terms of traditional public-interest criteria along the lines that the media should educate and inform as well as entertain the US system earns mixed grades. From the dozens of channels available, especially PBS, culture, education, and information are available. For many viewers, particularly the less educated, it tends to get lost amongst the babble of entertainment and the clutter of advertising.

The agencies create and place the bulk of advertisements on behalf of the advertisers. Between 1986 and 1988 there was a wave of mergers amongst the advertising agencies. A three-way merger between three Madison Avenue companies created the biggest advertising agency in the world, Omnicom. Then Saatchi & Saatchi in Britain bought Tom Bates to become number one. In 1987 WPP Group, made up of former Saatchi employees, bought the famous J. Walter Thomson agency to bring it under the WPP umbrella. The world of advertising was taking on a global structure as the television world did likewise. The next two chapters examine the changes in advertising and television in Europe.

Canada

Most of Canada's 24 million population live within 100 miles of the US border. Canada is also one of the most cabled countries in the world. Consequently over three-quarters of the population have access to dozens of US channels over cable or by satellite.[66]

Few countries have experienced US media and cultural imperialism to the extent that Canada has. Television has played a major role in the process. Not only are most cable channels filled with US broadcasts and cable services but Canada's own broadcasters in both the public and the private sector import many hours of US programming for transmission. They also produce their own imitations of US programmes to meet Canadian content requirements in addition to producing some truly Canadian programming. However, Canadian channels are at a casual glance virtually indistinguishable from US ones. US channels close to the border carry Canadian news and advertising in recognition of where a major part of the market they serve is found.

The Canadian television industry is controlled by the Canadian Radio and Telecommunications Commission (CRTC). The industry is a duopoly, but one with much competition from US imports not controlled by the CRTC. The public sector is the Canadian Broadcasting Corporation, which can trace its roots back to the 1929 Royal Commission on Radio Broadcasting. The Aird Commission concluded that broadcasting was a primary means of preserving Canada's fragile cultural identity. This same theme resounded through the pages of the Caplan–Sauvageau report of 1987, nearly six decades later. It said, ' . . . the overriding goal of Canadian broadcasting policy . . . [is] to establish a Canadian presence on television through programs that are made by Canadians, chiefly for Canadians, and good enough to attract Canadian viewers'.[67]

The CRTC also regulates the private sector of broadcasting, run by the Canadian Television Corporation (CTV), cable television, pay television, and all radio. The CRTC regulates both content and the times when Canadian programmes must be shown. However, it cannot control their quality, nor can it prevent unregulated US alternatives entering the country twenty-four hours a day, every day.

The CBC operates both a French and an English-language network across Canada. For the nearly 6 million people who live in Quebec there are no free programmes in French from the US, so there is very little import competition for CTV and CBC. CBC operates a northern service in the Inuktitut languages for native Indians. Canada was the first country to launch a domestic communications satellite, the Anik satellite, to reach its isolated communities. Such services have to be financed by the state and play a nation-building role similar to that of the state-run television systems in many developing countries.

The CTV network is the private network with many parallels to the British commercial channels. CTV networks reach 97 per cent of Canadians in both French and English. There are two other private networks. Global Television Network covers much of Ontario, and TVA is a French-language alternative. These stations have all enjoyed good reported profitability in part because of the economic rents enjoyed from their free use of the scarce public airwaves. As in Britain only nominal fees are paid for licences. In 1984 the CTV network and its affiliated stations earned a 71 per cent return on their working capital.[68] The Caplan–Sauvageau report also criticized CTV for spending too little on programming.

In Canada education comes under provincial jurisdiction. Five of the provinces operate their own educational networks. These are TV-Ontario, Radio-Quebec, Saskmedia in Saskatchewan, Access in Alberta and the Knowledge Network in British Columbia. The Knowledge Network uses the Anik-C satellite to broadcast to an area greater than Germany, France, and Britain combined and operates a television university degree programme. Channels such as the Knowledge Network show how a low-budget minority-appeal channel can be a successful supplement to the commercial channels. The Knowledge Network shows a mix of documentaries from around the world, educational programming from the US and Britain, and lectures and talks from the local universities.

There are also a number of pay services to meet other minority interests. Services such as Latinovision and Chinavision meet the needs of ethnic groups whilst the Sports Network and MuchMusic provide sport and music.

Canada's concern about media imperialism is not unique. In this Canada has much in common with many Third World countries. Although Canada can afford to supply Canadian programming the problem lies on the demand side. The majority of Canadians prefer to watch US sport and light entertainment. Canada has never tried to exclude the free US imports but could not even if she wanted. Indeed, one line of argument is that Canada enjoys a valuable free ride from the US television suppliers in the form of the latest network programmes. These are paid for by US advertisers but Canadians then choose to watch. The Canadian market is too small for advertisers to justify the $1 million per hour programmes the US networks offer.

The problem of media imperialism remains. The final chapter returns to this issue, but in Canada it has been proposed that in an era of television abundance the emphasis on control should be replaced by an emphasis on access. Canada was one of the first countries to discover that there is no effective control of outside broadcasts. Instead it has been proposed that access for Canadian suppliers should be improved. For example, the CBC might stop showing US programmes, and programme carriers might be separated from content providers. The CTV companies would then broadcast programmes which separate producers wanted to broadcast and which they paid the CTV to air so long as they met certain technical and content standards.[69] A similar system has had success in Holland.

Notes

1   *Business Week*, 7 December 1987.
2   Patricia Sellers, 'Lessons for television's new bosses', *Fortune*, 14 March 1988.
3   *The Economist*, 13 August 1988.
4   Booz Allen & Hamilton, *Subscription Television: a Study for the Home Office*, London: Booz Allen & Hamilton, 1987, p. 24.
5   One medium-sized automobile advertiser was the Japanese Nissan car company, which had experienced an erosion of its share of the US market throughout the decade. Nissan spent $150 million in 1988. Whether this expenditure actually sold any cars, or even whether the advertisements just reminded potential Nissan consumers to consider them, is hard to assess. Nissan cannot repeat history with more advertisements, in order to see whether there would have been any change in market share. Nissan has little idea about what influences consumers or for how long, but dares not cease trying to influence.
6   Children are a target of advertisers because they have a say in how household income is spent even if they have no income.
7   *Business Week*, 4 July 1988.
8   *Time*, 27 June 1988.
9   The cigarette manufacturers claim that the $160 million they spend on advertising each year just encourages smokers to switch between brands; in other words, advertising affects only market shares and not the size of the market.
10 The hispanic population grew 34 per cent in the 1980s and incomes rose by over 210 per cent.
11 *Business Week*, 6 June 1988.
12 Univision was formerly Spanish International Network and was once tied to the huge Mexican television company, Televisa. In 1986 after investigations by the FCC, and fearful it might lose its licences, Televisa sold Univision to Hallmark Cards for $600 million. Telemundo is owned by Reliance Holdings.
13 *Business Week*, 18 July 1988.

114

14 In 1987 HSN suffered a major setback when its telephone system, supplied by GTE, went awry. Forecast sales of $1 billion were not achieved and other home sales networks moved in. Meanwhile HSN sued GTE, its stock dropped, and some pundits claimed that home shopping was a temporary phenomenon.

15 *New York Times*, 9 September 1988.

16 *The Economist*, 24 December 1988.

17 Late in 1988 the highly respected *Christian Science Monitor* newspaper started a religious television station offering religious programming and selling advertising at $1,200 for thirty seconds.

18 *Business Week*, 12 September 1988.

19 One of the advertisements showed criminals going through a revolving door to remind viewers that Dukakis had been Governor of Massachusett's at a time when a criminal on leave had committed another murder. Another showed the polluted waters of Boston harbour with the message that Dukakis was not strong on the environment.

20 Rupert Murdoch has been examined as to his motive by a number of authors, who suggest that he is trying to lay the ghost of his late father's lack of confidence in him.

21 *Business Week*, 30 May 1987.

22 *Canada and the World*, May 1987, p. 23.

23 *Business Week*, 8 August 1988.

24 *Business Week*, 3 October 1988.

25 *Business Week*, 12 September 1988.

26 *Mother Jones*, June/July 1987, p. 58.

27 For the author his first exposure to seeing Atlanta television was amazement. It was like finding a New York station next to the BBC, totally unexpected.

28 Mark A. Zupan, 'Cable Franchise Renewals: do Incumbent Firms behave Opportunistically?' Unpublished paper, University of Southern California, April 1987.

29 *Business Week*, 26 October 1987.

30 *Business Week*, 28 October 1987.

31 *Business Week*, 21 March 1988.

32 Since 1985 the satellite owners have been allowed to sell the transponders, squeezing out the middlemen who used to buy long and sell short at a profit. One consequence has been a decline in the prices of transponders.

33 When there were limited numbers of dishes serving people with no access to cable, free riding on the signals was costless to the distributors. Once people began to use a dish to pick up a signal they would otherwise have paid for, the attitude of distributors became less tolerant.

34 Both Ed Murrow and Walter Cronkite had a liberal bias which irritated the US administration. Murrow was best known for his opposition to Senator McCarthy of Wisconsin in the 1950s. Murrow so impressed Winston Churchill with his coverage of World War II that Churchill invited him to be assistant director-general of the BBC after

the war, the only non-national ever to be so honoured. He declined. Cronkite was placed on a black list by the US Intelligence Agency in 1981 as unsuitable to represent the United States.

35 *Business Week*, 30 May 1988.
36 This was the result of a survey by Univision, the Spanish-language network, 1987.
37 This was the same survey by Univision and would mean a hispanic market in the United States larger than most European markets.
38 *Business Week*, 6 June 1988.
39 *Time*, 17 December 1987.
40 See chapters 3 and 4 for an analysis of the relationship between increased costs and increased revenues and the interdependence of demand and supply.
41 *Business Week*, 6 June 1988.
42 *Business Week*, 10 October 1988.
43 *Mother Jones*, June/July 1987, p. 58.
44 *Time*, 16 September 1985.
45 Rupert J. Taylor, 'Television: a version of reality', *Canada and the World*, May 1987, pp. 11–29.
46 By adding a crossword or a daily nude a newspaper does not have to delete the sports page or the classified advertisements. For example, at *The Times* of London Murdoch increased circulation by adding more business, crime, photographs, and games, but he did not remove the Court Circular column. All appeared in the same issue. In contrast, a television cannot be both a crime show and a game show at the same time.
47 *Christian Science Monitor*, 22–8 August 1988.
48 Either because of synergy, as a consequence of owning the magazine, or because of product improvement, Fox's new programmes for 1989, such as *America's Most Wanted*, were attracting high ratings in early 1989.
49 *US News and World Report*, 13 May 1986.
50 This observation does not mean that the news has to degenerate into all tabloid news. It does mean that it has to be entertaining to viewers, particularly high-income viewers.
51 The film *Broadcast News*, released in 1987, emphasized the point that news journalists are unsure about their true role, about whether they are journalists or entertainers.
52 This is discussed in some detail in the first part of chapter 10, under the sections on educational television in Latin America and Mexico.
53 *Business Week*, 31 August 1988.
54 The USA paid $300 million out of a total $410 paid to the Seoul Olympic Organizing Committee in 1988. The applicable analysis is that of a bilateral monopoly, in the case of the non-US countries, and a monopoly selling to competitive bidders in the case of the USA. In a bilateral monopoly the output is indeterminate but the buyer is usually better-off.
55 Fragmentation of the sports audience could mean that some major

events such as the NFL lose some of their audience. For example, a regional cable network could offer another event such as a local NHL game in the same time slot. This would lower the value of NFL games if NFL ratings fell.

56   This prevents the best teams from getting the most revenue and so becoming able to buy the best players. In other words, equal shares help maintain competition in the NFL.

57   *Los Angeles Times*, 30 December 1988.

58   *Time*, 4 January 1988.

59   These included *At the Movies, Tales from the Darkside, US Farm Report*, and *Soul Train*.

60   *Los Angeles Times*, 30 December 1988.

61   Home shopping still has to show that it can create profits for the shopping networks and hold customers in the long run. Many home shoppers quickly tire of the novelty.

62   *Business Week*, 14 December 1987.

63   From a letter to *The Economist*, 7 November 1987.

64   *Time*, 17 December 1987.

65   In the 1970s Alvin Toffler, a futurologist, examined the age of abundant communications and its effect on society in *Future Shock*, New York: Bantam, 1970.

66   *Satellite Entertainment Guide* listed the following US programmes every week in 1983: over fifty children's shows, over twenty-five game shows, over seventy family shows, and over fifty episodes of ten different daytime soaps. There were also many US news programmes, religious programmes, cookery programmes, and financial programmes. In other words Canada has been exposed to media imperialism for most of the decade.

67   This quotation and a summary of the report can be found in Ian Morrison, 'The state or the United States', *Policy Options*, April 1987, p. 19.

68   ibid., p. 20.

69   Frank Spiller, 'Electronic freeway', *Policy Options*, January 1987, p. 18.

Chapter six

United Kingdom: a declining role for Auntie

Before World War II the British television broadcasting industry enjoyed an early forced start because of state-provided financial support. Viewers paid for licences which were used to support the publicly owned British Broadcasting Corporation. At that time, in the 1930s, the American television industry looked upon the British approach with envy because it guaranteed adequate finance. Fifty years later, after much discussion and several government reports, Britain was on the brink of going over to a market system similar to that of the Americans.[1] This was despite British television's reputation worldwide amongst many critics of the industry for quality programming. Yet the truth was that with many competing demands for public finance the state was unable to afford the cost of supporting all the new media technologies. In any case the Conservative government of Mrs Thatcher was philosophically opposed to doing so. The British government decided that finance for cable and satellites, in addition to a majority of broadcasting, had to come from the private sector.

The major developments in British television history were the start of regular broadcasting by the BBC in 1936; the introduction of commercial television in 1955; the introduction of colour television and a 625 line system on BBC-2 in 1967; the setting up of Channel 4 in 1982; and the start of breakfast-time television in 1983 on both the commercial and the state-run systems. In 1980 Awdurdod Sianel Pedwar Cymru, the Welsh fourth channel authority, was founded and began transmitting in Welsh in 1982.[2] In 1988, therefore, there were two public and two commercially run broadcast channels operating. A 1988 White Paper promised significant further change, particularly in 1993, when the current commercial franchises expire. Funding for the BBC comes from the government, which collects the licence fees through the Post Office. The government sets the licence fee and is thus able to control the corporation's budget. From 1975 to 1986 the budget grew from £214 million to £933 million. This allowed the BBC to maintain a staff of 28,000 and to supply 9,700 hours of television broadcast in 1987. In

1975, by contrast the BBC had supplied 7,500 hours. Funding for commercial television comes from advertising. In 1975 ITV spent about the same amount on programming as the BBC, somewhat in excess of £200 million. Reflecting the growth of advertising revenue, ITV spent £1·7 billion in 1986, or nearly twice the BBC budget.[3]

Consumer, advertiser, and political demand

The British watch a lot of television. The average viewing time per person is twenty-eight hours per week. In 1988 only the Americans and Japanese watched more. The British watch television which only partly meets their demands. For example, VCRs, which were slow to take off in the United States, enjoyed rapid sales from 1980 to 1983 in Britain. VCRs were used to access the sort of programme material that was not available on the government-controlled systems and to shift what was available to times when there was little or no programming. For although Britain has had commercial television since 1955, and although advertisers are largely as uninterested in programme content as they are in the USA, the decision as to what is shown is not passed on to the viewer. Rather, for both state and commercial television, government-appointed boards determine the nature of television content, even if they do not actually select programmes. The reasons why this is so are examined below.

Table 25 Hours of viewing by individuals per week, UK, 1970–85

Year	All	BBC-1	BBC-2	ITV	Channel 4
1970	15.3	7.2	0·4	7·3	–
1975	17·3	7·6	1·3	8·1	–
1980	18·1	8·2	2·0	7·5	–
1981	22·1	8·4	2·3	10·5	–
1982	21·4	7·5	2·3	10·1	0·6
1983	20·4	7·4	2·1	9·5	0·5
1984	23·0	8·2	2·2	11·0	1·2
1985	26·3	9·2	2·6	12·2	1·6

Source: BBC Research Unit.

The British buy their television with both their money and their time. They pay an annual licence fee, if they are a colour television household, of £58 per year. Even those who claim not to watch the state television pay the licence fee. Since 99 per cent of households own or rent at least one television set, virtually all households pay for a licence. Many households hire television sets, a uniquely popular British phenomenon, rather than own them or buy them on credit. Consequently many Britons are used to the idea of paying a weekly charge as well as an annual one

Table 26 Television and VCR ownership in the UK as a percentage of households, 1969–86

Year	TV	VCR
1969	90·9	–
1974	94·6	–
1979	97·4	1·3
1980	97·4	2·1
1981	97·3	4·4
1982	97·2	6·7
1983	97·1	15·6
1984	97·2	22·8
1985	96·9	28·2
1986	96·6	35·4

Source: Booz Allen & Hamilton

to have television. Even as the numbers renting sets have declined in the 1980s the numbers renting VCRs have increased. This unique social characteristic will help ease the way to pay television should it be introduced as proposed in the 1988 White Paper.[4] Viewers also pay for television with their time by watching advertisements, although advertising is not as intrusive as in the USA. Advertising breaks on the commercial channels are limited to one break for every thirty-minute show or, by agreement with the state regulatory authority, six minutes per hour.

The rapid growth in sales and rentals of VCRs in the early 1980s reflected that consumer demand was not being met. By 1983 Britain had over 5 million VCRs, one for every fourth household, the highest penetration level in Europe. In 1988 there were over 10 million VCRs in use. The introduction of breakfast television in 1983 extended the number of hours of television transmission somewhat, but the round-the-clock availability of television which North Americans and Japanese take for granted was still not available. VCRs filled the vacuum, particularly the lack of daytime television, and VCRs were used primarily for time swapping.

Unfulfilled television demand was also met by video cassettes, whose sales exceeded £400 million in value in 1987. By 1986 the British video rental market was enjoying rentals worth over £1 million each day. This meant that more than three people hired a video that year for every one who watched a league football match or read a paperback book. In total 330 million video cassettes were hired in 1987.[5] As early as 1983 the piracy of programmes had become a serious problem and the Copyright Act was amended so that penalties for video piracy were greatly increased. Exporting pirated material became a criminal offence and a Video Copyright Society was set up jointly by the British Broadcasting

Corporation (BBC), the Independent Television (ITV) companies, and the Society of Film Manufacturers.

Other television substitutes are available in addition to VCRs. They take the form of radio, films, newspapers, and magazines. Although there are fifty commercial radio stations the majority of people still listen to the comprehensive and much respected BBC radio. The British also consume newspapers at one of the highest rates in the world, surpassed only by the Japanese. Most newspapers are morning papers and the majority are lightweight tabloids. Consumers use newspapers as a substitute for inadequate supplies of daytime television. With limited daytime television Britons read lowbrow newspapers during the day for light entertainment.

The film industry in Britain suffered heavily with the introduction of television. It is not clear why the fall in cinema attendance was so much greater than in France or the United States, nor whether the high propensity of the British to watch television was totally to blame. By the late 1980s Britain had only one-third as many cinema screens *per capita* as either France or Germany.[6] One reason advanced was the physical state of British cinemas in the 1970s and '80s. Their poor condition undoubtedly discouraged patrons. Based on this premise, the late 1980s saw new multi-screen cinemas built by American and Canadian investors such as Cineplex Odeon in the hope of attracting new filmgoers and encouraging new film makers.

The share of GNP devoted to advertising is less than in the United States but still the highest in Europe (see table 4). State control of television means that there are constraints on the supply side in terms of the amount of time available to advertisers to run their commercials. As a result in the 1980s as the economy enjoyed healthy growth rates some advertisers complained to the government about the high and ever rising cost of television advertising. A thirty-second slot could cost as much as £30,000 to reach an audience one-fifth the size of the North American market in terms of population and one-seventh the size in terms of income.

There are many other advertising vehicles available, so that although prices are high the sort of complaints regarding month-long delays before advertisements are shown which were made in the 1980s about some European countries do not apply to Britain. Rather the effect of supply-side constraints is to drive up price and divert advertising to newspapers, magazines, and other methods of promotion. Britain's large and vital newspaper industry rests on the advertising revenue it receives, and will be adversely affected as television is deregulated. As new television channels become available in the 1990s the newspaper industry, recently rejuvenated following reforms to eliminate costly labour practices, will come under further pressure. Plentiful daytime television will mean new competition for both readers and advertisers.

One spin-off from commercial television since 1955 and a strong economy in the 1980s has been the growth of the advertising industry. Advertising agencies such as Saatchi & Saatchi and WPP have enjoyed phenomenal growth and challenged the once dominant Americans. As Britain moves towards more commercial television there will be more demand for their services. As the world moves towards a global economy and global advertising, a move reflected in the rising concentration of the world advertising industry, further growth outside Britain in the over $150 billion industry can be anticipated. British advertising is often perceived as more subtle and humorous than the frequently hard sell of American advertisers.

One of Saatchi & Saatchi's greatest successes on its way to becoming world leader was in the 1979 election which brought Mrs Thatcher to power. Saatchi & Saatchi conceived the powerful slogan 'Labour isn't working', aimed successfully at the Labour government of the day.

Political demand for advertising plays a relatively small part in British politics and total expenditure on the 1987 election by all parties was £10 million. Election campaigns are much shorter than in the United States and the huge sums spent on the media in the United States to get elected have no equivalent in Britain. The law also guarantees equal time to each major party, including during the news, which requires laborious clock-watching by the broadcasters. The party political broadcasts – time slots given to the parties to put forward their position – have been traditionally rather boring, although a spectacular featuring the Labour Party leader Neil Kinnock by the producer of the film *Chariots of Fire* in 1988 was entertaining. The attitude of the television news producers, in contrast to the United States, is to report what the candidates say, often at considerable length and usually with little commentary. If that means poor entertainment, then the loss is regarded as the party's, not the television producer's. Since all channels carry the party political broadcast at the same time the viewer has no option but to watch it or turn off the set. Consequently the conflict between ratings and political coverage which leads to short sound clips on the US networks is largely avoided.

The government has a demand for advertisements in the public interest and purchases advertising time on the independent channels to place anti-commercials against 'bads'. For example, it has advertised against drugs, drunken driving, and holiday hooliganism by Britons in Spain. The government has learned from business advertisers that soft images sometimes have more success than hard-sells. Gruesome pictures of faces injured because those in accidents had not worn seat belts were rejected and ignored by the public in the 1970s. Calmer messages, such as quiet talk saying that 'drinking and driving wrecks lives' work better, statistics show. Argument against anti-social behaviour seems to work better than shock in Britain.

Political demand in terms of programme content also affects the basic conditions under which television operates. In the 1987 election Prime Minister Thatcher pledged her party to address widespread concern about violence on television. Polls showed that nearly 70 per cent of people thought that violence on television was a problem.[7] Much of this concern related to imported shows such as *The A-Team* and *Miami Vice*. A Rambo-style massacre in the village of Hungerford in 1987 convinced many people that there was a link between television and violence. Although a 1988 study commissioned by the BBC found that the acts of violence per hour in the 1980s were half those of a generation earlier, the government took action. It appointed a Broadcasting Standards Council with power to preview programmes.

Mrs Thatcher appointed the former editor of the *Sunday Times* and former vice-chairman of the BBC's Board of Governors, Sir William Rees-Mogg, a devout Roman Catholic, to head the Broadcasting Standards Council. Similar to a press council, the council was charged with creating a code of taste and decency for broadcasting.[8] Responsible to Parliament, it reflected the triumph of old Tory paternalism over Mrs Thatcher's free-market philosophy and her desire to deregulate the economy.

Political concern was immediately raised about the new board. The year of its creation, 1988, marked the 300th anniversary of the Glorious Revolution, which led to constitutional government and the rule of law. Britain has no written constitution and no explicit right to freedom of speech, and Parliament can pass whatever laws it sees fit. There is no Supreme Court to which appeals can be made. The link between television violence and actual violence has not been proved, while the potential of the BSC to encroach on to the areas of civil liberty and censorship is obvious. Sir William initially wanted the authority to preview just imported programmes. Many feared that this would spread to a preview of domestic programmes and open the door to political intervention. Television executives took the view that the BBC and the IBA boards of governors were competent to ensure that standards were maintained and that the BSC was superfluous. For Mrs Thatcher it seemed that free markets sometimes need a little regulating. For her television is more than a toaster with pictures, as the chairman of the FCC in the USA described it.[9]

Television in the 1980s also helped revitalize the political system. In 1985 the largely moribund House of Lords was startled into life when the television cameras were installed on a trial basis. The peers responded so well to their new observers that the cameras remained and the Lords began to exert real political pressure on such matters as health, education, and local government, even persuading the government to rethink legislation on occasion.[10]

Other demands that have a significant place in North American television are expressed in non-television media in Britain. For example, there is no direct selling on television. Nor is there much scope for religious demand to express itself on television. This is partly because religious groups cannot afford to buy time but also a reflection of the greater indifference of British society to organized religion. The demand for religious time comes from the established Churches, which are given limited coverage by both television authorities.

The current supply

Although television broadcast supply is state-controlled both the public BBC and the commercial ITV systems are run independently, at least in theory, of the government. The terms upon which they supply television are meant to guarantee that there is no intervention by the ruling party in the day-to-day operations of the broadcasters and certainly no interference for party political reasons. Those terms are set out in the licences under which they operate.

The British Broadcasting Corporation was founded in 1922 by royal charter and is responsible to the Home Office. The Home Secretary is empowered to license persons or corporate bodies to operate broadcasting stations. Conditions are laid out in the 1949 Wireless Telegraphy Act. The BBC is incorporated by royal charter and operates under a licence that runs until 1996, while the Independent Broadcasting Authority, which governs the ITV companies, operates under a licence which ends in 1992. The IBA operates under the 1981 Broadcasting Act, and was set up in 1954 under the authority of Parliament. The IBA selects and awards franchises which last for eight years and appoints the commercial ITV programme companies, each of which has a regional commercial television monopoly. The IBA was set up to provide a complementary, advertising-financed, service to the BBC's monopoly. A second BBC channel, BBC-2, was started in 1964. Both the BBC and ITV services are available to 99 per cent of the population.[11]

The forerunner of the IBA, the Independent Television Authority (ITA), was created by Parliament in 1954 with a mandate to supply a comprehensive service. In 1972 legislation renamed the authority and gave it control over commercial radio as well as television. The IBA has the vital job of deciding who shall have the licences for commercial broadcasting, Lord Thomson, one of the first franchisees, called them 'a licence to print money'.[12] The IBA grants the valuable franchises and then supervises those it has chosen. The IBA supervises programming, which by the 1980 Broadcasting Act must 'inform, educate and entertain'.[13] Franchises for the sixteen ITV stations are renewed every eight years. Like municipalities in the United States with the cable franchises, the IBA has one real hour of glory. That is the hour when they award the franchises. However, since the transmitters and the infrastructure are owned by the IBA it is easier for the IBA to throw out unsatisfactory performers and give the franchise to an apparently more deserving applicant than it is for American municipalities and their cable franchises. The IBA also controls advertising and builds and operates the transmitters used by the fifteen independent television companies. The IBA has revoked franchises in the past and so has demonstrated that franchisees must meet its standards.

A novel new source of supply appeared in the 1980s. Channel 4 was created by the 1980 Broadcasting Act to serve minority interests with programmes financed by a levy on the commercial television companies' profits. They in return were allowed to sell the advertising time on Channel 4. This experiment in television began broadcasting in 1982 and has worked with considerable success. Channel 4 has shown programmes of great interest to small minorities and critics have acclaimed highly much of Channel 4's programming. At the same time the channel has been an economic success and more than covered its costs.

The IBA is responsible for Channel 4, which provides a nationwide service, except for Wales. The IBA must ensure that the programmes on Channel 4 complement those on ITV and meet demands not normally met by ITV. Channel 4 broadcasts for over seventy hours each week. About fifteen per cent of programmes are educational and about half are categorized as informational. The majority of programmes are provided by independent suppliers.[14] In Wales the Welsh Fourth Channel Authority is required to ensure that programmes in the Welsh language are shown for twenty-two hours per week and that all programmes from 6.30 p.m. until 10.00 p.m. are in Welsh. For the rest of the time non-Welsh-language programmes are broadcast from Channel 4. The intent of the separate Welsh authority is to protect the Welsh language.

The structure of Channel 4 is of interest because it enables a commercially financed channel to circumvent the problems associated with the preference option. It means that in Britain a commercially viable method has been created of supplying quality minority programming in a world dominated by commercial television. Although the finance for Channel 4 comes from advertising, the link between revenue and ratings has been disconnected. Britain, it seems, has, 'stumbled on an extraordinarily elegant solution to the problem of financing broadcasting'.[15]

Although Channel 4 is an undoubted success the structure of Channel 4 is not without problems. The levy is imposed on the profits of the commercial stations. They earn considerable economic rents from their advertising monopoly and so the profits to finance Channel 4 should be assured, unless the government decides to auction off or sell the licences at a price approaching the capitalized value of the rents. However, the levy also creates an incentive to squander profits at the other commercial channels on high employee costs and wasteful practices. The levy, like any tax on profits, acts as a disincentive to earn profits and be efficient.

One consequence of the ITV advertising monopoly is that restrictive practices in the commercial sector are widespread. The disincentive effect of the levy for Channel 4 on profit maximization aggravates the problem. Restrictive trade practices in general outrage Mrs Thatcher but those at the ITV companies drove her 'beyond fury.'[16] Her government in 1988 decided to use the 1973 Fair Trade Act to eliminate them in television. In the 1988 White Paper the government also proposed auctioning off the franchises for commercial television to new entrants who would not be burdened by the entrenched high costs of the current ITV companies. As part of the process Channel 4 would be privatized. This is in spite of Channel 4's remarkable success in reconciling the problem of the preference option and meeting demand for minority programming.[17]

The IBA is also responsible for DBS television from high-power satellites, another planned new source of supply. DBS was intended to begin in 1989 but has been beset by problems. First proposed in 1979, the original intention was that the BBC would be responsible for DBS. The Department of Trade and Industry anticipated that DBS would be a source of new jobs.[18] As cost projections soared for the seven-year life span of the satellite the BBC got cold feet about its proposed monopoly. The next proposal in 1984 was that the ITV companies and perhaps a third partner should join the BBC. In return the franchises of the commercial companies were extended to run for an additional three years to 1992, guaranteeing them an additional £3 billion in revenue.[19] Then in 1986 the IBA concluded a contract with a private consortium, British Satellite Broadcasting (BSB), to provide three additional television services which could be received all over Britain.

The new consortium included the Australian entrepreneur Alan Bond, the French transport company Chargeurs, the retailer Next, the consumer electronics company Amstrad, the publishing company Reed International, an investment company from Luxembourg, and a London merchant securities firm. In 1987 Amstrad backed out in the face of cost problems and downward revisions of estimated revenue. Projected costs for BSB had risen to £650 million. As other European satellite projects were announced the prospects for BSB worsened.

BSB will not be the first satellite television over Britain. In 1984 Rupert Murdoch started a European satellite service on a medium-powered satellite with a footprint covering all of Britain. By 1985 there were two medium-powered satellites over Europe used for television. Both Intelsat 5 and ECS were primarily telecommunications satellites using spare capacity to carry seventeen broadcast channels, mostly in English, to

Europe. Programme suppliers for British markets on ECS were Rupert Murdoch with Sky channel and Thorn-EMI with Ten and Premiere. CNN was also available via Intelsat 5. In addition there were a children's channel, the Music Box channel of rock videos, and channels in French, German, and Norwegian. However, despite being allowed to own dishes, only a very small number of Britons had access to these channels and only 15,000 households owned dishes in 1988.[20] Sky channel is beamed from a private satellite, so, unlike terrestrial broadcasting channels, it is subject to a minimum of government interference. Satellite television's major competitor in the new media is cable. In 1983 half a million households received television via old relay cables capable of carrying just a few channels but the future of cable is in multi-channel cable and fibre-optic cable.

Following the recommendations of a House of Commons report a new Cable Authority was established and the first franchises for multi-channel cable systems were awarded in 1983. In 1984 two large television rental companies, Rediffusion and Visionhire, pulled out in the face of poor consumer response, and in 1985, when five more contracts were awarded, there was no competition for any of them. As a result one innovative franchisee, Cotswold Cable, was successful with a plan to lay the cables through the local sewers. To encourage new entrants to the industry not all the regulations proposed by the House of Commons report were implemented, but even so cable made slow progress.[21]

Cable in Britain in 1988 therefore was still in the experimental stage. By 1987 only eight of the eleven pilot projects had become operational and only about 100,000 households had signed up to be connected to multi-channel systems. These were in Westminster in central London, in Glasgow and Aberdeen in Scotland, and in Croydon, Coventry, Swindon, and Windsor. Meanwhile the number of old relay systems and upgraded relay systems actually declined as broadcast transmission in remote areas was improved. In 1987 just over 2 per cent of households were passed by any sort of cable, and of these only one in five was connected. This is a stark contrast to the US, where over half of all households were connected to a multi-channel system.

In 1989 the one per cent of households who had satellite dishes or who were hooked up to cable television could enjoy mostly sport, news, and general entertainment. It was possible to pick up some twenty satellite channels over Britain. In addition to these general-interest programmes, in the London area a cable operator carried an Indian channel, *Indra Dhnush*, while the footprint of a Middle Eastern channel made it possible to watch Arabic television via satellite.

Despite much interest, therefore, in the new media in 1988 the majority still relied on the four broadcast channels and VCRs for most of their video supply. The programmes they watched, whether from

BBC-1, BBC-2, or ITV were nearly all produced in-house by the programme distributors. These three channels bought in few programmes from independent domestic suppliers. In 1987 the new director-general of the BBC, Michael Checkland, announced that the BBC would spend more money on outside programming.[22] Out of a total budget of £1·1 billion for 1988, £20 million would be spent on outside purchases. In fact any casual viewer would conclude that the two duopoly distributors, the BBC and ITV, also produced all their own programmes except for the 15 per cent of obviously imported US programmes.

On the other hand Channel 4 is not vertically integrated and has been a source of minority programming and a market for independent suppliers. In 1987 360 independent suppliers sold programmes to Channel 4, which used them to meet its mandate to serve all the people part of the time. Channel 4 received £135 million from the levy imposed on the ITV companies' profits. Channel 4 has used this money to pay for new movies and programming, some of which have been an outstanding success. They include the award-winning films *A Room with a View, Letter to Brezhnev*, and *My Beautiful Laundrette*. One-third of all revenue returns to the ITV companies for programmes. These programmes purchased from the ITV companies help satisfy that part of the ITV mandate which requires them to produce educational material. Only thirty minutes of programming each week is produced in-house.

In terms of input costs, until the late 1980s the tight BBC and ITV duopoly allowed the vertically integrated broadcasters to put downward pressure on the costs of some inputs to their programmes. As an illustration, few entertainers or athletes received the high incomes that US entertainers and athletes earned. Indeed, many went to the United States, attracted by the possible financial rewards. The fact that the British market was less than a quarter the size of the United States market only partly explains the income disparity. Fewer channels in Britain mean that each channel receives a higher proportion of the total audience and, in the case of ITV, of total advertising. One would expect perhaps one-fifth as many highly paid entertainers and athletes as in the United States, on a *per capita* basis. Instead a powerful duopsony of the BBC and ITV hiring competing performers prevents performers from extracting the economic rents.[23]

In the United States competition between the networks in the 1960s and '70s allowed athletes, as inputs to television programming, to earn fabulous salaries compared to most British athletes. In the late 1980s this began to change in Britain. Increased competition for sports programmes for television increased the incomes of successful athletes and the organizations they worked under. For the nearly bankrupt football clubs satellite and cable appeared as angels of mercy in 1988. In 1987 the BBC and IBA paid the Football League just £3·1 million for the right to televise soccer matches. BSB offered to triple that to £9 million for each of the next two seasons just to secure the right to show matches once BSB starts operating in 1990. The offer was then raised to £39 million for four years in a co-operative agreement with the BBC. The agreement allowed them to choose what matches they wanted to televise.

Beginning in 1990, the Football League clubs anticipate revenue of £30 million a year, and if satellite television and pay television are really successful up to half a billion dollars a year from worldwide distribution rights. That would be more than double the revenue from gate receipts and other sources. With forty of the ninety-two clubs in the league technically insolvent after a long period of declining gates and rising hooliganism television could be the salvation of the national game.

The end of the BBC and ITV cartel could also restructure the game of soccer, just as television has changed other sports such as golf and tennis in the US. For example, the ITV companies made an offer to the league of £32 million over four years to let them televise only the top ten clubs in the league. The smaller and poorer clubs feared that such an arrangement would leave them out of the money as a super-league of the best clubs absorbed all the television funding.[24]

The future supply

Looking towards the next century, growth prospects for the new cable and satellite entrants to the television industry depend upon their success in an inevitable battle over market share. This was so even before the announcement of structural changes in the 1988 White Paper. Although in the United States by 1988 cable had appeared as the primary alternative to broadcasting for programme distribution to households, Britain is not bound to follow the example. Even the most optimistic forecast of growth for cable anticipated less than 50 per cent market penetration by the year 2001.[25]

The rate of growth of cable will depend upon the competition from broadcasting and satellite, and particularly the price and the price elasticity of demand for satellite-receiving dishes. In 1988, when dishes still cost in the region of £1,000, only 15,000 homes had one. At a price of £200 for a dish, satellite television would provide intensive competition for cable. Entrepreneurs such as Murdoch anticipated a million dishes in use within two years, on the assumption of dish prices falling to the £200 level and people being able to hire dishes at £10 a month. On the assumption that there would be cheap dishes, Murdoch contracted for four new channels on the Astra satellite, owned by the Luxembourg SES company and launched late in 1988.

Financed by advertisements, the Murdoch channels will include Sky channel, renamed Sky Television. This general entertainment channel will compete with BBC-1 and ITV. A second news and current events channel will compete for news with the established broadcast channels. The possibility of ITN, the independent supplier of news to the ITV companies, providing input has not been ruled out. Two other channels will supply feature films on one channel and sport on the other. By using the PAL colour system used by the broadcast channels in Britain the Murdoch satellite channels will be compatible with current television sets.[26]

For Murdoch satellite television is a back-door opportunity to supply television. In Britain he is excluded from owning television stations by virtue of his strong hold on the newspaper industry. The Monopolies and Mergers Commission would prevent his acquiring a commercial franchise. However, his newspapers can be used to publicize his back-door entry into British television whilst his American television and film companies supply programming. With five years of satellite television experience and £50 million sunk into Sky channel, Murdoch is highly qualified to run a satellite system profitably in Europe.

The other major entrant to satellite television in Britain, BSB, will bring DBS television from a high-powered satellite in 1990. For the viewer high-powered satellites permit cheaper, smaller dishes. They also offer the opportunity to use more advanced high-definition techniques known as D-Mac. However, the costs of BSB are staggering. As already mentioned, some expected participants such as Amstrad have backed out. As the US experience has shown, pay or subscription television of any description has a hard job finding a market in the face of plentiful supplies of free television.

The 1988 White Paper proposed other new supplies of free television. They included privatizing Channel 4, a new separate night-time service on ITV's channel 3, another commercial broadcast on what will be channel 5 in 1993, and possibly yet another broadcast channel, channel 6, to follow. The White Paper also proposes placing BBC-2 and Channel 4 on BSB. Whilst for a time they would also be broadcast the move would free two more terrestrial channels for commercial broadcasters. There is also talk of new local VHF stations and more use of the dead hours of the night for scrambled broadcasting.[27]

The shift of BBC-2 and Channel 4 to BSB would dramatically change the basic conditions of British television and influence the struggle between cable, medium-power and high-power satellites for market share. If consumers were to want BBC-2 and Channel 4 in sufficient numbers to pay for the dishes to access the more advanced technology of BSB, then the prospects for BSB and its backers, who include Virgin Group, Granada, Pearson, and Reed International, will improve. Table 25 shows the market share of these two channels. The move would create a lever to switch Britain to DBS. In areas without cable, which means most of the country, cable could thereby be pre-empted as a delivery vehicle.

Political motives played a part in the proposal to shift BBC-2 and Channel 4 to satellite. The Department of Trade and Industry Minister, Lord Young, was concerned that a fifth terrestrial broadcast channel would not be accessible to many Tory voters in the south of England. Freeing the wavelengths used by BBC-2 and Channel 4 would allow new advertising-based channels to start up. Lord Young surmised that many Tory voters would be angered if they could not get access to a new broadcast channel. Moving BBC-2 and Channel 4 to BSB would probably also benefit the government's media supporter, Rupert Murdoch. With an incentive to buy a dish to get Channel 4 and BBC-2, consumers would then have an incentive to buy or hire the hardware necessary to access Sky Television. Although the dish for accessing DBS reflects technology inversion and so is smaller and cheaper than that needed to access medium-band satellites, it is reasonable to believe that the current incompatibility of the two different dishes and the different costs is a surmountable problem. For example, in 1988 a flat dish was announced in the United States that overcomes the need to move the dish. With an increasingly affluent middle class in Britain a substantial market for the larger dish can be anticipated. In 1988 Murdoch's Sky Television announced plans to beam four new channels into British households in 1989 for twenty-four hours a day. Sky Television was planning to use a transponder on the medium-powered Astra satellite.

The experience of Super Channel, a pan-European satellite service, between 1986 and 1988 is sobering for all European satellite ventures. Super Channel was set up in 1983 with backing from six of the ITV companies. In 1987 Super Channel lost £19 million on revenue of under £4 million. Thirty-second advertising slots sold for just $150. As a result, in 1988 it was restructured, with injections of new funding from NBC, Turner Broadcasting, Virgin Group, and four of the ITV companies which have an interest in Super Channel. Super Channel's problems were aggravated when Europeans who were hooked up to cable dropped the English-language entertainment channel when offered satellite-to-cable entertainment in their own languages in 1987 and 1988. In 1988 the channel was reportedly for sale for £1.[28]

Structural upheaval and change

In 1988, despite the embryo satellite and cable industries and the important reform proposals of the 1988 White Paper, British television was still essentially a government-controlled duopoly. The state financed the BBC. The state granted the ITV companies a monopoly of local and national television advertising.

Although both the BBC and the ITV are regulated by independent bodies, and the government by and large does not get involved in day-to-day activities, there is a subtle form of government control. This results from the government appointing the members of both the BBC and IBA boards of governors. Most are fine, upstanding, worthy citizens and no lackeys of the government. Yet the point remains. The fate of those running the BBC and ITV rests on the decisions of the boards of governors, not on the market. The boards of governors of the BBC and the IBA are responsible for programme content. Although they do not usually preview programmes, their comments on previous programmes influence current programming. BBC and ITV officials must please the boards. Consequently, although the government of the day has no legal right to intervene in what is shown, it can and does bring pressure to bear on the management and boards. Cases of intervention are discussed below.

ITV consists of sixteen different franchises. There is one ITV company for each of the fourteen regions of Britain, except London. The London market is divided between two companies. Thames Television has a franchise to distribute programmes during the week, whilst London Weekend Television is responsible for the weekend. The sixteenth franchise, awarded in 1983, produces the commercial morning television show, TV-am.

The ITV stations rely on their own production companies for 75 per cent of the material they show. News for all the ITV companies comes from a separate production company, Independent Television News, which operates under contract from the ITV franchisees. ITN received £50 million in 1987 to provide twenty-four hours of news per week. This is about one sixth of a US network's cost for the evening news, although the comparison fails to take into account ITN's ability to repeat the news during the day. On a daily basis ITN's costs are half those of a US network to a potential audience one-fifth the size.

ITN still enjoyed one of the last untouched government-created monopolies in television in 1988. One consequence was that ITN produced a high-quality product at a high price. In 1982 a staff of 706 produced 365 minutes of news programming a week. In 1988 a staff of 1,067 was producing nearly four times as much news. ITN's contract to supply national news to the ITV companies lasts until 1992, but then it will face competition. After 1992 the ITV companies will be able to produce their own news or buy from other new entrants.[29]

Costs in British television are generally inflated. Particularly at the ITV companies, market power, economic rents, and lack of incentives to maximize profits have encouraged the system to develop fat, or X-inefficiency. The trade unions in particular have been able to capture some of the economic rents earned by the monopoly franchises. As new supply competitors in the form of cable and satellite begin to chip away at the duopoly enjoyed by the BBC and ITV there will be downward pressure on costs. Some indication of the extent of fat in the system is given by the case of Thames Television following a labour dispute in 1987. At Thames the same programme that had involved thirty technicians being paid triple time was produced with seven technicians paid time and a half.[30]

In 1987 Mrs Thatcher called the independent television companies 'the last bastions of restrictive practices'.[31] In 1985 union legislation introduced by her government had had the effect of rationalizing labour practices in Fleet Street, and she intended to achieve the same results in the ITV companies. The Conservative government planned to end restrictive practices and excessive wage settlements by weakening the power of the unions.

ITV and ITN had both signed generous agreements with the four broadcasting unions in 1987. One reason why the trade unions in the television companies were so strong was that each television company had a regional monopoly of advertising. This meant that inflated labour costs resulting from pay negotiations could be passed on in the form of higher prices to advertisers. Since new entrants who might have provided competition were barred from the industry, there was little incentive for the television companies to control costs. With a fixed supply of advertising slots available and excess demand for them there was little reason to resist trade union demands.

One part of the government's strategy for breaking the unions and lowering costs was to open the industry up to the new cable and satellite competitors. This meant that the television companies would no longer be able to afford the sort of restrictive practices that so appalled Mrs Thatcher. Reflecting the pressure of increased competition, all 229 technicians at TV-am were fired in 1988 over the issue of restrictive practices. Fewer than half were then taken back.[32] With jobs for technicians outside London scarce, partly because of the effects of such labour-saving technology as one-man cameras on the demand for labour, the technicians offered limited resistance to the TV-am management's conditions.[33]

Also in 1988 in an attempt to weaken the unions the Employment Secretary, Norman Fowler, instructed the Monopolies and Mergers Commission to investigate the working practices of the television and film industries. The Commission was empowered by the 1973 Fair Trading Act to investigate where restrictive practices existed and whether they acted contrary to the public interest. This case was of historic interest. It was the first occasion on which the 1973 Fair Trading Act had been used to investigate a trade union. This was clearly not the intention of the original Act, passed by a Labour government which was concerned with business firms' behaviour. The Commission was

133

instructed to examine the extent to which work was being carried out by non-trade-union people and the extent to which a specified number of workers were being allotted to any given task.

The new media distribution vehicles and the government's deregulatory pro-market philosophy had already lowered entry barriers and created the opportunity for new programme suppliers to enter the television industry by 1988. For example, new news sources developed. Specialized news services had begun in the early 1980s in the US with channels such as CNN. As the structure of the British industry changed, similar new services started up. News agencies such as WTN and Visnews began in the early '80s to supply instantaneous pictures of news events worldwide via satellite. Domestic independent programmers who buy the service, then edit the pictures and insert journalistic interpretation locally now have a market in which to sell their service. In 1987 Independent Screen News began to supply half an hour of news to London Weekend Television. In 1988 bidding for the right to supply two other new news projects also took place. The first was to televise the House of Commons. The BBC and ITN had shared coverage of the House of Lords since 1985 but coverage of the Commons was put up for bids. The second new project was to supply news to BSB.

Threat of entry to any oligopoly is often sufficient to cause firms in the industry to modify conduct. Such was the case in the news sector. In response to new threats of entry and better technology both the BBC and ITN improved regional news coverage and cut costs. In 1988 ITN released 142 staff and adopted more flexible working practices.[34]

The ITV companies, who were paying £50 million a year to ITN, had been under some pressure since 1985 to reduce costs as their revenues stalled. They are keen to buy their news at lower prices. For regional television the House of Commons will be a good low-cost news source, and an independent producer with non-union workers will have a cost advantage in covering the proceedings. Showing that it can lower supply costs and be competitive, ITN bid successfully to supply BSB with fifty-six hours of news per week for £10 million, one-tenth the cost per hour of the price to the ITV companies. Then BSB cancelled the contract. BSB feared that ITN would simply unload on to BSB the news feeds that the ITV companies had rejected. BSB concluded it could get a better deal from an independent supplier.[35]

Anticipating a different future environment for the television industry in the 1990s, with more competition, the ITV companies sought to diversify. The investment of six of the companies in Super Channel has been noted. Television South diversified by purchasing the American production company belonging to Mary Tyler Moore, MTM. Television South paid $320 million for MTM. MTM will give TVS access to both the American and the European markets as programming demand swells in the wake of privatization and cable and satellite systems in Europe. Two French media companies, Canal-Plus and Générale d'Images also bought 20 per cent of the company. MTM produced *The Mary Tyler Moore Show* in the 1970s and successful US shows such as *Hill Street Blues* and *St Elsewhere* in the '80s.[36]

The 1988 White Paper also proposed a radical change in the way in which the ITV franchises are allocated. The government proposed to auction off the franchises. The proposed method is a two-stage process. Potential franchisees first have to qualify in terms of the quality of the programmes they would broadcast. Qualified applicants then bid for the franchises. The IBA will be replaced by an Independent Television Commission, regulations on franchisees will be relaxed, and public-interest broadcasting requirements will be removed.

Auctions will allow the ITC to collect the economic rents from using a scarce public resource, the airwaves, for the public purse. The current franchising system encourages the franchisees, especially before renewal time, to spend money on new studios, programmes, and on other strategies that will please the IBA, and only possibly return some benefit to the public. Much of the rest of the rent is dissipated, as noted, in inflated costs. In 1992 the ITV stations will either be auctioned off, or possibly an economic price will be set for them. This is what the ITV companies want. They argue that the IBA should choose the best offer of programming made at the economic price.[37]

As regards the future of the BBC, the Home Secretary, Douglas Hurd, has said that the licence fee system is 'not immortal'[38] and that a pay-per-view system could replace the licence fee. Although the 1988 White Paper focused on the commercial companies, the indirect consequence for the BBC as new supplies develop will be a fall in market share. The government has also told the BBC that licence fees will increase at a slower rate than the retail price index and that the BBC can anticipate some financing from sponsorship and subscription. However, the White Paper also affirmed that the BBC will continue to be the cornerstone of the broadcasting sector.[39]

Restrained behaviour

In contrast to the United States the four British channels do not compete head-to-head in the way the three US networks compete for the same market. BBC-1 emphasizes light entertainment, sport, children's programming, and current affairs. BBC-1 also provides two and a half hours of morning television. BBC-2 emphasizes programmes for minority interests, including serious drama, international films, travel programmes, and documentaries. ITV emphasizes mass-appeal television and competes most closely with BBC-1. It also provides early-morning television of news information and light entertainment. Although the BBC earned its reputation as a world news service, BBC television news is sometimes seen as second best when compared to that shown on ITV and produced by ITN. Whilst the quality of ITN's news service was of benefit to the public it was also a means of enhancing its reputation with the IBA and the government. Meanwhile BBC-1 was successful in morning television, attracting over 9 million viewers, in contrast to 7 · million viewers of commercial television's morning show in 1987.

A survey of programming over the last thirty years finds some of the best drama in television history. The great dramas include *The Forsyte Saga* in the 1960s, *Upstairs, Downstairs* in the 1970s, and *Brideshead Revisited* in the 1980s, all of which were shown many times in the United States as well. The export revenue from such programmes is an incentive to produce more, so that overseas demand, particularly from the United States, is an important argument to justify their production. British productions are the main source of programme supply for US public television and are exported to all the English-speaking countries. The works of Shakespeare, Tolstoy, and Kipling were all made into programmes for prime-time viewing in Britain and subsequently exported abroad, where they were greatly acclaimed, for example in Japan.

British comedians such as Benny Hill, John Cleese, and 'the two Ronnies' continue to be enjoyed in export markets years after their shows were first produced. What is irrational is that for many of the programmes there are no follow-ups, so that *Fawlty Towers*, a great favourite on US public television, is repeated time and time again. This contrasts with the US approach, where a popular series, which means a profitable series, is extended for season after season. As market forces play a bigger part in Britain spin-offs and clones of popular programmes can be anticipated.

No similar comments about universal acclaim can be made about British game shows and soap operas. The problem has not been so much quality as the lack of quantity. Game shows are relatively few and are often based on intellectual knowledge rather than luck, thus excluding large segments of the population.[40] Likewise there are relatively few soap operas, although *Coronation Street* and later *Eastenders* have attracted big audiences. The success of *Eastenders* after *Coronation Street* had been running for nearly two decades demonstrates that Britons wanted more soap operas. More recently Australian soaps such as *Neighbours* have done well. There is no reason to believe that demand has yet been met and as new channels are started more soaps, possibly imports from the USA, Europe, or Latin America, can be expected to attract large audiences.

Conduct at the BBC is constrained by the need to please the board of governors. This may mean pleasing the public. The goal of the ITV companies on the other hand is to make profits by selling advertising space, subject to not alienating the board of governors at the IBA. Conduct, in other words, is explained largely by the terms of the licences under which the broadcast duopoly operates. Structure explains conduct.

Although the BBC and ITV stations must please their governing boards, they are theoretically independent in their day-to-day programming. The boards by and large do not preview programmes, and programme decisions are ultimately the decision of the Director General of the BBC or of the managers at the commercial companies. Some control is exerted, because the Home Office has a say in who is appointed to senior positions and who receives the franchises. However, the BBC has not generally been a government toady. In fact the BBC is often perceived as having a liberal bias. In general it has not succumbed to government pressure for self-censorship, and many programmes have outraged the government and many conservatives.

The BBC in particular must avoid antagonizing the government which controls its purse strings. Its coverage of the Falklands war, SAS killings in Gibraltar, bombings in Libya, and the Zircon affair are all thought to have brought budget retribution. These events merit discussion because they reflect conduct in the British television industry, where the fine dividing line between reporting that harms the government and reporting that harms the state is not always clear. Self-censorship so as to protect the state is more easily justified than self-censorship to protect the government.

The Zircon affair in 1987 involved a documentary produced by the BBC dealing with secret government operations. The programme, *The Secret Society*, revealed that in the previous four years the government had spent £750 million on a super-secret spy satellite, code-named Zircon, without informing Parliament. Top officials at the BBC subsequently decided not to show the programme on the grounds that it was potentially harmful to national security. The programme's creator then wrote a piece on Zircon for *The New Statesman*, a socialist weekly magazine. Officers of the Special Branch, the police intelligence division, soon afterwards raided the writer's home, the offices of *The New Statesman*, and the Scottish headquarters of the BBC. The 1911 Official Secrets Act was used to justify the raids on the grounds that a public servant must have leaked the information. The parliamentary opposition claimed, with some justification, that the Conservative Party was interfering once again in BBC decisions.

There was also a hostile government reaction in July 1985 when the BBC proposed showing in August a documentary, *Real Lives*, which included interviews with Martin McGuinness, a member of the outlawed Sinn Fein movement in Ireland, and Gregory Campbell, an Ulster loyalist. Both men admitted in the interview that they were prepared to use violence. On 16 July 1985 Mrs Thatcher had said that terrorists ought not to be given the 'oxygen of publicity'.[41] Two weeks later the Home Secretary, Leon Brittan, wrote to the BBC asking for the story to be suppressed and releasing a copy of the letter to the press before it had even reached the BBC. The Director General agreed to allow the board of governors to preview the programme, something they had not done for seventeen years, and they decided not to show it. This went against the tradition of the board of governors, that they do not preview programmes, because they are not qualified to do so, and anyway it is the job of the Director General and his staff to decide what is suitable. More importantly it undermined the BBC's tradition of independence.[42] Finally, when the programme was shown a month later it was rather dull and uncontroversial.

In 1985 the BBC confirmed that MI5, the counter-intelligence service, was vetting appointments to senior positions in the BBC. In 1986 the Conservative government was criticized for appointing Marmaduke Hussey chairman of the BBC. Hussey had been chief executive officer of Times Newspapers, an organization whose owner, Rupert Murdoch, is a strong Thatcher supporter. The resignation of Alasdair Milne as Director General in 1987 was also suspect. Although the government issued a statement denying that he resigned under pressure, his resignation followed a report by the chairman of the Conservative Party, Norman Tebbit, which was unflattering about the BBC's coverage of the US bombing of Libya. The report called the coverage anti-government and anti-American.[43]

In 1988 in one week the Foreign Secretary approached both the BBC and the ITV to stop them showing programmes which dealt with the killing of three members of the IRA in Gibraltar. The three men had been killed by the SAS, and it was suggested that the SAS had orders to kill. Since the case had been discussed in detail in the press the television programmes could have added little that was not already known. Nevertheless the request was made.[44]

None of these events shows that the BBC has been intimidated by government involvement in the corporation's activities. It appears sometimes that such involvement can have the opposite effect. The events do reflect a closer involvement by the government, a greater awareness by the broadcasters of government sensitivity, and a greater propensity to intervene by the government in what the BBC in particular broadcasts, as compared to the United States government and the three major US news networks.[45]

By and large commercial television in Britain has been fabulously profitable for the owners and their workers for over thirty years. Salaries and wages at the commercial stations are considerably higher than at the BBC. Even reported profits do not reflect true profits, because of X-inefficiency. Nevertheless there have been commercial failures. The first year of commercial television in 1955 led to losses. Lord Rothermere, the owner of the *Daily Mail* and Associated Television, sold out, having lost £600,000, a considerable sum at the time. TV-am, the sixteenth franchise awarded by the IBA in 1980, also lost money in its early days and was nearly bankrupt after seven months of operation.

TV-am was predicated on the idea that commerical television always makes money. The story of TV-am reflects the cosy world of British television up to the 1980s, when a protected duopoly escaped the discipline of the market. TV-am was started with £16 million. Of this the financial institutions supplied 70 per cent and six well known personalities provided the rest. The six included Peter Jay, described by *Time* magazine as one of 150 people likely to influence the world in the future and the 'cleverest young man in England', and well known broadcasters, including David Frost, Michael Parkinson, Robert Kee, and Angela Rippon. Jay said, 'I regard breakfast television as one of the least risky things ever.'[46] All had already made personal fortunes out of television.

TV-am had a 'mission to explain', according to Jay.[47] It employed a staff of 350, more than any of the American network news departments, and undertook an expensive news-gathering operation. The maximum potential audience was about 6 million viewers. With costs at £26,000 per hour and advertising revenue at less than half that forecast, TV-am lost £1·1 million per month. TV-am reflected much of what was wrong with British television in general; it produced programmes at inflated cost to please the educated middle classes who ran it. In this TV-am was undercut by the BBC. Three weeks before TV-am, with its mission to explain, began, the BBC started a light, easy-going, low-budget entertainment morning show called *Breakfast Time*. This attracted over three-quarters of the viewing audience, about 1·8 million viewers, and showed that bigger budgets did not necessarily mean better programmes and that private television is not inherently superior at producing what the public wants.

After two months the largest financial backers stepped in. Aitken Hume Holdings, run by some grandchildren of the press baron Lord Beaverbrook, dismissed the media personalities and instituted some business discipline. The unions agreed to cuts, programme schedules were revived, and audiences increased.

Incomplete performance

The basic day-to-day problem facing British television suppliers is not government interference in political coverage. Nor is it the frequent disregard of cost efficiency. The real problem is that the suppliers must please the boards of governors, who do not represent the common man.

In terms of consumer sovereignty British television is too high in intellectual quality. British television meets neither consumer demand nor, because of supply-side restrictions on the number of advertisements, the demands of advertisers. In the United States and Italy, where television content is relatively free of government interference, bored housewives, tired workers, sick patients, impoverished families, and retired old folks, given the choice, freely choose to watch hours and hours of cheap-to-provide, easily comprehended games, talk shows, comedies, and dramas. They do not choose documentaries about the IRA or plays by Ibsen even when these are offered.[48]

These quality programmes are programmes for the minority. In Britain that minority has probably been better served than anywhere else in the world up to 1989. That minority includes those who conclude that Britain has the best television in the world. On their own terms they are right, but in terms of maximizing consumer satisfaction such a conclusion is open to question. The masses in Britain, as elsewhere, prefer light entertainment and lots of variety. They do not want television to educate or improve them. They are quite content to give the advertisers 10-15 per cent of their viewing time in return for quality light entertainment. British television would be better able to claim it is the best in the world if it provided more light entertainment *and* continued to produce the sort of minority-appeal programming for which it is justly renowned. At the same time, exporting those quality programmes has made a useful contribution to the balance of trade.

The recommendations of the Peacock Report, the 1988 White Paper on broadcasting, and other reports reflect that the British television industry could improve its performance. They show that vertical integration of all channels except Channel 4 has led to the abuse of market power as costs have been driven up and entry forestalled. They show that a lack of head-to-head competition has not solved most of the problems of the preference option and that demand, especially for light entertainment, has not been met. They also show that if more broadcast channels had been made available, and if demand had been more fully met, then there would have been more jobs to create both programming and advertising.

Even without implementing the recommendations of these publications Britain will enjoy more light entertainment from satellites and new broadcast channels. In the future Britain will enjoy the same sort of choice as the United States. There will be dozens of light entertainment channels. However, the irony is that if the budget of the BBC is reduced and Channel 4 privatized, then the supply of quality entertainment, the very supply which Britain has enjoyed and taken for granted for decades and for which Britain is famous, will probably decrease and possibly disappear.

Notes

1 Britain has long claimed a special relationship with the United States in politics and economics in addition to sharing a common language. The television industry reflects these ties. British television has traditionally been more like that of America than that of any other European country. For example, nearly all imported programmes come from the United States, very few from Europe or the Commonwealth. Britain was also from 1955 until the early 1980s the only European nation to allow commercial breaks within programming and the only European country with significant television advertising.

2 *The Europa Yearbook 1988*, London: Europa Publications, 1988, p. 2883.

3 *The Economist*, 5 March 1988.

4 Great Britain, *Broadcasting in the '90s*, London: HMSO, 1987.

5 Robert Gertner, *International Television and Video Almanac*, New York: Quigley, 1987, p. 453.

6 *The Economist*, 28 February 1987.

7 A Rambo-style massacre in the village of Hungerford produced a spate of articles on the subject of television violence. *New Society*, 4 December 1987, concluded that the link between violence and television deserved a verdict of 'not proven'.

8 *Christian Science Monitor*, 20 May–5 June 1988.

9 This quotation was made in discussing the deregulation of television under the Reagan administration. *Mother Jones*, June/July 1987, p. 58.

10 *Christian Science Monitor*, 20–6 June 1988.

11 *The Europa Yearbook 1988*, London: Europa Publications, 1988, p. 2884.

12 Anthony Sampson, *The Changing Anatomy of Britain*, London: Hodder & Stoughton, 1980, p. 406.

13 *The Europa Yearbook 1988*, London: Europa Publications, 1988, p. 2883.

14 *Globe and Mail*, 21 January 1988.

15 The problem with this method is that it is viable only if the ITV companies who pay the levy earn sufficient profits, and that probably means they have to be given commercial licences at less than their full value. The levy is a transfer of economic rents from the ITV companies back to Channel 4 if Channel 4 advertising falls below the levy, which as competition intensifies is likely. The quotation comes from Alasdair Milne, talking to the *Financial Times* and reproduced in *World Press Review*, January 1986.

16 *The Economist*, 7 May 1988.

17 *The Economist*, 16 April 1988.

18 *Broadcasting*, 8 June 1987.

19 *The Economist*, 6 April 1984.

20 *The Observer*, 8 August 1988.

21 Among the investors in British cable were regional US telephone companies who are not allowed to own cable in the United States although they would dearly love to supply television there. In 1988 US West invested over $23 million in France and Britain, including a 25 per cent interest in Cable London. *The Asian Wall Street Journal*, 12 December 1988.

22 *The Times*, 22 October 1987.

23 This situation can be contrasted with the US networks bidding for the Olympics. A monopoly either as buyer or seller is usually able to capture economic rents. The BBC and ITV, like the Olympic Committee against the competing networks, gain the advantage.

24 *The Economist*, 16 July 1988.

25 Booz Allen & Hamilton, *Subscription Television*, London: Booz Allen and Hamilton, 1987, p. 34.

26 *The Times*, 8 June 1988.

27 Another suggestion is to use former radar frequencies for broadcasting. At the moment these are used for mobile phones.

28 In the end most of the original backers agreed to put in extra money. *The Times*, 12 June 1987.

29 *The Times*, 18 May 1988.

30 *The Economist*, 5 March 1988.

31 *The Economist*, 5 March 1988.

32 *Financial Times*, 3 March 1988.

33 *The Economist*, 15 March 1988.

34 *The Economist*, 16 July 1988.

35 *The Times*, 4 May 1987

36 *Business Week*, 18 July 1988.

37 This is not a totally unreasonable approach and would allow the government to capture most of the economic rents and to exercise some control. Overbidding at an auction could have detrimental effects on *ex post* conduct as the winner finds costs squeezed.

38 *Christian Science Monitor*, 4 July 1988.

39 *Sunday Times*, 8 November 1988.

40 In the 1960s when Britain had just two channels the programme *University Challenge* represented the sort of game shows put on the air. Only 5 per cent of those of university age went to university.

41 Mark Bonham Carter, 'Whose service?' *Index on Censorship*, August 1988, p. 28.

42 The analogy can be drawn with a newspaper, where the Director General is equivalent to the editor and the Board of Governors to the owners, or, since the BBC is state-run, the state. The case was important for the BBC, whose External Service on the radio had for years been the independent voice of radio around the world. Quality reputations can take years to build and are easily destroyed. In the coming years an equivalent external service on television via satellite is conceivable.

43 *Index on Censorship*, 8 August 1988, p. 28.

44 *The Economist*, 7 May 1988.

45 *Time*, 16 February 1987.
46 *MacLean's*, 19 December 1983, p. 32.
47 ibid.
48 Usually, quality shows such as these are shown on public television stations and are frequently British imports.

Chapter seven

Europe: Coke or champagne?

In 1980 only three countries in Europe had private television stations.[1] Except for Britain, Italy, and Luxembourg television was a state monopoly. Advertising demand for television was severely constrained, with limits on commercials in all countries except Italy. The broadcasting airwaves are finite in number and the states of Europe had decided at the outset of television that the government should control their use in the public interest. Eight years later, in 1988, the structure of the television industry throughout Europe had changed dramatically, and further change was inevitable. Beginning in 1985, a whole new market for commercial television opened up.

Industrial organization theorists have observed that the behaviour of firms depends upon the number of firms in an industry and the number and nature of potential entrants to the industry. Satellites meant that by 1988 the ability of national governments to protect their national television from new entrants was much diminished. Big media companies from both Europe and the United States looked at the prospects for a privatized European television sector and anticipated a growth market with considerable profit opportunities.

The new entrants and potential new entrants were attracted by the prospect of huge advertising revenues. In 1988 Europe had 330 million television sets, more than in all the USA. Europe was also a bigger market, with a larger gross national product than the USA. Yet European advertising expenditure in 1986 was equivalent to $6 billion, compared with $23 billion in the USA.[2] That amounted to one-sixth of the equivalent US sum per person on the same income. The scope for growth in the advertising sector and for television in particular as an advertising vehicle acted as a powerful magnet to new entrants. European and American firms, especially media and publishing companies, sought to gain a place in the market.[3] The experience of the United States, particularly the profitability of cable after 1985, suggested that the rewards in Europe for firms with the correct strategy would be impressive. The question in 1989 was which strategy would succeed.

Table 27 The nature of European television demand, various years

Country	Average adult TV viewing per day (hours/minutes), 1984	Annual TV advertising expenditure per head, 1983 ($)	TV advertising expenditure as a % of total advertising expenditure, 1985
West Germany	2·13	8·40	10·7
UK	3·10	26·10	31·0
France	2·9	8·30	17·7
Italy	2·4	11·20	49·6
Spain	3	8·30	31·8
Netherlands	1·27[a]	5·60	5·0
Sweden	2	*None*	−
Belgium	2·55	*None*	−
Portugal	3	4·90	47·0
Greece	3	7·10	48·4
Austria	2·18	12·60	27·5
Switzerland	1·34	9·60	8·0
Denmark	1·54	*None*	−
Finland	2	15·50	*n.a.*
Norway	1·18	*None*	−

Note a Evenings only.
Source: Booz Allen & Hamilton.

Table 28 Advertising expenditure in Europe, total and *per capita*, 1983

Country	Total advertising expenditure ($ million)	Advertising as a % of GDP	Advertising expenditure per head ($)
UK	5·84	1·27	103
West Germany	5·23	0·79	85
France	2·92	0·56	53
Italy	2·04	0·58	35
Netherlands	1·81	1·37	124
Spain	1·40	0·87	36
Finland	0·89	1·79	182
Switzerland	0·85	0·80	132
Sweden	0·67	0·73	80
Norway	0·58	1·05	139
Denmark	0·57	1·01	110
Belgium	0·45	0·55	45
Austria	0·34	0·51	45
Greece	0·13	0·38	13
Ireland	0·10	0·56	28
Portugal	0·05	0·23	4
Total	22.87	−	1,214

Source: John Tydeman and Ellen Jakes Kelm, *New Media in Europe*, London, McGraw-Hill, 1986. pp. 52–3.

The new media

The vehicles available to new entrants were privatized state broadcast television channels, newly licensed broadcast channels, satellite transmission, and a limited number of cable opportunities. Whether cable would be the vehicle of success in Europe that it was in the United States was not certain. The outcome depended upon technology, timing, and relative prices. Technology was increasingly making satellite dishes more powerful. The same-sized dish which could pick up a 200 W signal in 1977 from a high-powered satellite could pick up a 50 W signal from a medium-powered satellite in 1986 because of improved amplifiers.[4] The price of a receiving dish to access both high-powered and medium-powered satellites also continued to fall in the late 1980s. Forecasts suggested that cable would not pass 50 per cent of European households by the year 2000. Satellite television seemed to have an advantage in terms of potential market share. Even so, in 1987 satellite costs were ten times those of broadcasting, while cable costs were three times the cost of broadcasting.[5] In 1988 it was not at all clear which would be the winning technology.

A number of European countries are examined in more detail below, particularly with regard to cable and broadcast privatization. However, satellites are supranational. For all European countries the basic conditions of their industry were altered with the launch of Eutelsat 1-F10 in July 1983.[6] Although Eutelsat 1 was primarily a telecommunications satellite set up by a consortium of national PTTs (postal, telephone, and telegraph authorities) it was equipped to carry video too. It meant that Europe had its own means of distributing television by satellite. The ability to exploit the video opportunities offered by Eutelsat depended upon national regulations and the state of cable system development within each country. In 1983 the most cabled countries were Belgium, the Netherlands, and Switzerland. France and Italy were the least cabled, a situation little changed five years later, although France had ambitious plans to cable much of the country.[7]

Limited cable development and the relatively high price of satellite dishes did not prevent many new suppliers entering the television industry. There were few profits for them in the 1980s. Sky channel was the pioneer in satellite programming, starting in 1982, using the Orbit Experimental Satellite. Five years later, with an audience of 10 million, Sky was still unprofitable. In 1986 Music Box, started by the Virgin Group in Britain, merged with ITV's Super Channel because of low revenue. MTV Europe, owned by Robert Maxwell, Viacom, and British Telecom, started in 1987 with estimated costs of $15 million per annum and revenue of $1 million, based on a twenty-four hour schedule. In contrast, but as an indicator of potential profits, MTV in the United

States earned $110 million from 36 million subscribers. The question was when and whether Europe would follow in the footsteps of the United States.

Table 29 Leading European satellite-delivered basic cable services, 1987

Service	Reach (million)[a]	Description
Sky Channel	8·3	Light entertainment
Super Channel	6·1	Light entertainment
TV–5	4·7	French entertainment
RAI	3·6	Italian public service
3-Sat	2·4	General entertainment
RTL-Plus	2·0	General entertainment
Worldnet[b]	1·8	US news and information
Sat-1	1·8	General entertainment
Screen Sport	0·1	Sports
Children's Channel	0·1	Children's
Lifestyle	0·1	Women's
Arts Channel[c]	0·0	Cultural
Music Box	1·4	Music

Notes: *a* These figures are those reached, not those watching. In fact few watched Sky and Super Channel.
b Worldnet is funded by the US government.
c Arts Channel reached 12,000.
Source: Booz Allen & Hamilton.

With the launch of Eutelsat non-national broadcasting expanded. Most of the media giants were involved. Bertelsmann was behind RTL-Plus, along with Paribas and Hachette. Alex Springer and Burda-Verlag were involved in Sat-1. Most of the national public broadcasters from Europe are involved in satellite rebroadcasting so that their programmes can be seen by those speaking their national language anywhere in Europe. For example, RAI of Italy rebroadcasts as RAI. The British ITV rebroadcasts as UK Super Channel. The French-language stations in Belgium, Switzerland, and France rebroadcast as channel TV–5 and include Canadian material from Quebec. The German-language national broadcasters set up 3-Sat to a cool response from viewers, reflected in low audience ratings. These channels are aimed at a specific language market rather than at specific national markets.

Direct broadcast satellites got off to a poor start. The first to be launched was West Germany's TV-Sat 1 in 1987. This satellite was one of four which a joint venture, begun in 1980 between France and West Germany, planned to launch at a cost of about a quarter of a billion dollars each. The joint venture was a consortium called Eurosatellite.[8] A solar panel on TV-Sat failed to open and the satellite had to be abandoned.[9] Although in late 1988 France launched TDF-1, the first French satellite from the joint venture, the world had changed since 1980. Technology inversion meant that more powerful dishes and medium-powered satellites at about a quarter the cost could achieve similar or even better results. The medium-powered satellites could carry sixteen as opposed to four channels.[10] Table 30 lists Europe's DBS projects for 1989 and 1990.

Table 30 Europe's major satellite television projects

Name	Cost ($ million)	Main types of programming
TDF-1, TDF-2	500	French-language cultural and family shows
Astra	225	Broad assortment of channels from Rupert Murdoch, Robert Maxwell, and others
TV Sat-2	500[a]	German-language programmes
British Satellite Broadcasting	1,100	Sport, news, films, light entertainment
Eutelsat Four satellites after March, 1990	660	Existing state TV programmes plus private channels

Note: a Includes cost of TV Sat-1, which failed to function in orbit.
Source: Business Week; company reports.

Narrowcasting means targeting a specific interest group. Several new satellite channels were aimed at particular interests other than just common language. Table 29 lists some of the narrowcaster channels such as Music Box. Most of them are backed by big media companies and the ventures are largely experimental as they gather expertise and get a foot in the market.

The new entrants to television discussed above anticipate profits in supplying programming both to cable operators and direct to satellite dishes. European demand for programmes from cable and broadcast satellite by 1990 has been forecast as a quarter of a million hours per year, with 50,000 new hours per year.[11] However, there is uncertainty about the future pattern of development. The mid-1980s saw an increase in regulatory flexibility in Germany and France towards the cable industry, but the cost of cabling densely packed Europe with mostly underground cable would be astronomical. For these reasons it is estimated that by 2000 less than half of Europe will have access to cable and fewer still will be hooked up.

Most European countries have had some sort of cable for the last three decades. As in Britain, most of these early cable systems were of limited capacity, usually no more than four channels, and used only in areas where broadcast reception was poor. They were hooked up to a local master aerial. In Europe, except for Austria, Belgium, Luxembourg, and Switzerland, the PTTs control the laying of cable. The PTTs were initially very attracted to cable as a means of interactive television. Lack of enthusiasm for such services by the public and high costs curbed the enthusiasm of the PTTs too, and in Britain and Germany early schemes were cut back. By 1987 fewer than 20,000 homes were hooked up to cable in France, fewer than 10 per cent in Germany, and virtually none in Italy.

Table 31 Penetration of cable television in Europe, selected years

	1981	1985	1988
Belgium	73	81	89
Netherlands	60	77	77
Switzerland	47	51	55
Irish Republic	18	27	34
West Germany	4	8	12
UK	0	2	5

Source: J. Walter Thomson.

Amongst those firms which participated in the restructured European television industry in the 1980s were: CBS, NBC, Time Inc., Paramount, and News International from the USA; Berlusconi and Agnelli from Italy; TV Globo from Brazil; Thorne-EMI, Virgin Group, and Mirror Group from Britain; Bouygues, Hachette, Hersant, and Thomson from France; Bertelsmann and Springer from Germany; CTL from Luxembourg, and GBL from Belgium. Others clearly had an interest, even if they had not yet made investments in the industry. All were interested in programming to Europe rather than to individual countries. For many, a joint venture to spread the risk was an attractive strategy. Joint ventures included Bouygues and Mirror Group, Bertelsmann in West Germany and CTL of Luxembourg, Murdoch and Groupe Bruxelles Lambert (GBL), the biggest finance group in Belgium, Berlusconi and Maxwell in France, and cross-holdings between Agnelli and Hachette.[12] There were further cross-interests, so that GBL has a major holding in CTL while CTL is in a joint venture with Compagnie Lyonnaise des Eaux.

The first private non-PTT European satellite was Astra, launched in 1988 by Société Européene des Satellites (SES) of Luxembourg. Astra has sixteen video channels and is capable of supplying four audio channels for each video channel. However, as English is increasingly used as an international language, separate language channels may become superfluous for some markets, such as the all-music channel MTV, which began in 1987.[13] For others it may be necessary to broadcast in the four major languages: English, French, German, and, for Scandinavians, Swedish.

The European Community

Attempting to come to terms with the new basic conditions of demand and supply in the television industry, governments throughout Europe issued papers and reports.[14] Increasingly the decisions about television, as television more and more ignored national boundaries, went to the European Community's authorities.

The Treaty of Rome of 1957 established the basic approach for European television policy. It supports the free flow of goods and services within the Community and the free flow of information. Broadcasting has been ruled to be a service by the European Court of Justice. This has meant that leakage over national boundaries has been ignored even when the programmes contained advertising contrary to national regulations. Since 1950 the European Broadcasting Union has existed to encourage co-operation in broadcasting.[15] In 1981 all the Western European countries signed a non-binding agreement to try and harmonize national rules and regulations concerning television broadcasts.[16] However, there was little unity in 1988, and increasingly problems of advertising from other countries was a source of irritation and concern.

The advertising issue as advertising volume increases involves the ability of a country to determine its own cultural development. For countries which have chosen to go the market route and allow the new media to develop on the basis of advertising any restriction on advertising impinges on their choice. For countries subjected involuntarily to that advertising, which is exported as a service as defined by the EC, the advertising can be viewed as an imposition on their ability to control their own destiny.[17]

The advertising issue in geographically compact Europe has another characteristic. If a country refuses to allow or impose limits on advertising, then it is likely to experience a redistribution of income to those countries that do permit advertising. They will export advertising. Consequently the country with the ban still finds it incurs the social costs of the advertising, its availability on its screens, but none of the benefits in the form of a larger advertising industry. With satellites, therefore, once one country allows advertising it is hard for others not to follow. If there is bound to be advertising, then it might as well originate domestically and create jobs and incomes.

In 1988, recognizing that television is a Community problem, the European Commission recommended that 60 per cent of programming should be European, a clear indication of concern about media imperialism and the high level of American content. This protectionist approach would guarantee European sourcing, although by 1988 the Europeans had shown that they could produce very light entertainment game shows as inane as any from the USA. Meanwhile the Council of Europe in

Strasbourg stressed the need for rules as the privatization of Europe's television inevitably progressed. It noted the case in 1987 of a Swiss programme on prostitution appearing in Britain, two time zones away, at a time of peak viewing by children and families.[18]

As of 1988 these issues of advertising and programme content had not been resolved. While most countries had concluded that cable and satellite were too costly for the government to finance, only a few countries such as Britain and Luxembourg were willing to depend completely on the private sector. The experience of privatization and deregulation of broadcasting in Italy in the 1970s, which had led to chaos, was an example no country intended to follow. Yet the growth of the private sector of television in some format was inevitable and already much privatization was planned. Even Spain and Norway, which enjoyed two of the dullest television markets in Europe, had private stations planned, as had conservative West Germany and Denmark. The policy requirement was an orderly transition. The new markets would be defined in terms of languages and satellite footprints as well as traditional national boundaries. As of 1987 national markets still dominated, with $5.5 billion of the $6 billion television advertising expenditure being allocated on a national basis.

In summary, the new media in the 1980s in Europe had attracted many new entrants. Many lost money. Amongst the biggest gainers in the early years were the American exporters who supplied the bulk of the programmes which the new suppliers distributed and which Europe itself could not produce in sufficient volume.

Italy

Italy had no intention in 1972 of privatizing its state monopoly of television. Radiotelevisione Italiana (RAI) had been set up in 1936 as part of the Istituto per la Ricostruzione Industriale (IRI), in turn set up by Mussolini in 1933. Like all Europe's state television broadcasters, RAI was seen as a natural monopoly by which the state controlled the limited airwaves in the public interest.

In 1972 amid the familiar turmoil of Italian politics the mandate of RAI was unintentionally allowed to lapse. This opened the door for small local stations to start up. Entry was easy and costs were low. A small transmitter and an empty broadcasting frequency were all that was needed. Following a 1974 Supreme Court ruling against the RAI monopoly of local broadcasts, over 800 new stations began transmitting. As occurred in the United States in the late 1940s, when there was inadequate supervision, there was constant interruption of one channel by another. A total lack of regulation of the airwaves led to anarchy.[19] Programme content also left much to be desired. In several cases unsuitable programming such as that known as 'housewife striptease' was made easily accessible to children. Following a crackdown by the PTT some sort of order was introduced, an inevitable market-driven rationalization took place, and by 1980 there were fewer than 250 stations. Starting a station had proved easier than running one at a profit. The least efficient went broke or merged. Those remaining relied heavily on the United States for cheap programming, making Italy the second largest export market for US programmes, worth $150 million in 1981.[20]

By 1987 Italy was certainly wealthy enough to support many commercial stations. In 1987 the country proudly announced that it had a GNP greater than that of Britain. Italy in the 1980s enjoyed faster economic growth than either France or Germany and had clearly become an important economic power in Europe. At the same time the country's later economic development meant that Italy is a country without the newspaper habit.[21] Consequently demand from both consumers and advertisers is directed towards television, which by 1988 absorbed half of all advertising expenditure. This means that the potential for television as an advertising vehicle is greater in Italy than in northern Europe, where the press has a greater hold as a medium of entertainment and information as well as of advertising. Table 4 shows the proportion of GNP going to advertising in some of the Western countries, and it is reasonable to anticipate all countries moving towards the US level, given plentiful supply.

In 1988 Italy's public television sector was run by RAI and was financed by a budget granted by the government but derived from licence fees and from advertising. For 1987 RAI's budget was $310 million, about one-third that of the BBC or a quarter that of the Japanese state television system, NHK. RAI is run by a director-general and a board of sixteen members. Parliament's supervisory committee chooses ten members of the board and the IRI's board six members. With its budget RAI operates three channels, RAI 1, 2, and 3. These attract about 50 per cent of the audience. Programmes include a considerable amount of local programming and news. On RAI less than 20 per cent of programming is foreign in content. Advertising on RAI is transmitted both during and between programmes for about an hour a day in total.

The private sector by 1988 had been rationalized under the influence of the major investors in the industry. The most sensational television entrepreneur was Silvio Berlusconi. In seven years he came to dominate the private sector. Sometimes called La Sua Emitteriza (His Transmittance) by the press, in 1988 80 per cent of those watching private stations were watching Berlusconi's television.[22] He had created or gained control of three loose affiliations called Canale 5, Rete 4, and Italiano Uno. In 1987 Canale 5 alone generated advertising revenues of $325 million, equivalent to the budget of RAI. Berlusconi was also known as the gravedigger of the Italian film industry, an unintended complement to his ability to meet the video demands of the average Italian.[23]

Early and disorganized privatization of television broadcasting had the effect of forestalling the entry of other suppliers into the video industry. With a plentiful supply of private broadcast light entertainment by 1980 VCRs had little success in the Italian market. This reflects the fact that, in contrast to the rest of Europe, consumer demand for video entertainment was met by the hundreds of private stations. Even in 1988 the penetration level of VCRs in Italy was the lowest in Europe, despite Italians' increasing affluence.

Plentiful broadcast television had a similar effect on demand for satellite and cable television as it had on demand for VCRs. In both areas development has lagged behind the rest of Europe.

Berlusconi dominates Italian television but his ambition is to create pan-European television by expanding into other countries. Already he has television interests in Spain, France, and Yugoslavia. He holds a major share of one of France's commercial stations and owns Spain's largest studios. He has announced plans to deliver satellite television with multilingual sound tracks. He also attempted but failed to take over television in Monte Carlo as a base for broadcasting to the countries surrounding Italy. Nevertheless in 1986 Berlusconi was the fourth largest broadcaster in the world, exceeded in size only by the big three American networks, and his advertising revenues in 1986 exceeded $1 billion.[24]

Berlusconi developed his television empire out of a basement broadcasting station which he started in Milan in 1979. The station was called Milano 2. As his television stations expanded he integrated backwards into production and built huge studios in Milan. At the time he started in 1979 Berlusconi already had a fortune which he had made out of property. He also had media interests as a newspaper publisher which included ownership of the newspaper *Giornale Nuova* in Milan.

Berlusconi has powerful opponents both at home and abroad in the television industry. In Italy there are potential entrants to the industry such as Agnelli of Fiat. Agnelli bought the *Corriere del Sol*, a Turin newspaper, in order to ensure that the news about his companies received a favourable voice. He clearly has ambitions of extending his interests in the communications industry as part of a strategy to diversify out of the increasingly competitive car market.[25]

Berlusconi also has to be concerned about the government and possible changes in competition policy. His stations have weakened the RAI and he has skirted round the aims of the 1974 law on the state broadcasting monopoly. In 1988 Italy's anti-trust legislation was inadequate to deal with Berlusconi's empire but he had defences ready for an attack from that quarter. In 1985, after he had unsuccessfully attempted to take over

Telemontecarlo and been thwarted by a bail-out of Telemontecarlo by RAI and the Brazilian television giant Globo, he made a deal with Telecapodistra Yugoslav. This offers his empire protection in the event of his Italian operations being dismantled or limits being imposed on media advertising, as has been proposed.

Advertising on Italy's private stations is broadcast every fifteen minutes in blocks. Although the stations have agreed to limits on commercials so that they average about nine minutes per hour, in prime time there can be as many as twenty minutes of advertisements each hour.

Berlusconi and the other private stations filled the market gap that the public system had failed to satisfy. Many early stations provided pornography and similar fare but the real consumer demand was for light entertainment. This is what Berlusconi and the other successful stations provided. They imported American shows at low prices and filled the airwaves with them. They also manufactured their own light entertainment programmes. The successful stations were those which understood that despite all the talk of narrowcast the greatest demand was for light entertainment, what has been described as 'chewing gum for the mind'. Italia Uno carries 92 per cent light entertainment.

A second ruling by the Supreme Court in 1976 following that in 1974 which allowed the establishment of private stations determined that the RAI had a monopoly of national broadcasting. This made it very difficult for any of the private networks to broadcast any news. It was an important decision for RAI, since in Italy most citizens rely on television for their news. Consequently the RAI is able to differentiate itself from the private stations and so is able to maintain a significant market share.

To counter the private stations RAI has also attempted to change its programming, particularly on RAI-1. They have revitalized the Italian film industry by supporting films made just for television. The RAI, however, has been frustrated by the effect of the private stations on costs. Private stations have bid up the price of well known television personalities in order to attract them from RAI. This gives the private stations instant credibility. Even those who stay with the public sector want parity. In 1984 RAI agreed to a contract which paid the popular Raffala Carre over $1 million after Mike Bonjano had jumped to Canale 5 for a similar fee.

The RAI continues to have a monopoly of all national broadcasting, not just the news. The 1974 Supreme Court decision found that the private stations could broadcast locally, using recorded material. As a result there is a basic artificiality to Canale 5, Rete 4, and Italiano Uno as networks. They cannot retransmit material. Instead all their material is pre-recorded and all of it is physically transported to every station so that each station is in theory the original broadcaster. What in effect happens is that a show is produced in Milan, and video cassettes are then distributed by plane and motor cycle to every affiliate with instructions to run the cassette at a particular time.

Italy therefore provides an interesting view of what the rest of Europe can anticipate as privatization continues and new broadcast, cable, and satellite supplies become available. Italy shows that much demand can be met by broadcasting and that deregulation does not lead to widespread pornography as some have feared. Italy shows that the forces for concentration are strong but that there can be a role for a public sector to meet demand which a purely commercial system leaves unfulfilled.

France

Politics has always played a central role in the French media. In the 1950s President Charles De Gaulle said, 'My opponents have much of the press on their side, so I keep television.'[26] President Pompidou said that television belonged to the French, which he interpreted to mean that he as President should control it. President Mitterrand, a socialist, said that 'freedom needs to be regulated'.[27] Such regulation allowed the government to ban a film for television by Jacques Cousteau in which Cousteau criticized the way the French handled their industrial wastes. When in 1985 President Mitterrand, in an apparent turn of face, announced that he was going to privatize the television industry it was because privatization of the media was a good political strategy.

In 1982 French radio had been deregulated. Soon there were over a thousand radio stations broadcasting, and a chaotic situation comparable to that in Italian television in the 1970s had developed. The government decided that the transition to a private system in television should be more orderly. To that end it ordered the Bredin Report, which appeared in 1985. The Bredin Report recommended slow progress, based largely on projections of likely growth in the advertising industry. Too many new stations would mean inadequate support for all of them.

The transition was not slow, although it was more orderly than the privatization of radio. Privatization took place in a two-year period. With an election looming in 1987 which Mitterrand was not assured of winning, the privatization and deregulation process was hurried up. Additional supplies of television from any distribution vehicle were a vote-winner, and Mitterrand needed help. The polls showed him trailing behind his right-wing opponent, Prime Minister Chirac, also Mayor of Paris.

Although Mitterrand was a socialist who had been first elected in 1980, favouring nationalization of more industries and promising a 'break with capitalism', privatization of television had wide appeal.[28] For many workers who traditionally voted socialist free and entertaining commercial television financed by advertisements, such as was available in Italy and Britain, was widely welcome. State television was much criticized

because it was boring. For middle-of-the-road voters television privatization showed that Mitterrand had shifted to the right. If he won the election
it would be a successful strategy. It would also be successful if he lost.
A former Minister in the opposition said, 'The Socialists are making
sure they have a safe seat in the media from which they will denigrate
the [next] government.'[29]

Until 1986 there were just three government-owned channels
supplying the French public. There was no commercial television
available from within France. Two years later there were six broadcast
television channels and only two were state-run. In 1987, for the first
time in the world history of television, a state system was privatized when
the government sold off TF-1.

In 1988 the following channels were operating in France. The French
government still ran FR3, the regional television station, and Antenne-2,
the original colour station set up in the 1960s. TF-1 was the now
privatized and commercially based former state station. There were also
two new privately owned stations, La Cinq and TV-6. Finally there was
Canal-Plus, the first scrambled broadcast television service in Europe.
Canal-Plus was started in 1984 and by 1987 12 per cent of households
had signed up for it. Canal-Plus was 42 per cent owned by the state
advertising agency Havas and showed a mix of films, drama, sport, news,
and special events. In the light of the entry of the new free channels
the prospects of Canal-Plus, which lost $80 million in 1985, were bleak.

Operating a television station can involve losses for some time before
the advertising base is developed. The new stations and the privatized
state stations required the backing of large conglomerates able to finance
them until advertising revenue was capable of covering all the costs.
Particularly keen to get into the television media were the French press
giants Hersant and Hachette, which supply the bulk of French newspapers
and magazines. Robert Hersant produced *Le Figaro*, owned twenty-one
regional newspapers, and was France's largest newspaper publisher.
Hachette was a media conglomerate and France's sixty-eighth largest
corporation. Once again politics played a critical role in the allocation
of the new stations.

Hachette was a strong favourite to be allowed to buy TF-1. However,
Hachette had the support of President Mitterrand's opponent, Prime
Minister Chirac. Robert Hersant, on the other hand, who earlier in life
had been accused of wartime collaboration with the Germans, was a
declared enemy of Mitterrand and therefore politically ineligible for the
plum station with its established audience. This had been made clear in
1984, when a hypocritical and politically motivated anti-monopoly piece
of media legislation had been passed, targeting him. Even Hersant's
opponents conceded that the Bill was drafted specifically to undermine
him and prevent him from expanding his media interests further. The

Bill excluded the only other media organization that fitted the terms of the legislation, state television.[30]

To avoid any accusations of favouritism over the sale of TF-1 the government established the Commission Nationale de la Communication et des Libertés (CNCL) to decide who should be allotted TF-1. The establishment of the CNCL gave the impression of an arms-length transaction. Many concluded, given the recent media history of France, that it was only a cover to give the appearance of impartiality. Such was not the case.

The surprise winner of TF-1 was a non-media conglomerate called Group Bouygues. With $8 billion in sales in 1987 Group Bouygues's main interest was construction. The firm was a major contractor for the building of the Channel tunnel. The CNCL interpreted the statement by Group Bouygues that it was not a media company and had no interest in the day-to-day running of the station as a convincing argument for selling it the station. Group Bouygues offered the possibility that TF-1 could operate free of political interference.[31] The station was sold on a 10–40–50 basis, with 10 per cent going to the employees, 40 per cent to the general public, and 50 per cent to Group Bouygues, in partnership with Britain's Mirror Group.[32] Mirror Group is headed by the press magnate Robert Maxwell.

Table 32 France's new broadcast television suppliers, 1988

Station	Major shareholders
TF-1	Bouygues, Maxwell, public
TF-2	State-owned
La Cinq	Hersant, Berlusconi
Canal-Plus	Havas
TV-6	CTL, Lyonnaise des Eaux

The price of TF-1 was set at $750 million, and some critics argued that this was much less than TF-1 was worth. TF-1 was oversubscribed four times, and with advertising revenue in 1986 of $590 million critics suggested that a price tag of $3 billion would have been more realistic. However, the advertising agency Havas had pulled out of the bidding, believing the price to be too high.[33] This reflected their uncertainty over the size of the future advertising market in a television-liberated France and the risk and uncertainties over who the competing video suppliers in Europe might be.

The 1985 Bredin report had recommended a slow and regulated increase in the number of new stations. Jean-Dennis Bredin argued for two new national stations and sixty-two regional ones. He suggested that market growth, at $330 million per year, could justify only two new stations. Accepting many of the report's recommendations, Mitterrand announced the start of two new channels immediately. The first went to Silvio Berlusconi of Italy. Lacking French entrepreneurs willing, wealthy, and politically acceptable, the government invited him to start one new channel. Berlusconi led a group which included Hersant, so that each got a 25 per cent share. The second channel, TV-6, went to Compagnie Luxembourgois de Télédiffusion (CLT) and Compagnie Lyonnaise des Eaux.[34]

Hachette, blocked from broadcasting but determined to be part of the new media, invested in satellite television. The French government had signed an agreement for a joint venture with Germany to launch TV-Sat late in 1987 to provide DBS. Hachette, in co-operation with US companies and Telecom-2, planned to become a programme supplier on one of the five channels to be offered via TV-Sat. However, this strategy was temporarily foiled when one of the solar panels on TV-Sat failed to open.

The failure of TV-Sat meant that there was still no DBS in Europe in 1988. There were plans for new launches, so France will have French satellite television by 1990 from TDF-1 satellite. Meanwhile the footprint of Sky channel already covered France and in 1987 MTV Europe was beamed over the country.

Cable development in France has been slow. Although in 1987 private companies were allowed to start laying cable to add yet more competitors for France's limited television advertising expenditure, with so many other delivery vehicles in place the French cable industry faced a tough challenge.

In one area of interactive television, videotext, France leads the world in terms of consumer participation. In 1982 the French government introduced Minitel. This was at a time when around the world virtually all videotext experiments were failing commercially. They were too expensive and clumsy. But the simple-to-operate French system, in which the government provided the hardware, was a raging success. Initially a replacement for the phone book, allowing viewers on government-provided consoles to call up numbers automatically over the phone lines, Minitel was soon allowing private operators to use the system. Consumers only paid for the services they used. Soon there were over 4,500 consumer services available, including 100 dating services in which individuals using the phones could exchange messages.[35] If they wished, their video dates could exchange phone numbers and meet in person. Often they were just fantasy talks which, for an extra charge, could go private. Whilst dating services were the most talked-about service, Minitel allowed access to a wide variety of other private and public services. The French experience showed that, at the right price, if the equipment was consumer-friendly and the services offered were useful, consumers would use videotext.

In 1988 one commentator said that the French had been promised 'beaujolais television' and got 'Coke and fries television'.[36] The comment was appropriate. The six channels did not provide all new French television programmes. Instead, as in Italy and the United States, there was heavy reliance on quiz shows, game shows, and US network re-runs. Such shows were cheap to produce or buy yet were watched and enjoyed by many French viewers.

The pressure to supply low-cost programmes was increased by the small advertising base. The Bredin report had recommended that advertising should be limited to twenty-four minutes per day. In 1986 total television advertising revenue amounted to under $1 billion, less than 5 per cent of US levels. In 1987 it rose to $1.25 billion and in 1988 approached $2 billion.[37] Compared with Britain and the United States, a smaller proportion of advertising revenue went to television. In 1985 only 17 per cent of total advertising expenditure, in contrast to nearly a third in the other two countries, was devoted to television. The small advertising base meant a tight constraint on the finance available for television programmes.

The dilemma created by a limit on advertising time is that restrictions on advertising mean programmers must rely on cheap imports, often from the United States. Limits on advertising mean greater exposure to a basically American culture. This has created a controversial problem regarding the purity of French culture.

France has a unique and widely admired culture. French was for long the international language. Fifty years ago Somerset Maugham said that French was 'the common language of educated men'.[38] The French spend heavily on culture, and the Minister of Culture, unlike in most countries, is a senior position. However, in the twentieth century French as the international language has been supplanted by English, or more honestly American, and the anglicization of French has been widespread. The French have expressed great concern about cultural imperialism in general and the effect of television in particular. They have even set up government agencies to find French words to replace English ones. Yet despite the effort France seems to have had little more success than other countries in dealing with the problem of television and cultural imperialism.

French television even introduced a unique game show to help the cause, in which contestants found French words for English ones. A walkman became a *baladeur* and computer hardware *matériel*.[39] However, as satellite television beams in increasing quantities of English-language television it will take more than game shows to keep the language pure.

A different but also unique French programme is *Apostrophes*, a show about books. The show's host on Antenne-2 is the book reviewer Bernard Pirot, whose charm and telegenic personality enable him to attract 6 million viewers each week who tune in to see and hear him discuss books which he has recently read.[40] Antenne-2 is one of the two remaining state-run channels, and as host he is paid $160,000 per annum. Other channels have offered him four times as much. Although Pirot has not switched, saying that money does not bother him, he is unusual. One consequence of the new and privatized stations, as in Italy, has been a bidding up of costs in general and of salaries in particular.

Established performers on the state systems found themselves to be hot properties when the new stations sought instant credibility. Whilst the government thought that privatization would lead to more competition, lower advertising rates, and more choice, this has not been the outcome. Rather the price of inputs has been bid up as a result of the increase in demand. Meanwhile the new stations have adopted strategies based on the preference option. The new stations offer more of the same programmes. Advertising rates have not fallen. The French do indeed enjoy 'Coke and french fries' television.

Table 33 Typical day programme schedule for La Cinq, April 1987

John Huston film	(US)
Hill Street Blues	(US)
Mission Impossible	(US)
Kojak	(US)
Star Trek	(US)

The reasons are easy to understand. An episode of the highly popular drama *Chateauvallon* cost over a third of a million dollars per episode in 1985. The American-produced *Dallas* or its equivalent was obtainable for a tenth of the price and attracted similar audiences. The profit motive, in combination with consumer demand for television programmes at zero price, determines conduct in a privatized environment. With the incentives created by Mitterrand's privatization the outcome is exactly what economics would predict: lots of light entertainment.

Germany

Germany has the largest economy in western Europe. The potential advertising market for television is worth in the order of $5 billion, based on current US levels. The largest media company in Europe, Bertelsman, is larger than CBS and would like to supply private television. The government has stalled such plans and taken a very cautious approach to the new media. In 1979 Chancellor Helmut Schmidt said that he regarded television as more dangerous than nuclear power.[41] Reflecting similar views in the 1980s, the government has been slow to allow an expansion of the traditional networks. At the same time it has recognized the inevitability of the new media.

Television is operated by two state-run organizations: the Arbeits-gemeinschaft der Offentlich-Rechtlichen Rundfunk anstalten der Bundesrepublik Deutschland (ARD), a network of nine regional stations established in 1950, and Zweites Deutsches Fernsehen (ZDF), a second channel created in 1961 under an agreement between the *Länder*, the eleven separate states of West Germany. Since Germany is a federation, the individual states have a considerable say in what happens on television. Changes in the structure of the industry are subject to veto by the individual states, which tends to work in favour of the *status quo* as regards television.[42]

Television is supplied on three programmes, the first produced by ARD, the second by ZDF. The third is a cultural and educational service which operates in the evenings and broadcasts programmes from the different regional broadcasters headquartered in Munich, Frankfurt, Hamburg, Bremen, Saarbrucken, Berlin, Stuttgart, Baden-Baden, and Cologne.[43] Since a complete range of programming is supplied from each centre of broadcasting, German television fails to exploit economies of scale.

The state channels rely on licence fees and advertising for their revenue. Advertising is limited to forty minutes daily, in ten-to-fifteen-minute blocks, broadcast usually in the early evening. There is no advertising on Sundays. Consequently advertising revenue covers only a little over one-third of operating costs at ZDF and ARD. Since the regional stations are commercial-free, licence fees are the major source of finance.

Advertising in 1988 was inefficient. Not only was the time limited to blocks at the end of the day which many people ignored but prices for the limited commercial slots were regulated. This meant that there was excess advertising demand. Advertisers could not choose when to advertise, they could only select the month. With too many advertisers wanting to advertise at the fixed price, advertisers either had to go without or else wait for what might be an unsatisfactory or inappropriate time slot. Meanwhile, since revenue from the limited time periods was not maximized, licence fees had to be higher to make up the difference. Nobody benefited. Advertisers got poor service whilst consumers paid higher licence fees and still received the same number of commercials.

Germany has been slower than the other three large European countries to restructure its television industry. Consequently in 1988 consumer and advertiser demand still went unmet. In 1987 20 per cent of Germans owned VCRs, a good indication that they were not getting the television programming they wanted.[44]

Despite government and Cartel Office concern, Bertelsmann still plan to provide private television. Bertelsmann created a furore in 1983 when they bought into RTL to allow them to distribute television programming from Luxembourg. Subsequently Bertelsmann invested in programme supply by taking a share in Teleclub, a German-language pay-television channel.

The government stalled the development of non-state television. Attitudes such as those expressed by Helmut Schmidt, a basic conservatism, and the difficulty of achieving consensus in a federal political system explain this. As a result, when SaT-1 was started all three SDP states vetoed the distribution of SaT-1 on cable systems in their states.

There has been advance, despite the opposition of the socialist parties. Bertelsmann's purchase of 40 per cent of RTL in 1983 made it clear that Germany would be receiving new programming one way or the other. Worldwide sales at that time of $2·4 billion meant that Bertelsmann were a force to be reckoned with. Either more television would come from abroad by DBS or the government could have some control, with supply coming internally.

In 1984 the Bundespost undertook a $10 billion programme to cable the nation. Like other PTTs, the Bundespost saw interactive cable as a growth sector for a wide variety of business and financial services as well as television.

The first cable systems were laid in Dortmund, Ludwigshafen, Munich, and Berlin. They were financed by a levy on the monthly television licence. In 1985 in Dortmund, following a decision by the SPD government to allow private media, it was possible to view SaT-1, Sky channel, and Music Box. In Berlin, Dusseldorf, Hamburg, Hanover, and Stuttgart optical fibre was used in an experimental system called BIGFON. By 1988 10 per cent of households were reached by cable. However, since Germans had to pay for the cost of linking up their residence to the cable in the street, cable was expensive and many consumers were reluctant to sign up.

Other suppliers were waiting to exploit new distribution channels. In 1984 Bertelsmann began a joint venture with the American company RCA, which owns the NBC network, to offer a pay-television service. In 1987 Berlusconi of Italy purchased 45 per cent of Kabel Media Programmgesellschaft, a Munich-based satellite-to-cable company which operates Music Box. Berlusconi also owns a cable company called Telefung. Music Box will have to compete with SaT-1 and RTL-Plus, which are backed by the big publishers.[45] In addition several German states have released additional local frequencies for commercial channels. In Munich Franz Strauss, the son of the former Bavarian Minister, operates a commercial channel, and new channels have also been started in Berlin.[46]

In terms of conduct by 1988 German television was still failing to meet the demands of viewers and advertisers. Advertising was limited, making television an unexploited media for advertisers. Television programming for those who were not on cable still reflected the tastes of the official broadcasters. Although the soap opera *Schwarzwaldklinik*, a nostalgic programme about a doctor's life in the 1950s, was highly popular, there was a shortage of light entertainment. This was reflected in the low viewing hours *per capita* in contrast to the other three major European powers. News was the largest category of programming on ARD in the mid-1980s and culture and education on ZDF.

The prospects for Germany are similar to those of the rest of Europe. The state monopoly is under siege. VCRs, cable, satellite, new broadcast, and an acceptance by the broadcasting authorities that change is inevitable all mean the same thing. Germans too will have access to a wide variety of advertiser-based and pay-television channels. There may be some delay, and the change may be a little more orderly than in Italy and France, but the outcome will be very similar.

An indication of this is found in the bidding up of input costs. In 1988 Bertelsmann bid $80 million for the right to televise Germany's top soccer league, the Bundesliga. This was the first time that the state channels had lost the right to televise German football. They bid $40 million. RTL-Plus immediately agreed to pay $53 million for the first-time showing rights of the league. Bertelsmann promised to sell packages to the state channels. However, 10 million people in Germany are keen soccer fans and RTL-Plus sees soccer as a means of getting more than 30 per cent of Germans to sign up for cable. It will also offer packages of programmes to private cable operators.[47]

By 1989 cable and satellite penetration was approaching 30 per cent. Of those with access to cable or satellite 55 per cent watched ZDF and ARD. Nineteen per cent watched SaT-1, 10 per cent watched RTL-Plus, about one per cent watched Sky and Super Channel in English, and the rest was accounted for by private cable and other sources.[48] In other words, after a slightly slower start, and despite some opposition, West Germany too was coming to the age of abundant television.

Other European countries

Radio Luxembourg hurdled the national boundaries of broadcasting more than thirty years ago. Small countries have always been more exposed to the broadcast leakages of large countries than *vice versa*. In the new media age their experience is shared by larger, heretofore protected nations. For years Belgium and Holland were the most cabled countries in Europe and accepted the inevitable outcome that the majority of channels must originate from outside the country.[49]

In *Holland* in 1988 a third publicly operated broadcasting station, Nederland 3, began transmission. It was publicly funded and in competition with two other public channels but also with more than twelve channels from Britain, France, West Germany, and Belgium. There was also a huge illegal pirate movie industry, in part a consequence of a six-month protection given to films before they can be shown on Dutch television.

Dutch public television has a unique structure. Eight associations run the first two public channels. The associations represent the different religious and political groups. Each association supplies a certain amount of programming to suit the requirements of those it represents. Surprisingly, the outcome is that the Dutch watch predominantly Dutch television. Over 80 per cent of viewing time goes to the publicly funded, limited-advertising domestic channels. This lends support to the notion that for entertainment even multilingual people such as the Dutch prefer their own language.

Belgium and *Luxembourg* are bases for international conglomerates which intend to transmit television to the rest of Europe. Belgium's GBL, together with News International, has a major stake in Compagnie Luxembourg de Télédiffusion, better known as Radio Luxembourg. CLT has two transponders on TDF-1, so that it can beam programmes via satellite all over Europe. By joining with News International CLT gained access to the 2,500-movie library of Twentieth Century–Fox. Bertelsmann also have a major interest in CLT, so that through CLT two of Europe's largest media companies are linked in a joint venture.

In *Spain* Berlusconi of Italy owns the largest production studios, Roma Studios. Spain's 24 million people watch an average three and a half hours of television per day, one of the highest levels in Europe. The state still controls television, which is dull and does not fully meet consumer demand. By holding down advertising rates on television the government is able to lessen the viability of Spanish newspapers. This reduces both the efficiency of advertising and the satisfaction consumers could derive from the media. However, it helps the government control the Fourth Estate.

From Spain Berlusconi plans to use the output from his Roma Studios for satellite television. He will use it for programming in his joint venture with Robert Maxwell on the two transponders they control on TDF-1.

Spain planned to start commercial television in 1986 to complement the two national services, TVE-1 and TVE-2. The legislation to start three commercial channels was finally passed in April 1988. The state channels are run by the state organization Television Espanola. In addition to TVE-1 and TVE-2 there are also three regional services. The regional services serve the Basque country, Catalonia, and the Canary Islands. Commercial television was introduced as a response to the threat of satellites and also in response to complaints about excessive political and relgious content on the state channels.

There are no licence fees in Spain. Most revenue comes from advertising, to which is added a small state subsidy. Again, advertising is inefficient, with limits of under an hour per day and low rates for these spots. The result for advertisers is no choice over timing and a long wait to place advertisements. It also means a failure to maximize revenue to pay for improved programming.

In conclusion, southern European countries such as Spain and Italy, but also Greece, Turkey, and Portugal, have a potential for greater advertising growth and for a greater influence of television than northern Europe. This is because they have experienced the 'leapfrog effect'.[50] Because of political events and their later economic 'take-off', there has been limited development of newspapers. Although they do read magazines their people have never developed the newspaper habit, hence television faces one less powerful substitute for both advertisers and viewers. With the prospect of rapid economic growth in a free-trade Europe after 1992 the outlook for the new commercial television suppliers is promising.

For all of Europe the growth of supranational television spilling over national boundaries will require regulation. The responsibility for appropriate legislation will lie with the European Community as a whole. The form of that regulation will then have an impact upon industry structure and conduct.

Notes

1 *The Economist*, 17 August 1987, reports only two countries but Luxembourg has been broadcasting commercials for decades to neighbouring European countries.
2 *Business Week*, 2 May 1987.
3 The list of potential entrants included all the major US networks and broadcasters. In Europe they included Sir James Goldsmith, Albert Frere, Robert Hersant, Rupert Murdoch, the Rothschilds, Robert Maxwell, Silvio Berlusconi, Giovanni Agnelli, Carlo de Benedetti, Jean Lagardere, and firms such as Havas, Hachette, Alex Springer, Bertelsmann, and Pearson.
4 *The Economist*, 10 January 1987.
5 *Satellite Entertainment Guide*, December 1985, p. 5.
6 This replaced the Orbit Experimental Satellite, sent up in 1977. Satellites have a life span of about seven years.
7 Diana Green, 'Cable television in France: a non-market approach', *Quarterly Review*, August 1984, p. 16.
8 The two principal West German participants were Messerschmitt-Bolkow-Blohm and AEG Telefunken. The two principal French

participants were Alcaltel Espace and Aerospatiale.

9   *Business Week*, 14 March 1988.

10 Low-powered satellites are from 10 W to 20 W, medium-powered ones from 40 W to 50 W, and high-powered ones from 110 W to 230 W. For example, TDF-1 is 230 W while BSB guarantees to be over 110 W. Astra is 45 W.

11 *The Economist*, 10 September 1984.

12 *The Economist*, 26 December 1987.

13 It is not clear to what extent English will dominate. Although English is widely spoken in much of Europe this is not the case away from the cities, nor even amongst many working people. Even many who can make themselves understood in English have no desire or intention of being fluent enough to enjoy leisure-time activities in English. There is much reason, therefore, to anticipate that there will be a market for non-English channels well into the future.

14 A thorough discussion can be found in Don R. Leduc, 'Policy patterns in Europe and the United States', *Journal of Broadcasting*, spring 1983, p. 99.

15 The European Broadcasting Union deals with such issues as programme exchanges, tariff rates, technical standards, and the monitoring of programmes to ensure that national rules are not broken. It encourages programme collaboration, the most famous being the Eurovision Song Contest, which for years had the same glamour as the Oscars in the United States.

16 *The Economist*, 10 September 1988. The agreement also proposed a move towards 60 per cent European content, although some of the worst of Europe's light entertainment was as bad as anything that might be imported from the United States.

17 The Dutch have taken the view that cable operators may carry channels from outside Holland but that broadcasters outside Holland may not advertise in Dutch.

18 *World Press Report*, December 1986.

19 *Christian Science Monitor*, 3 December 1984.

20 *The Broadcaster*, August 1983.

21 Peter J.S. Dunnett, *The World Newspaper Industry*, London: Croom Helm, 1988, p. 157. In 1989 it was reported that a version of the game Portfolio in *Corriere* had doubled circulation to over a million within the space of a few weeks, which suggests that there may be more room for newspaper growth in southern Europe than had been realized.

22 *The Economist*, 12 September 1987.

23 *The Economist*, 3 October 1987.

24 There is a lack of financial information about Berlusconi, who works through a holding company called Fininvest, whose revenues were estimated at 1·4 trillion lire for 1987.

25 Until 1992 Italy will continue to enjoy the benefits of an agreement signed in the 1960s to limit imports of Japanese cars to 3 per cent of the market. Fiat will then lose its protection and must anticipate

fierce competition in the production of small and medium-sized cars. Diversification away from automobiles makes sense.

26 R. Williams, 'France: a revolution in the making', *Channels*, September 1985, p. 60.
27 Peter J.S. Dunnett, *The World Newspaper Industry*, London: Croom Helm, 1988, p. 147.
28 *Christian Science Monitor*, 16 June 1988.
29 Luane Parker, 'A TV debut in France', *Maclean's*, 3 March 1986.
30 Hersant had other problems in terms of TF-1. He employed ten national deputies in his media empire and there could be a conflict of interest if he controlled France's largest television station, which attracted nearly half the viewers. These deputies had been unable to prevent the passage of a newspaper Bill targeted at Hersant which limited the market share that an owner could have in Paris and in the provinces.
31 There was almost immediate interference. *The Economist*, 26 September 1987, reported that the popular show *Droit de Réponse* had been dropped because it had criticized a plan to build a bridge from Ile De Ré to La Rochelle in Paris. The builder was Francois Bouygues.
32 *New York Times*, 6 February 1987.
33 *New York Times*, 24 February 1987.
34 *The Economist*, 28 February 1987.
35 *The Atlantic*, July 1986.
36 Luana Parker, 'A TV debut in France', *Maclean's* 3 March 1986.
37 *The Economist*, 23 July 1988.
38 *Time*, 14 September 1987.
39 There is even a 1911 law which forbids the use of English words in business.
40 *Time*, 13 July 1987.
41 Andrew C. Bron, 'Europe braces for free market television', *Fortune*, 20 February 1984. In 1984 West Germany spent even less than France on television advertising as a proportion of total advertising. In 1984 it was about 10 per cent of the total.
42 Marcellus C. Snow, 'Telecommunications and media policy in West Germany: recent developments', *Journal of Communications*, January 1981, p. 13. The reason why the *Länder* have such power reflects a reaction to events under the Nazis. By giving the Länder considerable power over the media it is hoped that a repeat of history will not occur. The price in the 1980s is slow progress in all areas of telecommunications.
43 *The Europa Yearbook*, London: Europa Publications, 1987, p. 1186.
44 Booz Allen & Hamilton, *The Future of Broadcasting*, London: Booz Allen & Hamilton, p. 40.
45 *Die Zeit*, 6 March 1987.
46 *The Economist*, 12 September 1987.
47 *Business Week*, 6 June 1988.
48 *The Economist*, 17 September 1988.

49 Jean-Marie Piérinne, 'Monopoly and/or public service: the Belgian instance, *Journal of Communications*, October 1983, p. 206.
50 Peter J.S. Dunnett, *The World Newspaper Industry*, London: Croom Helm, 1988. p. 21.

Chapter eight

Japan and Australia: reaching the frontiers

Japan

In the 1920s the Japanese examined the public broadcasting system of Britain and the commercial system of the United States and concluded that Britain was a more suitable model for Japan. Nippon Hoso Kyokai (NHK) was set up to reflect that choice as a public corporation in 1926. Japanese television in the late 1980s still reflected that choice but operated under a structure inherited from the Americans in 1950. The Supreme Allied Commander, General MacArthur, bequeathed to the country a constitution modelled after that of the United States. The 1950 Broadcast Law established a television structure in which there was both public and private television, a mix between the public systems of Europe and the commercial system of America.[1]

In 1988 Japan dominated the world consumer electronics market and was a formidable economic power. The situation in 1950, therefore, warrants recalling. At that time it was debatable whether even the mighty US economy could generate the advertising necessary to support a commercial television system. For impoverished Japan it would be impossible. It was thought then that the public station NHK, based on licence fees, would dominate and that the commercial stations would play a minor role. By 1988 NHK was the wealthiest public television system in the world, receiving licence fees from over 30 million households and broadcasting to a population of 123 million, more than Britain and France combined. There were also four profitable major commercial systems based upon the advertising revenue generated by the second largest consumer goods market in the world.

There is strong consumer demand and the Japanese watch nearly four hours of television a day. Only the United States watches more. Given that all households have television, that population growth is slow, and that new consumer electronic diversions are constantly appearing on the market, it is clear that television audiences will not increase much in the future.

Table 34 Japan's advertising expenditure, by class (%)

Sales promotion	34
Television	30
Newspapers	25
Magazines	7
Radio	4
Total expenditure (¥ billion)	3,945

Source: Dentsu.

Advertiser demand is also fully developed, and attracts over 36 per cent of each advertising yen, more than in most European countries. In 1986 this was worth $5.8 billion. Although economic growth will inevitably cause overall advertising expenditure to grow, some of it will be siphoned off to the new media, most notably DBS satellite television. In other words the Japanese broadcast television industry is a mature industry with limited opportunities for growth.

Japanese television is the most technologically advanced in the world. The 1950 Broadcast Law required that NHK supply television to every household. This has been interpreted by NHK as a mandate to play an important role in hardware development. Japan is a mountainous country, and getting broadcast signals to some of the more remote regions is difficult. NHK has therefore been a pioneer in both cable and satellite television in the 1980s as well as, in co-operation with the major consumer electronics firms, high-definition television. This it calls Hi-Vision.

In 1986 4 million homes received their television by cable, the rest getting satisfactory supply from the six main channels via broadcasting. Very few Japanese had the large 1.5 m dishes used by many Americans to free-ride on medium-powered satellite signals, because relatively few signals are available and living space is limited. However, in 1988 a large number bought smaller 75 cm dishes to receive twenty-four-hour broadcasts from the world's first DBS satellite. The first Japanese DBS satellite was launched in 1987 and by late 1988 a million people were able to watch the new channel from NHK. Households sometimes joined together so that one small dish could serve two households. Between 1987 and 1988 the price of DBS dishes fell from $2,000 to $940. As the price of dishes falls further, and as new satellites are put into orbit in the early 1990s, DBS will increasingly take viewers from traditional broadcasting. For 1991 a consortium of the major commercial broadcasters and other large conglomerates put together by the government and called the Satellite Broadcasting Company plans to supply one channel of DBS. NHK will supply two others.[3]

A number of factors in Japanese society guarantee that in the future there will be a tidal wave of new television products available to consumers. Japanese affluence provides a huge potential market for any successful venture. The Japanese love of gimmicks and the latest technology also helps create markets for new products, as does a willingness to throw out comparatively new and still working if outdated appliances. The high level of HDTV sales in 1988 showed that the Japanese continued to be attracted to the latest technology. Their high level of education makes them open to change and new methods, and they have been termed information junkies. Their small houses and apartments and the limited outdoor spaces in Japan reduce the competition from other leisure activities possible, for example, in North America. These factors help explain why Japan is in the forefront of the consumption of new television technology as well as being the source of its creation and development. The Japanese lead in fibre optics, high-definition television, and digital television as well as DBS.

The Japanese have gained a reputation for producing quality products and as a society for being intolerant of poor quality. Digital television and high-definition television provide a higher-quality picture, and the Japanese consumer clearly provides a large captive domestic market for their production. HDTV first appeared in 1981 on an experimental basis. However, over the finite broadcast airband it absorbed all the available bandwidth. The MUSE bandwidth compression breakthrough in 1985 allowed HDTV to be more economical. Obviously DBS increases the supply of airbands multifold, making HDTV practical. Finally NHK is committed to DBS to meet the mandate of the Broadcast Law. This means that Japan is likely to have regular HDTV in the early 1990s. Meanwhile improvements in digital television techniques offer a comparable improvement in picture quality using existing broadcast technology.[4]

The raw materials of all the new technologies are the programmes. The new supply methods merely distribute programmes to the viewer. Ninety-seven per cent of programmes are currently produced domestically, although until the 1970s the Japanese used to import shows from the United States, such as *I Love Lucy*, which enabled them to enjoy vicariously the space and affluence of American life. The Japanese continue to import American movies. These are usually low-quality, low-price movies which are dubbed into Japanese and then shown repeatedly in off-peak hours. About 800 American movies are imported each year.

NHK is vertically integrated and employs 16,000 people. They produce most of NHK's programmes. Even for news the Japanese tend to rely upon their own overseas bureaus for most of the news they supply.[5] In terms of the sorts of programmes supplied, on the commerical networks the programmes supplied are those which the viewers select via the preference option. As in the United States this results in low-quality programming which reaches a level generally agreed to be below that of the United States. In other words much of Japanese television, for all the advanced technology with which it is delivered, is trashy entertainment. This is in response to the desires of the viewers and to the demand of the advertisers that their message reach as many viewers as possible.

Structure and conduct

Despite the rise of the commercial stations on the back of the economic miracle NHK has maintained a good share of the market. With economic growth it has been possible to raise the monthly licence fee to over ¥1,000 each month to provide NHK with a budget of over ¥2 billion in 1986. ($1 = ¥187 thou.) The huge Japanese market allows NHK to exploit economies of scale, as it serves a market two to three times the size of the largest European public corporations. Even so, NHK ran a deficit in 1987. In the course of discussions about raising the monthly licence fee NHK ran into opposition and suggestions that it should turn to advertising to raise revenue. Currently NHK is still advertisement-free, and in 1988 98 per cent of revenue came from licences, the rest from fees paid by political parties for air time.[6]

NHK is financed by the monthly fees paid by the owners of receiver sets. The 1964 report of the Provisional Investigating Committee on the Law relating to Broadcasting concluded that:

> Receiving fees should be considered as a special share, that goes under the name of 'receiving fee', that NHK is permitted by right to collect for the maintenance of services according to law . . . [T]he present NHK can be considered to have been established by the people, the receivers, by law as their own broadcasting body, and the NHK authorities should therefore be placed in a position to carry out their operations, having received the mandate of the people.[7]

Article 32 of the Broadcast Law requires that any person who owns a receiver capable of receiving NHK broadcasts must as a duty conclude a contract with the corporation. Fees have to be approved by the National Diet, which debates the annual budget for NHK and its operational plans in the Standing Committee on Communications of both Houses. These debates are made public in the *Official Gazette*. NHK must also submit its balance sheet each year to the Ministry of Posts and Telegraphs. NHK fees are paid bi-monthly, and collecting them is a formidable and inefficiently accomplished task. In technologically sophisticated Japan in 1986 over one-third of fees were collected by door-to-door calling. This was in spite of NHK being willing to take the fees by automatic transfer and even offering a ¥50 per month discount to those who paid by automatic transfer. Fully 18 per cent of the NHK budget is spent on running ninety-one collection agencies which employ canvassers and collectors who try to maintain contact with an increasingly mobile society. This is a reflection of the Japanese aversion to using credit cards and preference for cash transactions.

The 1950 Broadcast Law intended that NHK should make a fresh start as 'the people's broadcasting station'.[8] To maintain its independence it has a structure similar to that of its original model, the BBC. There is a board of governors made up of twelve persons appointed by the Prime Minister but with the consent of both Houses of the National Diet. The board appoints and dismisses the president and the chief executive officer as well as the auditors. This structure seeks to keep NHK free from political forces and helps keep it free from the forces of the preference option and the ratings game. Article 3 of the Broadcast Law states that 'Broadcast programs shall never be interfered with or regulated by any person excepting the case where he does so upon the powers provided for by law.'[9]

The Broadcast Law forbids the establishment of networks like those in the United States. Even so, there are the equivalent of four networks centred on the four big commercial stations in Tokyo which have organized groups for the distribution of their programmes. These four stations are all owned by media conglomerates and linked with the big newspapers.

The first commercial station was started in 1953, just a few months after NHK began television broadcasting again, and was intended to be an educational station. At the time it was hoped that television would be a vehicle for education, and the Nippon Educational Television Company (NTV) was given a mandate to provide 60 per cent educational programming. NTV did not meet this commitment because to do so was unprofitable and in due course was broadcasting mostly entertainment.[10] NTV was soon joined by other commercial companies in Tokyo. By 1987 metropolitan Tokyo, with its population of 36 million, was served by NHK on channel 1; NTV on channel 4; TBS on channel 6; Fuji TV on channel 8; TV Asahi on channel 10.

There are barriers to entry to the broadcasting sector as a result of the limited number of airwaves and the fact that four large conglomerates have the licences to use those airwaves in metropolitan Tokyo. As in the United States, once the major stations are held – in this case the Tokyo and Osaka markets – entry is virtually impossible. Tokyo is the dominant market, although Japan is divided into eight key regions: Tokyo, Osaka, Nagoya, Fukuoka, Sapporo, Hiroshima, Sendai, and Hokkaido. All eight are served by the big four commercial stations. In remote areas served only by one or two stations there are often cross-broadcast arrangements between the local stations and more than one major Tokyo broadcaster will supply them with programming.

Programme costs are considerably lower than in the United States. The reasons are partly efficiency, partly historical, partly the size of the market. Until recently Japan could not afford the level of American extravagance. Japan also has a smaller domestic market and limited export opportunities. There is also less demand for the glossy programmes that the United States produces, and the popular game and quiz shows that dominate programming are relatively cheap to produce.

Cable and DBS have opened up new opportunities and lowered barriers to entry. Since the Japanese PTT first permitted development of two-way cable and Nippon Telephone & Telegraph (NTT) was privatized in 1985 new suppliers have entered the cable industry. They include the major newspaper companies and broadcasters, Yomiuri Shimbun, Manichi Shimbun, Nihon Keija Shimbun, Fuji, and TBS, as well as the huge distributor Maribeni, the engineering conglomerate Mitsubishi, Tokyo Express Railways, and Odakijii Railways.[11] The broadcasters were also the first to join the consortium for a private DBS channel in 1991. Asahi, Yomiuri, and Fuji all have a stake in the private-sector Satellite Broadcasting Company.

The costs and risks are enormous, since Japan is the pioneer in cable and satellite television. NHK is determined to make HDTV a reality, and Japan is committed to cable and DBS. However, for all new entrants the capital costs are high and there can be no expectation of profits until the mid-1990s.

There is vertical integration in the Japanese television industry, with the major stations all producing their own shows. This is more like Europe than the United States. The stations do buy-in films but in 1988 the Japanese began to invest in Hollywood for the production of movies.

Related to vertical integration is the link between hardware and software production for television. In the United States in the early days of television the television producers started broadcasting in order to supply their primary market, selling sets to consumers, with programmes. Japan is now the dominant consumer electronic goods producer, turning out television sets for most of America and much of the world. In the 1980s the television and video-recorder hardware producers also began to diversify into programme supply from the United States. In 1987 Sony extended their media interests by buying CBS Records and in 1989 Sony was rumoured to be interested in buying MGM/UA.[12] A few days after the failure of this bid Sony successfully offered $3.4 billion for Columbia Pictures. The purchase of either would allow Sony to provide the software to programme HDTV and so allow them to sell HDTVs, currently selling for about $3,500 each. This is the same motivation that led the radio-set manufacturers into television over half a century ago.

Also related to integration is the role of government. Under Prime

Minister Tanaka in the 1970s it was clear that control of the television stations was in the hands of the newspapers. These were the same newspapers which treated the Prime Minister with great care in the '70s, failing to investigate and expose several financial scandals.[13] In television, as in most other parts of the economy, the relationship with the government is close.

The conduct of the public system in Japan, as in Europe, is different from that of the private companies. Out of 2,000 leading companies in Japan in 1985 NHK was voted the most trustworthy. NHK is 'sponsored by the nation' and this is reflected in the firm's conduct.[14] At the same time NHK comes under the same two pressures that affect the BBC in Britain. First, there is opposition to the monthly licence fee by those who claim they do not watch NHK. As in Britain the NHK is constantly under threat that its financial base will be reduced for political reasons. Second, there is always the threat from the commercial systems as they increase market share. For example, in 1985 a University of the Air was launched for 18,000 students which undercut what had become the NHK's monopoly of education, and so part of NHK's justification of state support.

Article 44 of the Broadcast Law sets out NHK's responsibility for programme content. It must satisfy the wishes of the people as well as contribute to the elevation of the level of culture; it must provide local programming; facilitate new cultures, and preserve outstanding cultures of the past. NHK must also be politically impartial and provide as many viewpoints as possible. It must present the news without bias. It must provide cultural and educational programmes as well as news and entertainment. It also has a responsibility to provide educational broadcasting in conformity with the schools' curricula. To this end NHK has set up standards of its own and established Broadcasting Consultative Committees. They are made up of people from all walks of life and attempt to provide NHK with the sort of input that will make its programmes widely acceptable yet free from the tyranny of the advertising market and the preference option. There are district consulting committees in Kanto-Koshin'etsu, Kinki, Chulu, Chugoku, Tohoku, Hokkaido, and Shikoku.

NHK conduct is a response to the non-market forces that are built into its structure. Programming reflects this. Much of it is of high quality, yet it still attracts large audiences. In terms of news NHK provides more news and news of higher quality than the four commercial broadcasters. NHK has sixteen overseas news bureaus and 156 local news offices. It puts out four news programmes each day. A morning news programme runs for an hour and a half in the morning; there is noon news, news at seven and another three-quarter-hour programme at nine. In 1984 NHK created a unique twenty-four-hour-a-day news link with New York.

The pride of NHK programming, however, is the NHK 'Specials'. Over a thousand of these have been shown since their inception in 1978 and they have won Emmies and Italia prize awards, the top international awards in television. They are documentaries shown three days each week following the nine o'clock news and cover a wide range of topics. Prize-winning programmes have included *Zen Buddhism, The Nuclear Holocaust*, and a documentary on the early years of a set of quintuplets born to an NHK employee. There have also been specials on housing in the USSR and on life in the imperial palace, as well as on that stand-by of most public television stations, wildlife. There have also been longer co-operative ventures with foreign countries. There was a thirty-part documentary called *The Silk Road*, made in co-operation with the Chinese and shown over a five-year period. There was a ten-part documentary on the Yellow River, also made with the Chinese. A programme on the Louvre in thirteen parts was made in co-operation with the French. A three-year project by the team that made *The Silk Road* involved an archaeological study of the wreck of an ancient trading ship found in the Bay of Tartus, off the Syrian coast.[15]

NHK acts as a window on the world for Japan. It is a member of the Asian Broadcasting Union, an associate member of the European Broadcasting Union, and of OIRT, the Communist Broadcasting Union. In 1984 NHK broadcast 757 programmes from thirty-three countries, including *The Adventures of Sherlock Holmes, Shakespeare Theatre, Masterpiece World Film Theatre*, and *The Origin of Mankind*. NHK exported programmes to 67 countries, including its NHK specials and the popular soap opera series *O-shin*. Even so, all this still makes up only a small fraction of total NHK programming.

O-shin was one of the TV serial novels shown on Japanese television every morning. From 8.15 a.m. onwards as many as 50 per cent of households watch television novels, and watching a morning serial is for many a Japanese custom. Another popular television novel was *Oshui*, which Prime Minister Yasuhiro Nakasone used to enjoy. *Oshui* was the sentimental story of a woman from the years 1920 to 1982. Other light entertainment includes a show called *The Popular Knockout Competition* which plays up to the Japanese love of singing. The show has been credited with the birth of *karaoke*, where Japanese sing to recorded background music. *Karaoke* has in turn been a major force behind the success in Japan of video-disc players.[16] NHK also devotes about two hours each day of its prime time to regional programming.

In 1959 NHK started its educational channel. The majority of Japanese high schools use television as a teaching vehicle and NHK provides educational television to complement and support classroom teaching. In addition the educational channel provides programming for farmers, fishermen, housewives, and senior citizens, and publishes texts which can be used along with the television material. There is also an NHK Citizens' University which provides university-level courses, including on-going programmes in seven languages, English, German, French, Spanish, Chinese, Russian, and Korean. These attract large audiences. There is a show called *The Sprightly Club* for the elderly as well as programmes on health and for housewives. With a separate channel devoted to education, educational programmes can be shown throughout the day. In contrast many other educational programmes such as the BBC's Open University show educational material either very early or very late in the day.

In terms of conduct NHK is a leader in technological innovation. This reflects a response to its structure and its mandate under the 1950 Broadcast Law. It has a mandate to improve service and to serve all the people.[17] This provides NHK with the motivation to introduce new technologies which may not be commercially viable. In addition to HDTV NHK has been an innovator in teletext, which it introduced in 1983. This enabled NHK to reach the deaf and the hard-of-hearing, in other words to serve all market segments. NHK has also taken the lead in providing a service in the event of earthquakes and disasters. There are television sets which turn on automatically in the event of a disaster so that NHK can broadcast emergency messages into the home. NHK has also experimented with still picture broadcasting so that photographs can be shown on television. This will make it possible for television pictures to be used in conjunction with fax machines. NHK also provides several hours a day of multiplex broadcasting, which allows for bilingual sound tracks, for example a sound track in Japanese and in English on an imported American movie. The point is that NHK's structure allows it a freedom to experiment which is not generally available to a commercial system that must answer to the market and a group of shareholders.

In the private sector the four commercial systems are driven by the same forces that drive American commercial networks. In Japan there are Program Review Boards as required by the 1950 Broadcast Law to control programme excess. By and large these are ineffective, especially in the evenings, when virtually anything goes.[18] Japanese television does not reflect the delicacy which many Westerners associate with Japanese culture. To attract large audiences there is violence, sentimentality, humiliation, appeals to xenophobia, and sex. To attract revenue there is even more advertising than in the United States. Advertisements are supposed to be limited to 18 per cent of air time, but the limit is not strictly adhered to. To conserve energy, television stations are asked to limit broadcasting to sixteen hours per day, but in fact NHK broadcasts for eighteen and some of the commercial stations for over twenty hours.

Japan is a unique and changing market. Thirty years ago viewers used to watch soaps and dramas, and until the 1970s imported shows from America. In the late 1980s the Japanese were information-hungry, and to meet this demand there was a constant stream of news and current affairs. NHK broadcast fifteen news reports each day and had twenty overseas news bureaus to supply material. The commercial sector also responded to the demand for information. TBS emphasized the market in investigative news reporting to develop a news market niche. TBS achieved scoops with the crash of flight 007 and with the assassination of Benigno Aquino.[19] For the most part, however, television news follows the model of Japanese newspapers. It tries to be uncontroversial.

Yet if Western imported shows are not popular Japanese-speaking Westerners are. Over 90 per cent of children recognized the name Kent Gilbert, an American lawyer who has become a perennial television personality. Also successful was a former Mormon missionary who had made a successful conversion to game-show host.[20]

The highest ratings go to quiz shows, followed by films and sport. At the bottom in highly educated Japan was education programming. Japan reflects the point, not always recognized, that even the world's most educated people want entertainment and escapism through television. In Japan that has led to some novel programmes remarkably lacking in good taste. *Naruhado za Worcido* is a show where the host of the programme flies around the world to examine quaint local customs and then make jokes about them. Fuji was able to rise from No. 4 to No. 1 in the ratings in the early 1980s with shows such as *Twilight Meow, Meow*, a show using Japanese high-school girls singing and playing around.[21] These shows are reminiscent of 1950s *Playboy* magazines, with parades of mascot girls both with and without bikinis. Japan is less sexually repressed than the West, and scenes with rape and nudity are more common.

Violence is also more explicit. This is surprising, since in reality Japanese society is much less violent than Western society. Nevertheless on most evenings there is a plentiful supply of samurai and ninja dramas with fights and battles where heads are broken and guts are spilled.[22] Television to some extent reflects the soul of a nation, and in Japan it has been noted that those instigating the violence are often the bad guys and the hoodlums. Good people are usually seen to be the victims and are the ones to get hurt. This is unlike *The A-Team* from the United States, where the good guys often instigate the violence. In Japan violence is rarely portrayed as a means of achieving success. This book is not intended as a sociological tract but the Japanese television case is interesting. It suggests that it is not violence *per se* on television that imposes heavy violence costs on society. Rather it is the nature of that violence. The Japanese message is not that heroes start fights. Nor is it that violence is without pain. Such television violence, it appears, does not lead to violence in the real world.

In the real world violence can shock even the Japanese. The case of Toyota Shozi led to 750 protest calls to NHK, and the telephone lines at TBS were blocked for four hours.[23] In that case the television news crews were outside the offices of a firm accused of stealing gold by false pretences. Two men arrived at the firm's headquarters with bayonets and announced to the news-film crews that they were going to murder the firm's principal. They went inside and appeared a short time later covered in blood, talked to the film crews, and then left, having committed a murder. TBS explained that it had removed the more gory scenes. The point was that in terms of Japanese *mores* the gold dealer was beyond the pale and had lost his right in status-conscious Japan to humane treatment, either in real life or on the television news.

Commercials also reflect the Japanese character. The hard sell of the United States is unknown. Advertisements such as that in America which showed a grimy shirt collar to embarrass the viewer into using a particular soap powder are not used. The emphasis is more upon image advertising. In a world where all products are quality products, by assumption, differences in image are often the difference between market success and failure. Commercials frequently reveal the name of the product only at the end of the commercial. Often commercials will try to link the product with a world which is unattainable for the crowded Japanese, a world of space and beauty.

There are few restrictions on the products that can be advertised. The Japanese can advertise cigarettes and hard liquor on television, unlike in most Western countries. They also use the audio section of the advertisement to effect by increasing the volume during advertisements to force the message on to the viewer.

With advertisements running about nine to ten minutes in the hour the price of an advertisement is determined by the market. In 1986 the price was about $50,000 per minute on one of the national channels in prime time. In addition firms could sponsor programmes. The cost of a sponsorship was approximately $1.4 million per month.

Performance and conclusion

The Japanese television industry has much to commend it in terms of performance. It has taken the best of the British model and the best of the American. The NHK serves the public interest and meets minority demands. It provides educational and cultural masterpieces on a regular basis. The networks provide lots of light entertainment. Even the violence is portrayed in such a way as to lessen violence in society as opposed to setting it as a role model for aspiring heroes. Advertisers are well served, with plentiful supplies.

In terms of standard performance goals Japan is a leader in progress, with satellite television and HDTV. Television creates jobs and contributes to economic growth. The major weakness in allocative efficiency is the licence fee collection system. A lack of aggressiveness in news coverage results largely from the culture, with its emphasis on form and good conduct and an unwillingness to embarrass or admonish.

Australia

Like Japan, Australia has a mixed system based on the UK model but influenced by the American. The closest affinity, however, is with the Canadian television structure. Both Canada and Australia have relatively small populations and huge land masses. Both are former British colonies and both enjoy a high standard of living and have a high propensity to advertise.

The main difference between Australia and Canada is that Australia does not have a huge neighbour beaming down hundreds of signals on her as the USA does to Canada. Instead Australia plays the role of cultural imperialist to the hundreds of islands and the 8 million inhabitants of the South Pacific.[24]

The 1942 Australian Broadcasting Act granted complicated powers and responsibilities to the Australian Broadcasting Control Board, which was replaced by an Australian Broadcast Tribunal (ABT) in 1977. The ABT consists of a chairman and six full-time members appointed by the Governor General of Australia. It is a quasi-judicial body with the power to grant, revoke, and suspend licences as well as to determine standards.

Unlike the Canadian CRTC the ABT does not set a programme format. For example, there are few rules on content, partly because Australia does not have Canada's huge neighbour but also as a reflection of the policy approach. The ABT assumes that if market structures are appropriate, then the correct conduct will follow. A former ABT chairman said, 'You can't have regulations which force people to supply programmes.'[25] There is in fact a requirement to programme 104 hours of Australian-produced prime-time shows a year but most of the stations offer considerably more than that.[26]

The television industry's private sector began a major restructuring following the passage of new legislation late in 1986. Since the inception of television the private sector had been dominated by the newspaper companies. As in Britain and Japan, when commercial television was first introduced preference in terms of allocating the licences was given to the newspaper companies. There were no cross-media regulations; instead the newspapers were favoured because they had the necessary finance and news-gathering ability. Nobody, not even the newspapers, was allowed to own more than two stations in the country. In addition owners had to be Australians. This meant that when Rupert Murdoch of News Corporation became a US citizen he had to sell most of his interests in the Ten Network. As a foreigner he could hold only 15 per cent.

The two-station limit meant that stations in Sydney and Melbourne became the most valuable, as those cities were the biggest markets. All the big four media companies, Fairfax, HWT, News Corporation, and Kerry Packer's Consolidated Press Holdings (CPH) acquired stations. So later did Australian entrepreneurs Alan Bond and Robert Holmes à Court. Following the 1986 legislation a shake-out began in which both HWT and Fairfax sold off assets. To meet the new regulations on ownership a restructuring of the media involving the buying and selling of both newspapers and television stations began.

The first network resulting from the new legislation was one put together by Alan Bond. He paid over A$1 billion for Packer's CPH. CPH owned stations in the desirable Melbourne and Sydney markets, to which Bond added his stations in Perth and Brisbane to create the Bond Network. The creation of networks such as the Bond Network should allow the exploitation of economies of scale and scope in the small Australian market and increase Australian content. For example, in 1986 *Miami Vice* cost Australian broadcasters $23,000 a show, whereas Australian productions cost about $200,000. Even so, Australia has had some success producing for export, particularly to the other English-speaking countries. For example the mini-series *Return to Eden* was well received worldwide, as the soap *Neighbours* and many Australian films have been.

With access to the Intelsat and Aussat satellites it became possible in the mid-'80s for the media companies to send their signals across the South Pacific, one of the last areas in the world to be reached by television. Although the market was small and not very affluent, Fiji granted a twelve-year licence to CPH in 1986. Meanwhile services were either planned or started for the Cook Islands, Tonga, and Papua New Guinea. The social consequences are inevitably going to be similar to those in independent Western Samoa, where people who used to spend late afternoons and evenings talking, singing, telling stories, and discussing family affairs as well as being involved in community and church activities now spend thirty-five hours a week watching television. In addition Samoan families hired on average twelve video cassettes a week. The effect has been a decline in the knowledge of history, genealogy, and all the vehicles which societies with an oral history use to carry their culture and identity.[27]

Notes

1 Jose Matekera, 'Government support or commercialisation: the Japanese Dilemma', *Media Development*, 2 February 1985, p. 18.
2 Nippon Hoso Kyokai, *This is NHK*, Tokyo: Audience Public Research Bureau, 1985, p. 3.
3 *Radio Japan News*, No. 8, 1986, p. 1.
4 In 1989 some experts argued that computer technology was advancing faster than television technology and that HDTV might be replaced in the fairly near future by true digital television delivered over fibre optic cable. In the *McNeil/Lehrer report* on PBS on 5 February 1989 it was suggested that the US would be well advised to ignore HDTV and invest in developing real digital television based on computer technology, in which the US still held a lead over the Japanese.
5 Nippon Hoso Kyokai, *This is NHK*, Tokyo: Audience Public Relations Bureau, 1985, pp. 85–1.
6 ibid., pp. 85–16.
7 ibid., pp. 85–12.
8 ibid., pp. 85–16.
9 ibid.
10 *Fortune*, 30 March 1987.
11 Tomohiko Masaki, 'Focus on new media', *Economic Eye*, March 1985, p. 15.
12 *Wall Street Journal*, 17 October 1988.
13 Peter J.S. Dunnett, *The World Newspaper Industry*, London: Croom Helm, 1988, p. 174.
14 Nippon Hoso Kyokai, *This is NHK*, Tokyo: Audience Public Relations Bureau, 1985, pp. 85–1.
15 ibid., pp. 85–6.
16 *Business Week*, 18 July 1988.
17 This is *NHK*, pp. 85–16.
18 ibid., pp. 85–12.
19 Ian de Stains, 'The medium and its message', *Japan Update*, autumn 1986, p. 8.
20 ibid., p. 10.
21 *Fortune*, 30 March 1987.
22 James Fallows, 'Japanese yearnings', *The Atlantic*, June 1987, p. 17.
23 *The Economist*, 22 June 1985.
24 Australia does not have a monopoly in the region, where the USA and New Zealand both transmit signals. New Zealand used to have a system based on licence fees but ten years ago allowed advertising to begin. By 1988 over ten minutes an hour went to advertising on the state system.
25 Barbara A. Moes, 'Regulation and consternation Down Under', *Broadcaster*, March 1986, p. 12.
26 The Kerry Packer stations have on occasion slipped below the 104 hour requirement and required a special dispensation to be allowed to continue broadcasting.
27 *Islands Business*, September 1986, p. 66.

Chapter nine

Communist countries: watch Big Brother

Much of the economic analysis which has been applied to the Western television industry is not applicable to that of the Communist countries. Under the planned systems of the Communist countries the decision about what hardware and what software to produce is made by the planners. The state decides how many television sets and VCRs to make available to the public and what programmes to make available to them. Government demand for television programming dominates consumer and advertiser demand. The state sees the media as an essential part of its system of control. To that end it is willing to finance television to the extent that it meets state goals.[1]

In Communist countries the decision about what to produce results from what state planners decide is in the social interest. The profit motive plays only a minor role. Western concepts of freedom of speech and freedom of information are not relevant. Hence even in China, where there are commercials and there is entertainment programming, the main driving force behind the supply of television is didactic. There are programmes about responsibility and about what to think and how to manage one's life in harmony with state goals. Television programmes instruct and moralize. Commercials and entertainment programmes are peripheral to television's main function, which is to propagate.

The 1980s have seen a dramatic change in the conditions under which Communist television supplies propaganda messages. The controversial 1980 McBride report, published by the United Nations Educational, Scientific, and Cultural Organization (UNESCO) did not even mention VCRs.[2] Without VCRs and DBS it was still possible for a state system to control what its citizens could view, unless they were in border regions such as East Germany, where Western programmes 'leak' over the border. VCRs and DBS undermine that control. The USSR has petitioned the United Nations for controls on DBS. The argument put forward is that 'Absolute freedom to inform other countries irrespective of their desires compromises their freedom. To be consistent the defenders of absolute freedom would have to allow that other countries be free to admit this information or reject it.'[3]

China

In 1987 there were believed to be 92 million television sets in China. This compares with 200,000 sets in 1976. In other words, during the 1980s television became available to the vast majority of Chinese under a programme started in 1979 to ensure that television-set production was greatly increased. In 1988 China even exported a million television sets to Europe, and by the year 2000 it will be the biggest television market in the world in terms of viewers.

Demand for television is made up primarily of the state demand discussed above, but also consumer demand for entertainment, news and information, and advertiser demand.

Advertiser demand comes from wholesalers and retailers, most in 1988 still run by the government, and from overseas suppliers of goods and services. For Western producers the notion of a billion potential consumers in China has long been attractive. Although few Western companies have had much commercial success so far, China is a huge potential market. For that reason many Western suppliers want to get their name known, even if there is no immediate possibility of creating a market for their products there.

Commercials on Chinese television were first begun in 1979. They are shown in two blocks each day, lasting between five and twenty minutes. In 1984 the revenue generated by commercials was approximately $125 million, and by 1987 it had risen to a quarter of a billion dollars. Westerners bought about $15 million worth of commercials, less than 10 per cent of the total. Many of these were image advertisements, so that the picture of a deluge of Western commercials creating unfulfilled dreams in Chinese minds is easy to overemphasize. At the same time Western producers and Western products are familiar through advertisements. So long as the relatively liberal economic policies of Deng Xiaoping continue, so more and more will television be a vehicle by which Western consumer products become known.

The evidence suggests that advertiser demand is met. Until Western producers can export more products to China it is unlikely that they will want more advertising time. One programme which attracts an incredible 300 million viewers was unable to sell all its advertising spaces in 1987 at prices which appear very low by Western standards. The *One World Show* offered 194 half-minute slots for $450,000 and could not sell them all.[4] That is half the cost of a single half-minute slot for a US Super-Bowl commercial to reach an audience five times as large as the SuperBowl audience, albeit much poorer. This emphasizes how, under any commercial system, it is not viewer enjoyment nor the number of viewers that matters. The key driving force behind advertising demand even in China is the income per viewer.

The structure of the television industry is simple. Almost all television is supplied by the state. The Ministry of Radio, Film and Television runs Central Television, which was founded in 1958. However, in Guangdong (Canton), near Hong Kong and Macao, the Chinese can receive television from those two islands. Their presence and influence have been one factor in the rapid growth and relative economic success of Guangdong during the 1980s. Even so, the government frowns upon this cultural imperialism. In 1987 it ordered all party cadres to cease watching television from Hong Kong and Macao. It also ordered people to remove the aerials which can be seen in vast numbers wherever there is leakage from the islands.[5]

Yet Deng is committed to economic development, and television is an important vehicle for the opening up of China. This is apparent in terms of conduct by the state television organization. Western commercials and Western advertising are encouraged, subject to state controls. The *One World Show* discussed above reflects the government's policy of openness.

One World Show is produced by Yue Sai Kan, an independent New York producer. It is shown on Central Television and is a travel documentary. It covers such topics as ethnic life in New York, Japanese festivals, and English stately homes. The programme, which is broadcast on Sunday evenings at 10.00 p.m., is reputed to have the largest audience in the world, reaching some 65 per cent of the population of Beijing and Guangdong. Despite this Kan could sell only four out of the permitted six commercials allowed with the show in 1986 and lost money. The show was cross-subsidized by *Asia World*, which was shown on independent stations in the United States.

Other Western shows shown on Chinese television in 1987 included a CBS one-hour show along the lines of CBS's highly acclaimed and very successful show in the United States, *Sixty Minutes*. The BBC and Walt Disney also supplied programmes, which carried commercials. These commercial slots sold for between $10,000 and $13,000 per minute. Advertisers from the West on these shows included Boeing, Colgate, Revlon, Mary Quant, Christian Dior, Coca-Cola, McDonald's, Pepsi-Cola, and Campbell's Soups from the United States. Sanyo, Toshiba, Seiko, and other consumer electronics firms advertised goods from Japan. There was even rivalry in advertising between Kodak and Fuji and Nescafé and Maxwell House.[6]

Kentucky Fried Chicken also advertised and had an outlet in Beijing. Experience there reflected the nature of the market which these Western suppliers hoped to reach. At the Beijing outlet a Kentucky Fried Chicken meal cost $1.89. This represented nearly two days' income for the average Chinese worker wtih a typical income of $300 per year. Coca-cola, still using the jingle of the 1970s, 'I'd like to buy the world a Coke . . . ', sold 30 million cans in 1987. That represents one Coke per Chinese per lifetime, compared to about one a week in the United States.

The Western programmes are indicative of economic change in China. However, they constitute only a few hours of programming each week. Each week Central Television broadcasts 170 hours of programmes. In Beijing there are three channels, 2, 6, and 8. Much of this is educational or propagandistic to create the right attitudes and inform society.

Educational programming includes lectures where the lecturer uses a blackboard to make his points. These and documentary-type programmes cover such topics as science, computers, and farming. There are practical programmes on life skills, including foreign-language programmes in English, Japanese, and French from the BBC, NHK, and AFP. The BBC's programme called *Follow me* is hosted by Kathy Flower, who has perhaps the best known face of a living Westerner in all of China.

There are many programmes about citizens' responsibilities. There are also programmes characteristic of most public television stations, dealing with topics of historical interest, of economic and social change, and about nature. Finally cartoons are broadcast for children for a full twenty hours per week. They have self-explanatory titles such as *Good Friends* and *The Proud General*.[7]

Entertainment programming to meet consumer demand is dominated by movies, which make up about 50 per cent of entertainment content. Ballet, opera, music, drama, and sport are also supplied, reflecting how all public-service television shies away from meeting demand for frivolous, time-killing programming. Chinese television is intended to encourage self-improvement and not decadent self-indulgence. A controversial programme in 1988 was *River Elegy* a six-part portrayal of China's history which attempted to create a historical rationale for the country's open-door policy by reinterpreting some of China's traditional history.[8] The programme began as a collaboration between NHK of Japan and the Television and Broadcasting Ministry.

Finally there is a lot of news programming. The Chinese use the format of a male and female news team to supply the news that the government wishes the people to see and hear.

In terms of performance the government has achieved its goals of making television available to the bulk of the population in the 1980s. It has successfully used television for didactic purposes to educate society for the twentieth century and to emphasize responsibility and self-improvement. In 1988 the government reduced the number of places in the universities for graduate students and instead introduced a series of instruction programmes over television.[9] At the same time the threat of satellites and VCRs undermining state control, with a few exceptions such as broadcasts from Hong Kong, was just a threat in 1989.

As regards meeting advertiser demands, demand was met. State producers had only limited use for commercials in a system which still saw salesmanship, service to the consumer, and sales commissions as contrary to society's interests. Foreign suppliers had a limited demand for advertising until the likelihood of developing markets in China increased. In terms of consumer demand, demand was probably not met. Whilst the 170 hours of programming and choice offered in Beijing are vastly improved over the supply at the beginning of the decade, and whilst more television sets and colour sets are available, it seems unlikely that the average Chinese, any more than the average citizens of all other countries where pure entertainment television is available, would not watch entertainment television if they could.

The Eastern Bloc

Glasnost in the latter 1980s introduced new policies into the Russian economy and with it repercussions for the other Eastern Bloc countries. The use of free markets and market incentives increased. Television was one means by which the party could pass on information about the new policies. One Muscovite who watched the coverage of the proceedings of the Communist Party Congress in the summer of 1988 commented, 'I am hearing things on television that three weeks ago I would never have whispered over the telephone.'[10]

There was certainly room for improvement. In 1979 the Communist Party Central Committee lashed out at the state-run system. It was criticized for its 'formalism, verbosity, propagandistic clichés, grey commentary style and mechanical repetition of official truths to the detriment of creative interpretation'.[11]

At the same time, throughout the Communist world, the forces of technology were working to supply alternative programming to that of the state monopolies. Although the 1980 McBride report did not even mention them, VCRs were already starting to undermine the state monopoly on television. This was critically important in a system where control of the means of information was a key element in the control of society. The Russians, for example, spent $3 billion per year just to jam foreign radio broadcasts. Transistor radios had earlier been nicknamed the underground telegraph. Together, therefore, technology and *glasnost* brought about a major change in the structure and conduct of Eastern Bloc television.

In terms of formal structure all the Eastern Bloc countries have similar state monopolies on the supply of television. For example, in Russia the State Committee for Television and Radio of the USSR Council of

Ministers controls the state broadcasting system, Gostelradio. In 1985 it operated 115 television centres throughout the 8 million square miles of the USSR. A national network penetrated to over 90 per cent of the population, who owned over 80 million television sets, about one set for every four people. From Moscow, Moscow I and Moscow II broadcast thirteen and a half hours of programming each day. The programmes were then rebroadcast four times each day to the four different time zones. Within Moscow itself there were thirteen channels.[12]

In terms of conduct Eastern Bloc television serves the interests of the Communist Party. Its chief function is to meet propaganda demand from the state. Lenin said that 'Ideas are weapons' and television was seen as a propaganda weapon in the Cold War.[13] To that end it had a reputation until the late 1980s for being boring and full of propaganda, continuing on video the war of words that had dominated radio for decades.

There was very little demand for advertising by state suppliers of consumer goods in a system unable to meet consumer demand for most products. When there was surplus of state-produced consumer goods, which happened on occasion, the state could use television as a means of unloading them. For example, in 1986 there was a surplus of refrigerators, and television was used to let consumers know. Other goods that have been advertised on the instruction of local Industry Ministers include health spas, rugs, state-run lotteries, and do-it-yourself car radio kits. Advertisements were accompanied by the following message on the screen: 'Dear customer, If you have questions about the products that are advertised, you will have to ask your local authorities about their availability.'[14] Blocks of advertisements are shown about twice a week for about a quarter of an hour on the Second Programme, the entertainment channel.

Advertisements are produced by the state agency, Soiuztorgreklama. They can reflect Western influence and Western decadence. The advertisement for a Tula motor cycle first dwells on the bike as an object of desire. It then shows three brothers in pursuit of the local beauty. One has a bicycle, one a horse, and one a Tula. The Tula arrives first, the girl is impressed, and then, along with the viewer, is told the name of the bike. The advertisement has all the subtlety of hard-sell Madison Avenue.

Programmes about consumer products such as *Better Products* can be used, therefore, both to criticize suppliers and to increase demand for products in excess supply. Nevertheless their primary purpose is to serve the government, even if they appear to have the interest of the consumer at heart.

As regards consumer demand for programmes, it was not met. The state made available those programmes which it thought its citizens should watch, not what they might like to watch. This was reflected in the popularity of VCRs even though they cost the equivalent of a year's income to buy. In 1986 two-thirds of the programmes on Channel One, the only channel broadcast to all of the USSR, were of an educational nature. They included some very good children's programmes.

The best television in the Eastern Bloc traditionally came from East Germany. In 1961 Walter Ulbricht, former leader of the Socialist Unity Party (East German Communist party), referred to the class enemy sitting on the roof. The reference was to the television aerials which East Germans erected to pick up the leakage from West German television. In 1987 some 80 per cent of East Germans watched television from the West. Only in areas around Dresden in the east was it not possible to pick up the signals. This area was known as 'westblind'. It was reported that people would refuse promotion which involved a transfer to Dresden because it meant they would be deprived of Western television. Faced with this competition, East German television had to provide programmes which attracted its own citizens. Competition also forced the East German media to discuss issues it might have preferred to ignore, since its citizens were informed about them by the West German television channels. [15]

Whenever television fails to meet consumer demand VCRs are used to circumvent inadequate broadcast television. VCRs have been immensely popular in the Eastern Bloc despite attempts to control them. [16] In Bulgaria they have to be registered. The VCR technology used in the USSR differs from that used in the West, so that Western tapes are incompatible with USSR-made machines, thus maintaining some state control. Even so, the price of those produced by Elektronica in the USSR is high, about 2,500 roubles. [17] Thus high prices are used as a means of rationing supply in combination with import controls on Western machines. Quality is also poor, and the Japanese Ministry of Trade and Industry quashed an attempt by the Russians to import Japanese technology.

Many VCRs are imported by officials such as diplomats who bring back Western VCRs to the Eastern Bloc when they return from duty. Banned Western tapes of movies are very popular when and where available. For example, *The Deer Hunter*, a film about Vietnam, was very popular in Moscow in 1986. As well as making the forbidden fruits of the Western entertainment media available VCRs are also used for political purposes. One of the first of these was the use of tapes by Solidarity in the early 1980s in Poland. By 1986 it was estimated that there were over 300,000 VCRs in Poland. [18] This was possible despite the dire state of the economy because many Poles had relatives in the West who provided them with the hard currency necessary to obtain the machines.

189

There is government opposition to the widespread use of VCRs, especially Western VCRs which can use Western cassettes. Rather than oppose them on the grounds that they circumvent censorship they are officially opposed on the economic grounds that they involve profiteering in addition to using up hard currency. To meet demand in a controlled format the USSR has increased production at Electronika, which began production of VCRs in 1984, and set up hire shops. In addition VCRs have been supplied to remote areas where television is still not available.

When Mikhail Gorbachev came to power one of his first moves was to replace the long-time head of Gostelradio. There was no change in the structure of television, which continued to be a state monopoly whose goal was to serve the state. Under Gorbachev programming changed as he attempted to convert the Russian people to his *perestroika* policy.[19] Gorbachev clearly appreciated the critical role television had to play.

As a consequence conduct improved enormously by traditional industrial organization standards as new programmes met consumer demand. Programmes became more entertaining, even if the motivation for supplying them was political. Shows such as *View (Vzglyad)*, broadcast once a week, seemed like the equivalent of any Western news entertainment programme, for example *Meet the Press* in the USA or *Panorama* in Britain. *View* tested the limits of *glasnost* by covering such topics as neo-Nazism in the USSR, the role of the Czars, Stalin's atrocities, and economic issues such as wasted resources and shoddy products. There were Western-style interviews asking personal questions and open discussions of problems such as the environment and alcoholism. A popular night-time show called *Before and After Midnight* was introduced, and music videos and the wearing of jeans became commonplace. Even full-frontal nude go-go dancers as well as Michael Jackson and Madonna were shown.

All this was much more entertaining for the viewer, although it reflected government demand. Rock music videos were an easy and quick way to gain popularity, whilst the news could be used to advantage. For example, when the television news showed a man in Siberia shouting at Gorbachev that there was nothing at all available in the shops he could be presented as giving support to the Premier's economic reforms.[20] None the less these shows, which attempted to increase Gorbachev's popularity, also met consumer demand.

In terms of exports there is very little demand outside the Eastern Bloc for most Soviet programmes. Some USSR television is shown on satellite television in North America for information and as a curiosity. In 1987 the USSR signed a contract with Proton, a US company, to put three satellites in space. This will increase exports of programmes. The one large Western market for Eastern Bloc programmes is sport. Viewers in West Germany tune in to East German television for the soccer matches, and newspapers in West Germany print the TV schedules of East Germany for this reason. Finally, in 1988, under the spirit of *glasnost*, the Russians allowed Western television suppliers into the USSR to provide a picture of the Russian way of life for Western viewers. In 1988 NBC *Sunrise* was transmitted in part from the USSR to the USA, and all the US networks enjoyed greater access to the USSR.

While from the standpoint of viewers in the USSR there was a revolution in television, the revolution was restricted to the sort of programming being transmitted. By providing more light entertainment and complete news – for example, the 1988 earthquake in Armenia was covered much more critically than one in Kazakstan in 1985 – the USSR was becoming more normal in terms of how most other television systems in the world behave. In terms of structure and motivation, however, there was little change in the television system of the USSR. It still met the goals set for it by Lenin at the beginning of the Communist era. Lenin described the press as 'the Party's strongest weapon, the organizer, agitator and educator of the masses'.[21]

Conclusion This brief chapter has illustrated how in a state system market forces are replaced by planning. As a result the economics of television are fairly simple. The government authorizes the funds necessary to support the programmes it deems necessary to meet state goals. The goals may allow entertainment on television if it will encourage support for some particular policy, such as *perestroika*.

Notes

1 The problems of estimating any USSR expenditure are legion. Since there are no markets, prices do not reflect costs. Even the Russians have difficulty estimating economic growth and defence expenditure. When in 1989 economic growth figures were revised it was suspected that the Russians were simply recycling Western estimates. The most controversial area has been USSR defence estimates, which range anywhere from 12 to 20 per cent of GNP. Consequently expenditures on television have little meaning.
2 The McBride report is discussed in some detail in Peter J.S. Dunnett, *The World Newspaper Industry*, London: Croom Helm, 1988, p. 19.
3 David Marks, 'Broadcasting over the Wall: the free flow of information between East Germany and West Germany, *Journal of Communications*, January 1983, p. 47.
4 *Business Week*, 19 January 1987.
5 *Far Eastern Review*, 17 September 1987.
6 *Business Week*, 25 January 1988.
7 Joe Reizen, 'China tunes in on television and radio', *Journal of the Royal Television Society*, October 1985, p. 251.

8   *Far Eastern Review*, 30 September 1988.
9   *The Economist*, 30 April 1988.
10 *Time*, 11 June 1988.
11 *World Press Review*, December 1986.
12 *The Europa Yearbook: a World Survey*, London: Europa Publications, 1977, p. 2723.
13 *Time*, 9 September 1985.
14 *Forbes*, 7 September 1987.
15 David Marks, 'Broadcasting over the wall: the free flow of information between East Germany and West Germany', *Journal of Communications*, January 1983, p. 53.
16 *Index on Censorship*, March 1986, p. 20.
17 ibid., p. 18.
18 *Manchester Guardian Weekly*, 30 March 1986.
19 *Time*, 10 October 1988.
20 *Business Week*, 17 October 1988.
21 *The Listener*, 7 April 1988.

Chapter ten

The developing world

The television industries that serve the 3 billion people who constitute the Third World are characterized by the following common features. First, there is an inadequate advertising market to allow television to be viably financed commercially. There must be some sort of government financial support. This may take the form of state finance and control, state subsidies and grants, or a state-granted monopoly. Second, there is a high degree of government control and interference in the supply of television programming. The prerequisites of democratic traditions and affluence which permit television to operate free of government interference in much of the developed world do not generally exist in the developing world. Third, governments in the developing world often have some secondary goals, for example education for the masses, which they wish to achieve through television. Government influence on structure, conduct, and performance is therefore pervasive. Finally, VCRs are widely used to enable customer demand to be satisfied in spite of governments' desire to control what people see. Their impact has been greatest in Africa, the Middle East, and the Far East wherever electricity is available.

The 1980s saw a dramatic change in the basic conditions of the television industry of the developing world. Growth in demand was exceedingly rapid. VCRs, which were virtually unknown in the '70s, became commonplace even in remote rural areas. The number of television sets in countries like India increased many times over. VCRs and satellites transformed the ability of television to reach the people and the terms on which they were reached. VCRs proved hard for governments to control, and once people had viewed Western shows on VCRs they were less inclined to accept the humdrum material that their political masters might prefer them to watch.[1]

In response to the constraints of limited democratic traditions and a weak advertising market different governments have pursued different policies governing the terms and conditions under which their own industry operates. The following survey contrasts the variety of responses by different governments and the consequences for industry performance.

Latin America

The two largest countries in Latin America, Mexico and Brazil, have highly successful vertically integrated commercial suppliers who produce some of the most interesting and widely followed television in the world. Brazil, with a population of nearly 150 million people, is by far the largest country in Latin America. It has the sixth largest population in the world. Mexico has a population of around 85 million, and together the two countries make up about two-thirds of the population of Latin America. Brazil represents three-quarters of the world's Portuguese-speakers. Mexico is the largest Spanish-speaking country in the world, and represents about a quarter of the world's Spanish-speakers. Neither country is rich. *Per capita* income in Brazil in 1987 was $1,500 per year. Yet parts of Brazil's economy are highly developed and Brazil is a major supplier of armaments, aeroplanes, and automobiles. Mexico likewise has a substantial manufacturing sector despite a *per capita* income of $2,000 per year. Both countries have huge urban centres. The populations of Mexico City and São Paulo are both over 15 million and that of Rio de Janeiro is over 10 million.

Brazil

In Brazil TV Globo dominates the supply of television. In 1925 Roberto Marinho started a four-page newspaper with a circulation of 15,000. It developed into the newspaper *O Globo*, which in 1988 was the best-selling newspaper in Brazil with a circulation of over half a million. In 1966 he founded TV Globo and because international programmes and films were too expensive he decided that 'we must do it ourselves'.[2]

By the mid-1980s TV Globo had invested in huge studios and production facilities and was producing sixteen hours of programming each day. It included news, variety shows, children's programmes, drama, and educational programmes. The network's speciality, however, is the production of TV *novelas*, soap operas, which Globo exports to forty-five countries worldwide, including Kuwait, Iceland, and Australia.[3] The *novelas* are so popular in Brazil that the Council of Ministers has been known to take a break in order to catch critical episodes. Of the 20 per cent of programmes that TV Globo imported in 1986 the majority were films and US television series, which were shown at off-peak hours. In Brazil the home-made product attracted larger audiences than the US programmes which are overwhelmingly popular in most of the Third World.

The *novelas* are a major cultural experience for a large sector of society.[4] A prime-time *telenovela* can attract an audience of 50 million to 60 million. There may be as many as fourteen *novelas* daily to choose from, but the prime time for *novelas* is between 5.00 p.m and 10.30 p.m. A series may run up to 370 episodes. The *novelas* are studio productions, which keeps costs low. They can generate $25,000 of revenue for each episode, although production costs are usually below $10,000. This means that home-produced *novelas* are cost-competitive with US imports once the cost of dubbing is taken into account.

The topics covered by *novelas* vary. Although they may deal with politics and scandals, themes about love, upward social mobility, class conflict, success, and detectives are more usual. *Novelas* tend to follow the formula of least objectionable programming so as to maximize audiences. To maximize revenues, *novelas* also use the technique known as merchandising. Heroes and heroines in the story will plug products from foods to underclothing.

Unlike American daytime soaps, where 90 per cent of the audience is female, soaps in Brazil are the dominant format for prime time, much as situation comedies are in North America. *Novelas* have been credited with unifying the country by making Portuguese the national language. In every little town and village in the 1980s groups of people would gather round a concrete block on which sat the community television. The television set and the *novela* had become the meeting place of Brazilians from all sectors of life.[5]

There is television censorship. The threat or actuality of military rule is ever present, and TV Globo, which started in 1966, a year after the army seized power, operates at the government's pleasure. The government uses the threat of censorship to control TV Globo so that the television network exercises internal censorship. This extends beyond politics to sexual content and controversial matters of all kinds. Marinho is a realist who has said, 'We are trapped between the political powers, who give us our permit to run the station, and the power of audience opinion. So long as the politicians remain stronger we will continue to support them'.[6]

In turn Rede Globo is a powerful media conglomerate. With its headquarters in Rio de Janeiro, Globo has interests in newspapers, radio stations, books, and records. The Globo network of five broadcasting stations and thirty-six affiliated stations can reach two-thirds of the population. In 1986 the company had a turnover of over half a billion dollars and enjoyed considerable power and influence. Marinho uses this power to achieve his own object. Each evening between the two prime-time *novelas* there is a thirty-minute news programme called *Journal Nacional*. This assures Marinho of a large audience, to whom he says, 'We give all the necessary information but our opinions are in some way or other dependent upon my character, my convictions, and my patriotism.'[7]

In fact TV Globo has been a propaganda vehicle of successive military regimes. The end of formal censorship in the 1970s made little difference to the news on the *Journal*. In 1984, on behalf of General Joao Figuerdo, TV Globo supported the opposition candidate, Tancred Neves, for first civilian President because the general did not like the ruling party's nominee. The Communications Minister in 1987, Antonio Magathaes, was a close friend and business partner of Marinho. He ensured that a new constitution drafted by the congress excluded any mention of broadcasting regulation. When in 1987 there was public dissatisfaction with President Sarney, Marinho banned the words 'direct elections' from his media interests. This helped the public discontent die.[8]

Yet Marinho is no lackey. The state–broadcasting relationship is a matter of common interests. Marinho wants to tell Brazilians what they should know and think about the world. To that end his own interests accord with those of the right-wing governments of the last twenty-five years. He hires staff who know that they must play down labour unrest and left-wing politics and play up all efforts to strengthen the government and the economy. Reflecting his view of his contribution, in 1984 he said, 'We have made television into a true form of popular culture. Our channel is programmed for Brazilians. It is not one of those international *pot-pourris* with no real identity, as most television networks in the world have become.'[9]

There are other commercial television suppliers, although TV Globo is by far the largest. Radio/TV Bandeirantes has a television network with twenty-three stations across Brazil, while TV Manchette operates a station in Rio de Janeiro, and TV Record operates Canal 7 in São Paulo.[10]

In a country as poor as Brazil a deprivation effect can be generated internally, and such accusations have been made against the top-rated daytime *Xuxa Show*. It features a very beautiful hostess who leads a four-and-a-half-hour daily show of dancing, singing, and cartoons, and promotes consumer products. In a country where less than half the population get eight years of schooling the majority of the viewers have no chance of being able to afford the products pushed on the programmes.[11]

As a vehicle of development the government requires that all broadcasting networks transmit educational programmes for two hours per day. One channel, TVE mea, was started by the State of Cearas in 1972 to serve *telescolas*, television schools. TVE mea distributes educational material by microwave and video cassette to remote regions of the country. When there is no teacher available the parents may act as monitors, although much of TVE's material is aimed at adults. Papers are sent to the Ministry of Education for marking. As in much of Latin America, however, *telescolas* have had only marginal success.[12]

Mexico

Since the revolution of 1910 leftist governments have favoured government control of industry. Until 1988 Mexico was virtually a one-party authoritarian state, and it might be expected that there would be a state television monopoly. Instead Mexico has a structure similar to that of the United States, with a large private and a small public sector, although there is more control and censorship.

Televisa is the private company that dominates television. It was formed in 1973 as a result of a merger between Telesistema Mexicana (TSM) and Independente de Mexico (TIM). It brought together four private Mexico City stations and seventy other stations under a single administration. This was in fact a return to the *status quo*. Before 1968, when two new independent channels, Channels 8 and 13, were started, there had been no competition with TSM. TIM was never profitable and the alternative to a merger between TIM and TSM was the take-over of TIM by one of the state agencies such as SoMex.[13]

Between the 1973 merger and 1983 Televisa was run by the former owners of TIM and TSM. In 1983 the O'Farrills, a Mexican family which has extensive holdings in many sectors of the country's industry, took control.[14]

Televisa was started in the 1920s by Emilio Azcarraja, the father of the current president of the company, Emilio Azcarraja junior. In the 1920s the founder sold records throughout Mexico. He then formed a pro-government radio station and built it into the top radio network. When three television concessions were handed out in 1953 they went to the president's family, a newspaper firm, and to Emilio Azcarraja. In 1965 the three television stations merged to form a television monopoly, the forerunner of Televisa. In 1987 a senior Televisa executive was the son of the former President of Mexico, cementing Televisa's close relations with the government.

The state approved the 1973 merger on the grounds that competition had been a destructive force, reflected in a decrease in the quality of programming as stations attempted to maximize advertiser reach. A merger, it was argued, meant that a Mexican formula for television could be implemented. With co-operation from Televisa the state could ensure that television was programmed in accord with national objectives.

Two Ministries in particular influence the conduct of Televisa. The Ministry of Communications and Transport is responsible for licensing and technical aspects of broadcasting. The Minister of the Interior regulates content and authorizes the production of government programming. Government programming is shown over the government's own channel and on the free time which is made available to it on the commercial television. These programmes are produced by a state agency, Production Nacional de Radio y Television, set up in 1977. Formally the state and the industry interact through a national Chamber of Radio and Television Industry, but informal links are more important. Although there is much co-operation there is a basic conflict. The state wants television to help it meet social goals. Televisa wants to make profits from advertising. Nevertheless there has been successful co-operation, not just in programming but also in cable television and satellites for telecommunications.

Channel 13 is the government's own commercial station, which consistently loses money. Its weakness can be blamed in part on Televisa's success. However, the balance of power between Televisa and the state rests in the state's ability to control Televisa. In 1982 the state nationalized the banks when their co-operation was deemed inadequate, so the threat of similar treatment is always there should Televisa ever fail to please the government.

Televisa is possibly the most powerful private conglomerate in Mexico. It is something of an anachronism in a country where for decades politicians using revolutionary language have created a suspicion of private enterprise. The revolution was supposed to eliminate monopolies from the economy. Yet Televisa is a true multinational which sells soap operas and variety shows to the United States, to all the countries of Latin America, and to Europe. It even owned the biggest Spanish-language station in the United States until 1987, serving an audience of over 20 million hispanics there. At home Televisa has interests in films, records, books, video-cassette rentals, and sports stadiums, and owns the country's top soccer team.

Televisa's control of the medium enables it to dominate television news in a country where few people read newspapers and many are functionally illiterate. Its only competition is the losing government station, which achieves low ratings. The basic truth is that Televisa is so close to the government that nationalization is unnecessary. It collaborates with the government and ignores the opposition. It gives high priority to the President, denounces demonstrations, and plays down bad news. In return the government allows Televisa to function as a sort of ministry of culture, education, and truth in a country where television is ubiquitous and illiteracy pervasive.

Televisa, like Globo in Brazil, produces *telenovelas* at low cost and attracts huge audiences both in Mexico and in its export markets, which include the United States and most of the smaller Latin American countries. *Telenovelas* are not only profitable for Televisa but also help the state achieve its social goals.

198

The use of *telenovelas* to promote the state's social objectives began in the 1960s with a *telenovela* called *Simplemente Maria*. Recalling the failure of *telescolas* in economic development, the impact of *Simplemente Maria* is of interest. The story was that of a girl from the slums who goes to work for a rich family. There she develops her talents as a seamstress; she moves on to become a famous fashion designer. The effect of the simple story line was a dramatic rise in the sales of Singer sewing machines. Singer bought all the pre-show and post-show advertising spots. When the *novela* was exported to other Latin American countries Singer enjoyed soaring sales.

Mexican *telenovelas* have exploited this experience. They have become a soft sell for all sorts of role models and to achieve desired social outcomes. The story *Ven conmigo* was credited with persuading or inspiring some one million adults in Latin America to enrol in adult literacy courses. Rather than teaching literacy, television was used to show how a poor person who attends literacy classes can break out of poverty and achieve success.

Televisa, however, is in business to make profits. In return for supporting the government and its social policies it is able to exploit its market power. One example of this was the 1986 World Cup, the biggest event in the world for the most popular sport in the world, soccer. Twenty-four countries participated. The United States is one of the few where soccer is not a major sport. Even so, the game's potential for television encouraged the United States to seek to hold the World Cup there in 1989.

In 1986 Televisa exploited its monopoly to the full. It built superb accommodation for the event which it then rented at exceedingly high rates to visiting broadcasters. For the sportscasters it built a magnificent art-filled atrium. For the facilities that broadcasters need it put up another building. It hired out much of the broadcasting equipment, too, so that foreign broadcasters ended up paying rents of $1,000 per square metre during the event. There were 150 countries with broadcasting rights. Some threatened a boycott over the high prices charged by the state-sanctioned monopolist. It was thought to be the biggest television spectacle in the world, with over 3 billion people watching some part of it. For Mexico, which had hosted the games in 1970, it meant thousands of tourists and millions of tourist dollars. For Televisa it meant huge revenues on a production provided free by the International Football Federation.[15]

Mexico and Brazil are the major suppliers of programming to Latin America. Although US programmes are available at very low cost – for example, an episode of *Dallas* costs around $1,000 – they have to be dubbed. Mexican productions do not have to be dubbed. Brazil and Mexico are the two dubbing centres of Latin American, and they attempt to act as gatekeepers on imported programmes from outside the region. They have been able to erect a barrier to entry based on accent. The accents of Chicanos in the United States are generally unacceptable to Mexican broadcasters, so that the dubbing into Spanish is done in Mexico for American programme producers such as Lorimar.[16]

Mexico and Brazil export to most of the Latin American countries and are the major suppliers of programmes to Peru and Argentina. Chile restricts imports from Mexico and Brazil to one hour per day but does not restrict imports from the United States. Consequently more US television is seen in Chile than elsewhere. There are some co-operative efforts, so that Televisa and Globo show imported Latin American shows in return for shows bartered and traded with the rest of Latin America.

Ecuador

Ecuador provides a case study in the way in which a private television industry operating within a non-democratic form of government is likely to behave. Behaviour will likely be pro-government even if there are no controls on conduct. This is because the state can create barriers to entry by firms which are potentially unsympathetic.[17]

In 1984 a company called Ortel signed a contract with the government to start a new, politically independent television station. The new administration of President Leon Febres Cordero was opposed to Ortel and instituted a programme of harassment. Import permits were withdrawn. Banks were encouraged to be difficult about loans. Land needed for a transmitter was suddenly unavailable. When a retired general offered Ortel the use of his land near by, his cancer treatment, paid for by the government because he was a national hero, suddenly ceased. When the general refused to give in, his land was declared a security zone. Since the Ortel contract stipulated that broadcasting operations must begin within 270 days after signature, the government simply intended to prevent equipment being installed.

However, during a soccer match Ortel slipped its equipment past guards preoccupied by a broadcast of the match and began transmitting. The next day military personnel destroyed the equipment. When Ortel protested, the congress voted in favour of the company. However, the final blow was struck by the government. It appealed against the decision of congress and set in motion a process of appeals that would last as long as the administration held office.

Educational television in Latin America

Thirty years ago educational television (ETV) seemed the answer to Latin America's need for education to foster economic development. The first

ETV was started in Uruguay in 1958, following initial experiments with educational television in Europe and the United States. By the late 1980s empty ETV studios were to be found in the Amazon, Caracas, São Paulo and all over Latin America. Between 1968 and 1973 the number of ETV stations rose from three to fourteen but then declined.

In hindsight the reasons are straightforward. Television is not a good teaching vehicle, even if it can be a useful tool for use by a live teacher. The problems faced by ETV in Latin America were many. It was often claimed that there was inadequate state finance, although it is not clear that additional money would have changed the outcome very much. There was competition from the commercial systems, which feared they would lose viewers. There were problems of maintenance with the VCRs and television sets in uncertain climates and conditions. Transmissions were not reliable. The monitors would often learn the lessons and make the television sets redundant. There was cynicism and lack of interest. The timetables were often inappropriate and at the wrong hours. Local teachers feared and opposed television to the extent that in El Salvador they went on strike over ETV. Perhaps most important is the conclusion of research that in fact the pictures are a distraction. Radio and books are more effective, and success from ETV is generally based on the audio segment.[18]

By 1980 in all of Latin America there were some 30 million illiterates and 20 million more who had not completed primary education. There were just 100,000 registered *telescola* students. The only success story of merit was the *telesecundia* programme in Mexico, where 30,000 students took secondary school via television and achieved results in the national exams which exceeded those of the average high-school student.[19] This success pales in comparison with that of soap operas such as *Con venmigo*, discussed above.[20]

Religious television

The 1980s in Latin America also saw significant religious demand. Jimmy Swaggart, a leader in television evangelism in the United States, spread his ministry to Latin America. There, through translators on television, he was instrumental in Protestant expansion in a Catholic region. In a decade the number of Protestants rose from 12 million to 30 million. In 1987 Swaggart's hour-long weekly programme was shown on 511 Latin American stations. Although the programmes meet some religious demand they also have an element of political demand. The evangelists usually avoid overt political statements, but by failing to criticize economic and social conditions they support and in turn are supported by many political leaders. President José Napoleon Duarte met Swaggart and admitted to watching the programme. While in Chile Swaggart prayed for General Pinochet. Politicians also like the welfare provision such as education and medical care that the US evangelists bring to Latin America.[21]

Latin American television, dominated as it is by private corporations which exercise considerable monopoly power, provides a contrast to the rest of the developing world, where state ownership is more prevalent.

Africa

This section focuses on the two wealthiest nations, Nigeria and South Africa. Nigeria has had television since 1958 and was the first African country to begin television broadcasts; politics lay behind the decision. Politics likewise lay behind the South African decision not to start television.

In terms of economics Africa is not a good market for television. It is poor, it is rural, and it has many more urgent economic priorities. Terrestrial broadcasting to a geographical area nearly three times the size of Europe would be hard to finance, whether from licence fees, commercials, or state grants. Finally, in terms of meeting consumer demand for entertainment VCRs became very popular in the 1980s amongst the small minority able to acquire them. In other words VCRs have played a pre-emptive role in parts of Africa.

They have been a source of frustration to African leaders, who realize that VCRs can undermine their power and influence. In Nigeria Segun Olusola said in 1986 that video had 'become the enemy in our backyards . . . [Nigerians] had tuned out broadcast television.'[22] Instead they watched cassettes. Of course in many parts of Africa there is no broadcasting to tune out.

In Africa until the introduction of VCRs broadcast television was seen chiefly as a means of nation-building and of spreading the political philosophy of the government. This reflected the fact that the African experience with broadcasting was based largely on the legacy of the former colonial rulers. The Empire Broadcasting Service from Britain was a colonial government-provided vehicle to meet the information and educational needs of the ruling classes. Although there is a private press in countries such as Nigeria, Kenya, and Ghana, the mass media are dominated by the state. In Africa commercial television is neither commercially viable nor in many cases politically conceivable. The major issue is not private versus public television but public versus state-controlled television. Government-regulated and financed television is the norm.[23]

Nigeria

Western Nigeria was the first region of Africa to have television. It even had television before radio. Western Nigeria Television (WNTV) was started when an opposition leader was refused access to radio to express his political views there. Chief Awolowo, head of the Action Group for Government of Western Nigeria, responded by using the regional broadcasting rights granted under the McPherson constitution of 1951. In co-operation with Overseas Rediffusion of London he started WNTV in order to have a political voice in a land where few people read newspapers.[24]

WNTV provided the chief with considerable prestige and a means of reaching the affluent who could afford television. WNTV was financed by commercials and government grants. It was not a financial success; the advertising base was inadequate, and in 1961 Rediffusion pulled out. In the years leading up to the Biafran War in 1966 WNTV built additional transmitters so that it could reach into Lagos as well as serving the 12 million population of Ibadan and the Yoruba people with informational, educational, and entertainment programming. Clearly WNTV served only an elite who could afford television in the 1960s and no audience figures are available.

In 1976 WNTV was taken over by All-Nigeria TV Service (NTV) as part of a programme to stress national unity and play down tribal discord. Consequently content changed. Foreign programming fell from 80 to 20 per cent as the government sought to nation-build. However, viewers cannot be forced to watch. Whether it be Kenya or Nigeria, VCR owners rarely tune in to local television, where the President can be seen nightly. Instead they watch American movies.

To compete, some African countries have begun to provide more entertainment. For the most part programming is characterized by a lack of creativity and timidity. Highly centralized television systems which receive either no, or very small, revenue from commercials and licence fees serve the government, which provides the budget, first. The fact that in *coups d'état* the first institution a new government takes over is the broadcast media demonstrates this primary function of television in Africa.

South Africa

The South African government feared the effects of television on their *apartheid* policy and resisted its introduction until 1975. The South African Broadcasting Corporation (SABC) is based on the model of the BBC in being a public corporation. However, there is much control of news and current affairs, and there is censorship of programmes that might be contrary to the policy of *apartheid*.[25] Hence sex and violence are permitted but shows such as *Roots*, discussing the heritage of blacks, are not.

However, *Roots* was shown on Bophutha Tswana Television (Bop-TV), which was started in 1984. Bop-TV is an attempt to introduce *apartheid* television. South Africa would like to make Botswana a separate country but the International Telecommunications Union (ITU) does not recognize it as such and so does not allocate it broadcasting frequencies. SABC has therefore made a channel available to Bop-TV which is beamed to Soweto, twenty miles outside Johannesburg.[26]

Bop-TV has had some interesting economic consequences. First, it has demonstrated that the dry fare supplied to white South Africans does not meet even white demand. Viewers in Johannesburg who are able to pick up the Bop-TV channel because of spillage pay nearly $200 to erect special aerials so that they can receive Bop-TV. It was estimated that in 1985 over 100,000 white South Africans tuned in to Bop-TV. In addition Bop-TV has affected property values. A house that can exploit the spillage and receive the channel is worth about R1,930 ($1,000) more than one which cannot. Second, it has shown the problem of the current structure. When Bop-TV showed clips from the African National Congress and interviewed Winnie Mandela South Africa protested and threatened to close the channel down. Bop-TV operates conditionally, therefore, even though it is in a separate homeland. Undeterred, South Africa still plans to start up separate channels for the other nine homelands.

SABC operates two other channels for blacks. They were started in 1982 and broadcast in the tribal languages. This is despite the fact that 80 per cent of city blacks use English as their daily language. Commercials also have to be in the native language, and this creates difficulties. As the French language has been anglicized with expressions such as *le french fries*, so Zulu has adopted the English words for toothpaste and potato crisps, which came to them through the English-speaking whites. Writers of commercials therefore have to make up Zulu equivalents for the words on advertisements on the black channels.

Perhaps the most bizarre television in Africa is that found in Libya. African governments finance most television and use it primarily to foster national unity and national development. To that end, when revolution swept Colonel Gadaffi to power in 1969, he took over the television service that had been started three years earlier. In 1975 the Al-Watan-al-Arabi broadcasting station was established. Based heavily on news provided by the Libyan news agency, JANA, all news programmes begin with extracts from Gadaffi's *Green Book* of quotations and philosophy. There are three television channels, a general channel, a foreign channel, and a third channel devoted entirely to the *Green Book*. In 1984 Gadaffi cancelled all elementary education, making television even more influential. In fact many Libyans avoid Al-Watan-al-Arabi and rely upon broadcasts from Egypt and Tunisia for news of the outside world and for entertainment.[27] Libya also has the most gruesome television: in 1987 it showed public hangings of those accused of plotting against Gadaffi.[28]

The Middle East

The effect of oil on the Middle East was to transform a society little removed from the Middle Ages into part of the modern world. The written word, except for the Koran, is not trusted in the same way that it is in the West, so that the potential for video to affect society is considerable. Recognizing this, President Nasser spent heavily to promote Egyptian state television in the 1950s. He recognized that television fitted in well with Islamic family values, as well as meeting his own political demands. In the 1980s Egyptian television was still coming to terms with the conflict between traditional and modern views.

In 1988 the more fundamentalist followers of the country's most popular religious leader on television, Sheikh Muhammed Metwalli, attempted to ban music, dancing, and singing during the holy period of Ramadan. Many of their more puritanical views are inspired by Muslims from Saudi Arabia. In 1988 demonstrations and protests caused the state-run television system to modify its programming and include more religious content during Ramadan.[29] Although Egyptian television has never aired shows such as *Dynasty* because they have homosexual characters, other popular US programmes such as *Knots Landing* continued to be shown, as did belly-dancers and an Egyptian-made programme called *Ramadan Quiz* which was filled with music and dancing.[30]

Saudi Arabian television began in 1965. The government wanted to act as gatekeeper of what Saudis watched and to use television for encouraging what they saw as the appropriate sort of social development. Saudi is tightly controlled by the ruling princes of the Saud family, who are members of the fundamentalist Wahabi sect of Islam and regarded as the keepers of the faith. However, in the early 1970s wealthy Saudis returning from the West brought back US standard Sony half-inch U-Matic video-cassette recorders. The machines were meant for commercial use, but the Saudis liked the freedom they gave from government control of what they watched, as well as providing more variety and control of programming. Some Saudi leaders as a result declared their country the first video society and the first country to demonstrate that the government's gatekeeper role was over.

All other countries in the Gulf soon experienced VCR-delivered programming. Guest workers from Egypt returned with VCRs, and by the mid-1980s VCRs were to be found everywhere in Egypt where there was electricity. When the government banned the film *Sadat* on television it was still circulated widely on video.

The effect of VCRs has been a loosening of political ties. In Iran in 1979 VCRs were credited with permitting the distribution of anti-Shah material and contributing to the success of the revolution. The Shah's extravagant wedding was shown on television with all its Western excess and was thought to have helped turn Iranians against the regime. Although Khomeini and his successors used television to promote the fundamentalist Muslim world view, his successors must be concerned that the technology that allowed Khomeini to undermine the Shah will be used against the current ruling party at some time in the future.

India

An Indian who had emigrated a decade earlier recalled a return visit to his village in 1987 as follows. Having made the journey by jet and train, he took a bullock cart to his village. In the morning the milk was delivered by bullock cart exactly as it had been in his childhood and for generations earlier. However, the milkman now delivered VCR and video-cassette rentals along with the milk. India is a country of contrasts, and its television is no exception. In the most backward rural villages traditional life styles and the latest satellite television technology came together in the 1980s.

The population of this huge country is comparable to that of Europe, North America, and the USSR combined. There is a middle class of over 100 million, and during the '80s it enjoyed an economic growth rate of around 4 per cent per annum. Many of its leaders, following the example first of Prime Minister Indira Gandhi and then of her successor Rajiv Gandhi, are committed to thrusting India into economic development. To that end, particularly following the public relations opportunities which occurred at the 1982 Asian Games, held in India, the government has undertaken a commitment to increased supplies of the new media.

In 1983 India launched the satellite InSAT-1B, which gave television access to remote areas and created the infrastructure necessary for development.[31] InSAT-1B has bearer channels on it which, under India's sixth economic plan, provide a national hook-up for Doordarshan (Televiewing), the state's broadcasting authority.

Despite the fact that India is the world's largest democracy, the ruling Congress Party has resisted all pressure to hand the broadcasting media over to an autonomous body. Although there is a free press, broadcasting is a state monopoly. Doordarshan has a director-general, but unlike the

Director-General of the BBC he is a civil servant and does what the Information Committee of the Cabinet tells him.

The structure of Indian television has given rise to concern that television will be used for indoctrination rather than education. In general this has not been the case. There is control of the news, and local news is poorly covered, although the latter fact reflects financial constraints as much as political motives. In 1987 the government, however, raided the offices of the vocal and critical newspaper *India Express* when it exposed the fact that Indian middlemen had received pay-offs from foreign companies which had sold military equipment to India.[32] This reveals how sensitive the government is to criticism and why it wishes to control television, a medium potentially much more powerful than newspapers in a country where the majority are still illiterate. There is also a tendency to self-censorship, so that Doordarshan ignores topics such as suttee, the burning alive of widows, and bribery in the Congress.[33] Late in 1988 the director-general was transferred to the Ministry of Culture as Rajiv Gandhi prepared for the 1989 elections. The suspicion was that the Prime Minister wanted a director-general who would work harder to build Gandhi up and criticize his opponents.[34]

Doordarshan runs two state channels, with commercials shown on the entertainment channel. Most programmes are in either Hindi or English, although there is broadcasting in six of the sixteen major languages. Despite the fact that English is the mother tongue of only 0.25 per cent of the population and is spoken by only 3 per cent, its use is prevalent in broadcasting. This is partly because those who can afford television tend also to be those who speak English but also because 10 per cent or more of programmes are imported from the West. English remains the language of the elite, and television is likely to keep it so.

Access to television has grown dramatically in the 1980s. In 1983 India produced 50,000 colour television sets; in 1986 it produced 800,000. Since 1982 the government has allowed the production of television sets without special manufacturing licences and this has led to competition, increased quality, and lower prices. Prices fell from around $5,000 to $800.[35] There has also been a shake-out amongst television-set producers.

Television received a fillip from the Asian Games, which the government wanted to use as a showcase to as many Indians as possible. Licences, taxes, and import restrictions on television sets and VCRs were reduced, so that by 1984 there were over half a million VCRs and 5 million television sets for the country's 800 million people. These made television available to a substantial proportion of the population. Whilst the affluent would buy a television set and a VCR, the middle classes were more likely to rent them. The lower classes in both rural and urban areas could go to video theatres. There, for about two rupees, they could watch an Indian or American movie on video. In comparison a cinema ticket cost five rupees (about 38¢). Consequently the huge Indian film industry as well as the cinemas experienced a decrease in demand as viewers switched to video theatres which generated no revenue for the film industry.[36]

Whether the Indian film industry will find that a secondary market grows, as the US film industry found with VCRs, exports, and television remains to be seen. In 1988 in conjunction with Britain's Channel 4 a remarkable film was made called *Salaam Bombay*. It portrayed life on the streets of the city and used street children to play the parts. The film portrayed the grim world in which India's 135 million child labourers live and shows how television can become a medium of economic and social change by raising public consciousness.

VCRs and video theatres also gave rise to concern on the part of government. To control them the government introduced measures including powers to confiscate, to censor, and to impose entertainment taxes. However, even these measures can only curb the use of VCRs. By 1988 there were reports that passengers were refusing to use long-distance buses that were not equipped with a VCR. It was also reported that there had been several accidents involving buses, when the driver was preoccupied with changing the cassette. Evidently whole Bombay apartment blocks were sometimes wired for VCRs. Within just a few years VCRs had had a dramatic and irreversible effect on Indian society and upon India's film industry, still the largest in the world.

Partly to offset the influence of VCRs, but also for propaganda and educational purposes, Indira Gandhi mounted a campaign in 1984 to broaden television coverage from 23 per cent to 70 per cent of the population. This required the building of new transmitters as well as the use of satellites. It was also in 1984 that India began commercial television. This development was an outcome of the policy of broadening television coverage and using it to encourage family planning.

Television advertising in India has its origins in educational television. In 1984 S.S. Gill, the Secretary of Information and Broadcasting, wanted to imitate the success of Mexican soap operas as a means of achieving social goals. He wanted a commercial company to sponsor the production of a soap opera advocating family planning. Eventually the Swiss company Nestlé agreed. The soap opera, in Hindi, was called *Hum Log*. When it received a lukewarm reception the plot was altered. Family planning was abandoned and the show adopted a working-class theme. It achieved great success and ran long enough to attract over 200 advertisers. With this success other commercial organizations were attracted, and commercial television took off.[37] Between 1985 and 1986 total advertising revenue on television rose from 4 billion to 6.3 billion rupees. At the equivalent of $1,500 for a thirty-second slot or $6,000 to sponsor a half-hour programme advertising seemed a bargain, even if most viewers were too poor to buy the products advertised. By 1986 up to twenty minutes per hour of commercial messages were being broadcast by firms such as Nestlé, Colgate, Vicks (cough drops), and Maggi (noodles). In 1987 the going price for a thirty-second commercial spot had risen to $18,000.[38]

Alarmed by the social implications, S.S. Gill, the instigator of commercials on television, became an advocate of a ban on advertising, such as that imposed by Indonesia in 1981. It was too late. By 1988 India's huge middle classes were reluctant to abandon their pursuit of Western consumer life styles. Advertisers too liked the new means of competition. Commercials on television had become a permanent fixture. For example, the most popular advertisement-supported soap opera, *Buniyaad* (*Foundation*), was shown twice a week and commanded an audience of 23 million loyal supporters.[39]

As an education medium television has not had the success that was initially hoped for. The older direct approach of educational television was first tried in the 1960s, and India was one of the first countries to use satellites to beam education to remote areas as an experiment, using Intelsat, in the 1970s. With much enthusiasm from sponsors, satellites and television seemed the ideal way to take education to the remote villages. However, just as in Latin America, the problems of breakdowns in equipment and teacher opposition, added to apathy among villagers, proved overwhelming. *Hum Log* failed to inspire family planning by the subtle indirect means of dramatic example. Television, as elsewhere, has not fulfilled its potential as a tool of economic development.

South East Asia

Much of what has been said about Latin America, Africa, and India applies to the countries of South East Asia. The freedom of the press and the independence of the Western media are not found. Rather, governments seek to control television, either directly or indirectly. There, too, VCRs have undermined that control and allowed uncensored programmes and politically subversive material to be circulated. VCRs have created problems for the Asian film industry, threatened the ability of governments to 'build' their nations, and challenged the governments' ability to act as gatekeeper of public morality. They have also helped meet consumer demand.

South Korea

South Korea is one of the four 'dragons' or 'tigers', one of the fastest-growing economies in the world and a challenge to the economic might of Japan. Government control over the whole economy is tight as it pursues economic development. There was still in 1988 widespread opposition to the government of President Roh Tae Woo. In an attempt to maintain control over the media the South Korean television industry was restructured back in 1980.[40]

Restructuring in 1980 took the form of the government forcing the consolidation of the two private companies, TBS and Dong-A, with the state authority, Korean Broadcasting Corporation (KBS). TBS had been owned by the Samsung Group, which produces television sets and VCRs. Dong-A had been owned by the *Dong-A-Bilbo* newspaper. Another station, Munhwa Broadcasting Corporation (MBC), was forced to sell two-thirds of its stock to KBS, whilst the Christian Broadcasting System (CBS) was forced to cease all non-religious broadcasting.

The motive for the restructure by the military regime of the then President, General Chun Dwoo Hwan was to create a public network along the lines of the highly respected BBC in Britain and the NHK of Japan. Like them KBS was initially financed entirely by subscription fees. However, affordable subscription fees in a relatively poor country – *per capita* income in 1988 was still only US $2,000 per annum – were insufficient to fund a quality network. Within a year KBS was accepting advertisements in order to generate sufficient revenue. By 1986 only half of all KBS revenues came from subscriptions of about US $2.85 per month. Advertising provided the rest.

In terms of conduct KBS was not criticized for bowing to commercialism, to the preference option, despite the dependence on advertising.[41] Rather, KBS was criticized because it showed state bias. It was too close to the government. News and public affairs programming was biased. Reflecting this closeness, a former president of KBS was appointed Minister of Culture and Information. Newspapers and the opposition party, the NDKP, urged viewers to boycott KBS and to refuse to pay their subscriptions. In the eyes of many South Koreans, according to *Dong-A-Bilbo*, licence fees had become a quasi-tax.[42] Although Koreans were used to propaganda, they found it particularly aggravating to have to pay for it.[43]

The 1988 Olympic Games were held in Seoul and in many countries the games became a 'media event', dominating every media outlet and overwhelming most of the competition. In 1983 in Korea another such national 'media event' occurred, but in this case spontaneously. In 1983 KBS prepared an anniversary programme to commemorate the Korean War. In a show called *We Are Still Separated* it interviewed wartime survivors. On the show a male survivor began crying when describing his heartache over his missing children.[44] In Korea the war had caused an estimated 10 million families to be broken up and their members to be separated.

KBS decided to run a two-hour follow-up programme in which they asked for volunteers who wished to be reunited. A thousand applied, with signboards and details of the missing. That evening thirty-six reunions took place but such was the interest that the programme was continued. It was continued for sixty-five hours over eight days. The programme was telecast to a US television station belonging to the ABC network in Los Angeles and to a station in West Germany. It then continued on a weekly basis for six months, at which time, after 453 hours of programming, some 10,189 families had been reunited. This heart-warming example shows that at times, for both good and ill, television can have outcomes which are beyond price.

Thailand

Thailand, formerly Siam, was the setting of the movie *The King and I*, with Yul Brynner, and royalty still dominates life in Thailand, including television.[45] The news begins each evening by recounting the activities of the royal family that day. Although none of the nine channels is a government channel, the government exerts strong direct and indirect controls over all the stations.

Thai television was started in 1955, making it one of the oldest systems in South East Asia. Broadcasting is in the hands of the Public Relations Department (PRD). The Mass Communication Organization of Television, a government agency, is responsible for the day-to-day management of television. Four channels operate in the capital, Bangkok. The Army Signals Corps runs Channel 5 and leases out another channel. Thai Television also operates one channel and leases out the other. The two leased channels are Channel 2, run by Bangkok Television, and Channel 3, run by Bangkok Entertainment. Together Bangkok's television systems serve an audience of over 15 million viewers. Thai Television's other four channels broadcast to the provinces.[46]

Conduct in Thailand in terms of programming is uninspired, and most programmes are imported. Many come from the United States and are dubbed into Thai. There is a general lack of public-affairs and educational television. Instead game shows, Chinese martial arts programmes, imported Western shows, and Western soap operas dominate. This is a direct result of cheap prices for imported material. In 1980 Thailand was paying under $200 to import many such programmes. In those circumstances would-be domestic producers faced insurmountable competition.

Imported programmes keep expenses low. This is essential, since revenues are obtained from commercials. These in turn are limited to ten thirty-second slots per hour. Since the average Thai income is still only $4,000, even though in the late 1980s economic growth was very rapid and earned Thailand the title of the fifth tiger, the slots do not command a very high price.

There is censorship.[47] The Radio and Television Administration Board is headed by a military general and does most of the censoring. The news each evening reflects this. After the events of the royal family's day comes the domestic news, and finally the most interesting, foreign news via satellite. Broadcasters who have outraged the censors have been rounded up and stations have been closed for showing unacceptable content.

Malaysia

Malaysia's television must serve one of the most heterogeneous audiences in the world. Five different scripts are used in the newspapers: Malaysi, Roman, Chinese, modified Arabic, and Indian. The population of about 16 million, with an average income of $1,500 per year, enjoys living conditions which vary from those of tree dwellers to modern city-dwellers.

If tamed producers in Thailand use their television stations to support the royal family, in Malaysia there is special concern to make Bahasa the national language and to promote Islam, the state religion. The authoritarian environment makes broadcasting journalists timid, and state television is reduced to a public-relations operation for the government. Censorship of racial, religious, sexual, and intimate behaviour ensures that television follows the government's plans for social and economic development.

Censorship and regulation are widespread. For example, the Jonestown massacre, in which over 900 people died, was not reported on television. Shows have frequently been banned because of sexual content. Both *Roots* and *The Holocaust* were banned because they dealt with race. All commercials must be filmed in Malaysi and made in Malaysia. Commercials dealing with liquor or cosmetics and those involving kissing are all forbidden.

In 1984 TV-3, a private station, was started in Kuala Lumpur, to supplement the state-run system. However, its ownership is linked with the establishment. TV-3 is owned by Sistem Televisyen Malaysia, which in turn is part of the Fleet Group, which owns the *New Straits Times*. Finance Minister Daim Zainviddi has a controlling interest in Fleet Group. Local banks and the MIC are also owners.[48]

TV-3 provides a more appealing programme line-up than the state-run Radio-TV-Malaysia (RTM). When it started in 1984 many viewers abandoned RTM in favour of TV-3. However, as in much of Asia, Malaysians were already using VCRs to avoid the bland material on state television. By 1985 there were over a thousand video hire shops, and

Western and Hong Kong films were the main fare. TV-3 relied heavily on US imports and popular entertainment shows to attract audiences from RTM. However, when Muslim extremists complained about decadent Western shows TV-3 increased its local content.

Cultural imperialism is normally associated with Western programmes to the Third World. The experience of the independent states of Brunei, Sabah, and Sarawak with Malaysia suggests otherwise. Since 1980 Malaysia has used Indonesia's PALAPA satellite to beam down programmes on to those countries in English and Bahasa Malaysia. This threatens the local languages.

In Brunei, surrounded by Malaysian transmitters, the Sultan responded to the threat from Malaysia. He believed that Malaysia had designs on his territory. First he started colour television broadcasts to compete with Television Malaysia. Second, for Ibans in very remote areas, he used helicopters to deliver small petrol generators so that they could receive community television in their longhouses. Finally, he instituted a programme of interest-free loans for colour television sets and aerials. Consequently in Bandar Seri, where most houses are built of mud on stilts in the river, colour television aerials can be seen. Since Brunei cannot afford much local programming, viewers squat and watch much the same material that viewers watch in New York. The head of television for Brunei commented, 'It has grieved me that we have robbed them of their culture overnight . . . [but] if we took no steps that might be wrong.' Economics meant that the choice was not between cultural imperialism and no cultural imperialism but between American and Malaysian cultural imperialism.[49]

Singapore too has been a victim of leakage from Malaysia. When TV-3 started, aerials to pick up the signal began to appear all over Singapore. TV-3 filled consumer demand that the state-owned SBC failed to meet.

Singapore

Singapore Broadcasting Corporation (SBC) is derived from Malaysia's broadcasting structure, since Singapore was formerly part of Malaysia. Although SBC is an autonomous body rather than a government department, the government exerts tight control through the Ministry of Culture and Subsidies. SBC broadcasts in four languages to a population of 1.5 million whose small size constrains expenditure on programmes. There is little quality programming, and cheap foreign imports account for 60 per cent of programmes. Among Chinese viewers, more than half watch video cassettes rather than television.[50]

Singapore is very development-conscious, with one of the fastest growth rates in the world. SBC was first used for development purposes in 1968 in the first campaign to keep Singapore clean. Visitors are always impressed at the cleanliness of Singapore, where a cigarette end is never seen. SBC has played an instrumental part in spreading the message of the Prime Minister, Lee Kwan Yew. Education and informational programming constitutes 26 per cent of air time. All material shown is conservative and highly censored. For example, in 1973 it was announced that for three days a week there would be violence-free television, meaning in effect a ban on violent US shows. When those living in public housing wanted to put up aerials, so as to pick up TV-3 from Malaysia to meet their demand for light entertainment, the government quashed the plan on the grounds that such aerials would be inappropriate in public housing.[51]

Hong Kong and Macao

In 1997 Hong Kong becomes part of China, and in 1998 Macao likewise returns to China. Both countries continue to develop their television systems. Both countries continue to exercise tight censorship of the media.[52] In 1989 Hong Kong invited tenders for cabling the island, whilst in 1987 Macao privatized its television system.[53] Both islands can broadcast to mainland China as well as to each other. Chapter 9 noted how the Chinese had ordered cadres to stop watching Hong Kong television, and in 1987 Hong Kong in its turn experienced some unwanted television leakage.

In Hong Kong uninvited and unwanted spillage was reported in 1987 from Macao, the nearby Portuguese colony. The Hong Kong government had for years wanted to ban cigarette advertisements from the colony's two television channels, one in Chinese and one in English. However, television advertisements generated revenue of over US $25 million in 1987, and the Chinese-language channel, Asia Television, depended upon cigarette advertisements for commercial viability. The English-language station Television Broadcast (TVB) would not have been threatened commercially but the ban implied a loss of advertising revenue and lower profits.

The problem developed when Macao decided to split Teledifusao de Macao (TdM) into two channels in 1987. The channel in English and Portuguese was retained by the government but the Chinese station was auctioned off late in 1987. Bidders included Rupert Murdoch, Portugal's television company, which won the bidding, and a company from mainland China.

When it was announced that advertisements would be banned in Hong Kong in 1990 the newly privatized TdM announced that it was increasing the power of its transmitters. This would allow it to beam its programmes, which are uncensored as to sex, violence, and politics, to Hong Kong. TdM would also carry the cigarette advertisements which were forbidden to the Hong Kong channels. There was some irony in the situation, since for years the people of Macao had preferred Hong Kong television to their own.

In Hong Kong television is at the centre of other worries over economic imperialism. Hong Kong has expressed concern that TdM shows horse racing, which threatens the betting and attendance at the Royal Hong Kong Jockey Club, and has threatened to retaliate by opening a casino to attract gamblers from Macao. Casino revenues account for half of Macao government revenues.

Hong Kong therefore is only receiving a bit of its own treatment. Hong Kong in its turn has exerted a powerful influence on mainland China and Macao, and the problem of economic and cultural imperialism can be expected to continue until both former colonies are returned to China.

Indonesia

Indonesia is a huge country of 170 million people, the fifth largest population in the world, with a *per capita* income of only $500 per year. Indonesia also has a history of unusual television policies which, from an economic standpoint, are irrational.

In 1976, at vast expense for such a poor country, Indonesia became the fourth country in the world to launch its own domestic satellite, PALAPA. The policy goal was national unity. Commentators suggested that the major beneficiaries were the government, from propaganda, and the Western multinationals who supplied the technology.

Indonesia took the unusual step in 1981 of banning all advertisements. As much of the rest of the world moved towards commercially based television Indonesia, in order to increase government control over the media, moved in the other direction. All television is controlled by the Ministry of Information through the Director General of Radio, Television, and Film. Economic development and national unity are constant themes, and the ban on advertisements was prompted by the effects of commercials. It was thought that they created consumerism and unreasonable expectations, and encouraged migration to the cities. The ban also deprived advertisers of an outlet and the government of a source of revenue.

TVR-1 does not meet all consumer demand for news and entertainment. This is reflected in the popularity of an Australian radio service, as one of the main sources of uncensored news, and the use of VCRs.

The Philippines

Under the corrupt regime of the late President Marcos television in the Philippines was privately structured but owed its existence to him.

Following martial law three of the five stations in metropolitan Manila were run by Marcos's close friend Roberto Benedicto. He control led Radio Philippines Network (RPN). He also had an interest in the other two stations, Banashaw Broadcasting Corporation (BBC) and Inter-island Broadcasting Corporation (IBC). Under Marcos he had been allowed to import new studios and broadcasting equipment duty-free and to hire a transponder from PALAPA to beam his television throughout the archipelago.

In 1987 the Philippine government recovered $5 billion worth of property from the Marcos family. This included eighteen television stations. Under the Aquino government the structure of the television industry did not change very much. In 1988 the same television stations were operating as in the Marcos days, although ownership had changed. In 1988 there were five major stations: BBC, RPN, IBC, and two others, GMA Radio Television Arts and the Makarlika Broadcasting System.[54]

In terms of conduct, in Manila BBC and IBC broadcast the news in Tagalog. English-language broadcasting is extensive during the daytime because of its low cost. There is also heavy use of evangelical broadcasting, again because of its low cost. In the evening Filipino-produced soap operas are very popular.

Conclusion

Some common patterns can be discerned amongst Third World countries. Most important, the competition of Western programmes sold at discriminatory prices well below the cost of production undermines the opportunities for local producers. As a result Third World countries are exposed to cultural imperialism whatever the structure. More than any other medium television creates an implosion of cultural values. Since the beginning of civilization cultures have developed away from each other along different lines.[55] In the late twentieth century the revolution in communications has caused a cultural implosion. The structure of the world television industry has been a significant factor. This survey has shown that, whether state-run or privately run, the forces to open up to the influence of Western television cultures are considerable. Brazil is one exception in providing a competitive supply of products, but few countries have so large a population over which to spread the costs of production. Even where governments attempt to close the door to outsiders their attempts can be circumvented by VCRs or by powerful aerials. The final chapter examines the implications of cultural imperialism further.

Notes

1 Douglas A. Boyd and Joseph D. Straubhar, 'Development impact of the home VCR on Third World countries', *Journal of Broadcasting and the Electronic Media*, winter 1985, p. 5.
2 *World Press Review*, October 1984.
3 *Time*, 20 July 1987. The dramas are sold for prices ranging from $8,000 to $800,000, depending upon the size of the audience.
4 Everett M. Rogers and Livia Antola, '*Telenovelas*: a Latin American success story', *Journal of Communications*, January 1986, p. 24.
5 Irene Penacchioni, 'The reception of popular television in north-eastern Brazil', *Media, Culture and Society*, October 1984, p. 336.
6 *World Press Review*, October 1984.
7 *The Economist*, 4 July 1987.
8 ibid.
9 *World Press Review*, October 1984.
10 *The Europa Year Book*, London: Europa Publications, 1988, p. 10.
11 *Times-Colonist* (Associated Press report), 18 November 1988.
12 John W. Tiffin, 'Educational television in the Third World', *Broadcasting in the Third World*, November 1983, p. 261.
13 Elizabeth Mahan, 'Mexican broadcasting: reassessing the industry-state relationship', *Journal of Communications*, April 1984, p. 66.
14 *World Press Review*, December 1986.
15 *Wall Street Journal*, 30 May 1986.
16 Everett M. Rogers and Livia Antola, '*Telenovelas*: a Latin American success story', *Journal of Communications*, January 1986, p. 24.
17 *Index on Censorship*, June 1987.
18 To show how little content the typical television news programme contains, Walter Cronkite, the long-time anchor man of *CBS Evening News* in the United States, once held up his script for the evening. A half-hour news show contained just one typed page of written material.
19 Thirty thousand out of 30 million illiterates is a very small proportion, and the relative success of this programme reflects the fact that entrants were literate, it was secondary education, and that some participants were from urban areas where the advantage of an education is more apparent.
20 John W. Tiffin, 'Educational television in Latin America', *Broadcasting in the Third World*, November 1983, p. 261.
21 *Time*, 16 March 1987.
22 Mike Egbon, 'West Nigeria television service – oldest in tropical Africa', *Journalism Quarterly*, summer 1983, p. 329.
23 Paul A.V. Ansal, The role of the state in broadcasting in Africa', *Media Development*, February 1985, p. 8.
24 Mike Egbon, 'Western Nigeria television service – oldest in tropical Africa', *Journalism Quarterly*, summer 1983, p. 331.
25 *The Economist*, 20 December 1987.
26 Allister Sparks, 'Forbidden television', *Channels*, May/June 1985, p. 46.

27 *Index on Censorship*, May 1987.
28 *Time*, 2 September 1987.
29 *Christian Science Monitor*, 2–8 May 1988.
30 The programme *Dallas* was dropped because it became too popular and a national obsession. *The Economist*, 21 May 1988.
31 *Far Eastern Review*, 6 September 1984.
32 *The Economist*, 5 September 1987.
33 *Far Eastern Review*, 14 April 1988.
34 *The Economist*, 15 October 1988.
35 John A. Lent, 'Videos in Asia: frivolity, frustration, futility', *Media Development*, January 1985, p. 9.
36 ibid.
37 James Traub, 'New Delhi gold rush', *Channels*, July/August 1986, p. 34.
38 *World Press Review*, December 1986, p. 21.
39 *Time*, 20 July 1987.
40 *Far Eastern Review*, 8 May 1986.
41 Publicly run commercial networks such as the CBC in Canada are frequently criticized, justifiably, for putting ratings before the public interest and minority broadcasting.
42 ibid.
43 The government-controlled MBC channel, which relied totally on advertisements, was exempt from this criticism.
44 Suk-ho Jun and Daniel Dayan, 'An interactive media event: South Korea's televised family reunion', *Journal of Communications*, spring 1986, p. 75.
45 *The Economist*, 24 October 1987.
46 *Far Eastern Review*, 23 May 1985.
47 John A. Lent, 'ASEAN mass communications and cultural submission', *Media, Culture and Society*, October 1981, p. 163.
48 *Far Eastern Review*, 28 February 1985.
49 John A. Lent, 'Mass media in east Malaysia and Brunei', *Gazette*, September 1982, p. 106.
50 John A. Lent, 'Videos in Asia: frivolity, frustration, futility', *Media Development*, January 1985, p. 6.
51 *Asiaweek*, 6 December 1985.
52 *Far Eastern Review*, 8 January 1987.
53 Possible builders included the US telephone companies, the 'baby Bells', who, excluded from the home market, were building systems throughout the world. Hong Kong's densely packed population made it very attractive as a cable proposition.
54 *The Europa Yearbook 1988*, London: Europa Publications, 1988, p. 2879.
55 William McNeil, *The Rise of the West: History of the Human Community*, Chicago: University of Chicago Press, 1970, p. 9.

Chapter eleven

Conclusion

> I'm not interested in culture. I'm not interested in pro-social values.
> I have only one interest. That's whether people watch the programme.
> That's my definition of good, that's my definition of bad – *CBS vice-
> president, 1987*[1]

Adam Smith observed more than 200 years ago that it was out of self-
interest that producers supply the goods and services that consumers
demand. He went on to observe that the invisible hand would work in
the public interest only if producers could not combine against the public
interest. In other words, motives, however crass, are not particularly
relevant if performance is satisfactory, and monopoly is usually detrimental to performance.

Recent developments in the field of industrial organization stress the
importance of preventing collusion. In the 1960s and '70s anti-trust policy
in the United States emphasized industry concentration, although the
Europeans and Japanese have always been more tolerant of monopoly
per se. Recent contributions from the Chicago school and contestability
theory argue that many potential new entrants to an industry are likely
to make it hard to establish a monopoly, therefore the emphasis should
be on preventing collusion against the public interest. This book has
shown that throughout the Western world there are many potential
entrants to the television industry and there is plenty of rivalry among
most sectors of the industry. It has shown that although outside the
Western world many government, state, and private broadcasting
monopolies remain, VCRs have created alternative supply sources
everywhere.

This conclusion examines whether the consumer is being well served
by the television industry. The focus must ultimately be upon the
consumer, and not the advertiser who pays for so much television, nor
the government which seeks to control it, nor the suppliers. As the
television industry moves from a state monopoly system or a tight
oligopoly to a loose oligopoly in many parts of the world, Adam Smith's

observations about the unimportance of motives and the importance of preventing monopoly and collusion are still relevant. The world is moving to a situation where a number of profit-motivated media conglomerates will provide much of what the world watches on television.[2] As long as there is rivalry between suppliers and as long as there are potential entrants waiting to contest existing suppliers, then, industrial organization studies suggest, the public is likely to be well served.

From the point of view of performance media conglomerates are not generally a threat to the public interest, or to economic efficiency. Media conglomerates exist to make profits. By and large an entrepreneur like Rupert Murdoch does not care about the programmes his television carries nor the news and editorials in his newspapers. He does care if people stop watching his television programmes or buying his newspapers. He appoints producers to his television and editors to his newspapers who are good at the job and philosophically not opposed to him. However, since most media entrepreneurs are fairly apolitical, it means that producers have virtually a free hand in television and on newspapers as long as they provide what the public wants and meet their budgets. As long as there are enough other media conglomerates supplying programmes and news, then each should keep the other efficient economically and each should keep the other from suppressing news or opinion.[3]

In terms of the standard performance criteria set out in Table 1 the television industry in the Western world in the 1980s has performed satisfactorily. Many monopolies or tight oligopolies, whether in the private sector or the public sector, have been demolished or are in the process of being demolished. These include the US networks, the UK ITV companies, and many European state monopolies. The process encourages more efficient operations and encourages the use of additional resources to increase supply and product variety. There have been new products and new applications of technology so that progress has been satisfactory. New jobs have been created and X-inefficiency has been eliminated in many countries.

In terms of equity, television has always been a great leveller, contributing to equity in the sense that a princess and a bus driver both have access to the same television. On the other hand there is a regressive element in that advertisers rank households in terms of the size of their income and this influences the sorts of programmes to which princesses and bus drivers have equal access. It also has ramifications on the Third World and television viewing there. Cheap imports at marginal cost allow developing countries to enjoy programmes they could never afford to produce and release resources for other uses where they have a comparative advantage. However, industry structure means that they have little input into the nature of the programmes made available to them.

In the Communist countries the goals set for television are different from those set out in figure 1, so the industry must be judged on different terms. The Communist television systems seek to help the party achieve its ends. Consequently, although recent years have seen a dramatic change in the apparent conduct of the television systems of many Communist countries, the structure and performance criteria are unchanged. The new programme format is certainly an improvement for the consumer. Whether the party is better served is not known.

Turning to the public interest criterion, the Western tradition is that a better informed society with more sources of information is a better society. Full and free information contributes to economic efficiency. It also helps build and maintain democracy.

Regulation and intervention in the public interest are justified when there is market failure, and this is usually the case with any public good. Two questions help assess whether any specific regulation of television really is in the public interest. Why regulate television? Why is television regulated?

The first question can be answered in terms of market failure and suggests remedies for such problems as too many stations trying to use the broadcasting frequencies, or unsatisfactory product quality such as violence, pornography, or excessive advertising.[4] Reasonable people can debate and disagree on the form of interference, but the reason for interference must always be in the interests of the consuming public. The second question is useful because it casts light on the fact that much regulation is not in the public interest at all. Capture theory argues that regulators are sometimes captured by those they regulate – for example, because the regulators deal with the regulated on a day-to-day basis and have little contact with the public they are supposed to protect. Regulators may then identify not with the consuming public but with the procedures. An alliance between regulators and regulated may then work in both their interests, providing both with jobs and security, rather than working in the public interest.[5] For many years the cosy regulated duopoly in Britain served the producers well. They in turn believed they produced the finest television in the world. Only the public disagreed and rushed out to buy VCRs when they became available.

The book has stressed that two key sources of market failure associated with the television industry justify intervention. First, market failure arises from the fact that if a single source of finance is adopted not all demand is likely to be met. This arises from the fact that television has some characteristics of a public good and that television cannot be sold efficiently as a private good. Second, television creates external effects, some positive and some negative. Market failure is only a necessary condition for intervention, not a sufficient one. Intervention must avoid non-market failure, in other words the intervention must remedy, not

221

aggravate, the market failure. Some things, even if not perfect, are best left alone.

Market failure and television finance

Advertising pays for much television. On the surface this seems to mean free television for the viewer. It was shown that this is not the case. Game theory and the analysis of Kaldor, along with a superficial examination of much television or any magazine, shows that there is probably too much advertising. This may mean higher consumer-goods prices, although that is not certain. Advertising may allow economies of scale and scope which lower consumer prices enough to offset the cost of the advertising. These comments, however, apply to all advertising. Banning television advertisements would lead to a reallocation of resources towards the other media and other methods of sales promotion. This would probably be an inferior alternative, given that for advertisers television is the medium of choice.

If television advertising is banned, as it has been in Indonesia, then alternative means of financing television must be found. All the alternatives have weaknesses.

State funding and licence fees mean that all television owners pay, whether they want the state services or not. Such funding methods also often lead to the wrong incentives for suppliers, so that the services the supplier thinks the consumer should see, not what the consumers want, are shown. Pay services also have drawbacks because they create a loss of consumer surplus, a deadweight loss. However, if the pay programmes are later shown again, free, the lost consumer surplus is probably small.

Other methods include finance by pledges, lotteries, which are a form of voluntary tax, and auctions. Pledging is inefficient and boring and allows free-ridership by those who do not pledge. By auctioning off the licences for commercial television the state is at least able to capture the economic rent derivable from owning a station for the public purse. A little late in the day, since increased competition is reducing the size of the economic rents, this has been proposed both in the United Kingdom and the USA. By 1989 the economic rents of the ITV companies and the US networks were being eroded by new suppliers.

In conclusion, no single method of financing television is able to provide totally satisfactory performance. Advertising means that television ignores the intensity of desire for a programme, as shown in figure 2. Licence fees and state provision prevent the viewer from revealing his preferences to the supplier. A pay-per-view system that is set up so that programmes shown are later available free on another channel would also be satisfactory, though experience to date suggests it might not be commercially viable and might not meet all legitimate minority demands. Therefore a mix of an advertising system and a non-advertising public service system set up to attempt to fill the unfilled demands ignored by a commercial system is a second-best solution, a first best not being available.

A different argument to support a public television service not financed by advertisements can be put forward on political grounds. Much of the literature on industrial organization in the 1980s argued that monopolies are likely to be undermined by new entrants, or the threat of potential new firms entering the industry. From a political standpoint, however, there may be a need for regulation and a public service on the grounds that people want it because they simply do not trust unfettered capitalism. Public policy in the form of regulation and a public service are then themselves a public service to help support democracy. On similar lines it is arguable that developing countries should have a national television system so that their national identity and culture can at least be represented amongst the cacophony of Western programming received by satellite and VCR.

This book has argued that public-service television best serves the public interest if it is not a direct competitor with commercial systems. Therefore advertising is a poor form of finance. Advertising links the public service to the ratings game. In New Zealand and Canada the need for ratings to raise adequate finance has forced the public systems to attempt to compete for large audiences. A public service best serves the public interest if it supplies the shows that a commercial system will not. Preferably such a channel should not be vertically integrated and should be an outlet for independent suppliers. Trends in several countries suggest that this is the way that public-service systems will move, although the BBC is toying with the idea of going over to advertising. Commenting on such a proposal, Roy Hattersley, shadow Home Secretary, said, 'It is a great retreat from the concept of public service broadcasting'.[6] Earlier chapters argued that the BBC did not always serve the public interest as well as it sometimes claimed, but a retreat into advertising would be a move in the wrong direction.

Positive and negative externalities

A second issue that arose many times in previous chapters was the problem of exernalities supposedly generated by television. These range from declining US educational standards, to the purity of the language in France, to Samoans watching television for thirty-five hours a week. Clearly the magnitude of the alleged negative externalities involved cannot be measured. However, some comments can be made.

1. The first relates to the cultural imperialism issue. Communications

are a major contributor to the implosion of cultures that has taken place in the last few decades of the twentieth century. This implosion follows thousands of years of cultural diversification after the emergence of the first civilizations in the Middle East, India, and China. Television has played an important part in the implosion process. However, even without television, international travel for the masses, telephones, radio, films, and magazines would all have allowed the process to occur, albeit less rapidly. The negative externalities claimed for television are sometimes externalities associated with the whole information revolution. The programmes on television may appear awful and inappropriate and the cause of the externality, but the real culprit is the technology. The medium is the message, as Marshall McLuhan observed a quarter of a century ago.

Further, the effects of media imperialism, particularly US media imperialism, as it relates to television may be overstated. There is limited information about what people in the Third World watch and how they react to it but studies have shown that VCRs in Asia are used mostly for watching Asian films, not US video cassettes.[7] Much of the huge black market in the Third World is for Asian pirated material. Obviously there are no reliable statistics on the size of that market.

In addition, it is not certain that viewers in the Third World necessarily believe that *Dynasty*, for example, represents the USA any more than most Americans or the French believe it does. Television is light entertainment and escapism. Even where television does modify a culture, as in Samoa, the loss may be more perceived by the observer than felt by the native. The comparison has been made with the fat man preaching to the starving. However, there is still a sense of deep loss over the change involved, whoever that loss may be to. Sometimes the loss may be more imagined than real. In southern Italy television is thought to have brought an improvement in the reactionary local culture.[8]

Smaller developed countries such as Canada are also concerned that their culture will be crowded out or homogenized by US television. Yet Canadians are as aware in 1988 of not being American as they have ever been. In discussions in the debate over free trade with the USA the point was made that a culture that cannot survive free trade may not be worth saving. English Canadian culture has survived thirty years of US television and French Canada has survived 200 years within English America. The point is that cultures change but are surely not so fragile that television programmes from the USA, as opposed to the whole revolution in communications, will destroy them.

2. The portrayal of violence on television, often imported with US programmes, creates another externality. If advertising influences viewers it is hard to believe that violence on television does not. Television may be entertainment but it still has influence. There are often regulations about explicit sex on television, and more control of explicit violence

might be implemented, particularly on how violence is portrayed. A lot of violence seems gratuitous, violence for its own sake with no redeeming merit. Singapore has required that television be violence-free on three days a week. Britain has established a Broadcasting Standards Council. Neither solution is ideal, and no country has found a really satisfactory and acceptable way to regulate a code of conduct.

3. Consumerism, materialism, and a deprivation effect, particularly among children and people in the Third World, are another negative externality created by television and television advertising. The costs can never be determined. Some would claim that they are sufficiently large to condemn television outright, offsetting all its other benefits.

The externalities problem must be examined in the context of the net costs or benefits of television. However much one may lament the situation in Brunei or Samoa as native peoples watch *Miami Vice*, there are also benefits. Offsetting the cost is the effect of improved information on social, economic, and political freedom around the world. Some of the benefits from this include the following.

1. On the positive side, television as part of the communications revolution helps increase the flow of information. The advantages of the free flow of information are widespread but include the opportunities created for progress and improvement, for the making of rational decisions, and for preventing abuse by governments, corporations, or individuals. Full information is essential for the efficient working of an economy as well as for a political system. Denial of information is a form of censorship. Both the Berlin Wall and the Great Wall of China were built to keep information out, and television has leapt both walls, bringing information and new opportunities.

Journals such as *Index on Censorship* repeat over and over again stories of events that deserve more coverage in the media. A frequent criticism in that journal is that freelance journalists find their stories rejected or given limited air time on US network television or on the national news in other countries with public systems. They also report attempts to control their ability to get information about events in countries like the Sudan and Israel out of the country. They never complain that there are too many news agencies wanting stories. The news supplies are available if they can get access to television. What is needed is more news distributors and more channels carrying news. CNN has improved the quality of the news in Japan since it has been available there by stimulating competition, and the same can be expected around the world as new distributors seek programming. New sources of news can contribute to an improvement in human rights. Since such news stories are often cheap to buy, they should be popular with profit-motivated distributors.

New sources of supply should have the effect of dispersing the flow

of information to provide a greater variety of information. As a consequence television will probably become more like the print media, where
a great variety of sources means that no single source, be it the government or a media conglomerate like TV Globo, exerts undue influence.
The ability of the Doordarshan in India or KBC in South Korea to censor
their opponents and keep their faces, names, and voices from the public
view will be reduced. These are considerable benefits.

2. The story about family reunification in Korea illustrates the
contribution to social welfare that improved information can make. The
story of *Ven conmigo* showed how television can encourage literacy.
The *Live Aid* concert joined together 2 billion people and raised awareness
as well as money about the plight of the starving. Television helped spread
the news about AIDS and then quickly informed people how to avoid
the disease. Television brought people the news about a hi-jacking in
1985 of TWA flight 847 in Beirut and then made it virtually impossible
for the hi-jackers to kill the hostages. Other positive externalities include
the ability of television at least to provide many people with a minimum
knowledge of world events and how other people live.

3. Finally, most obviously, television produces huge amounts of
apparently free popular entertainment. Much of it is mindless rubbish
that is nevertheless enjoyed by many. Some of it will deservedly disappear, but some will no doubt endure. In the past much popular entertainment in the theatre, films, and books was likewise mindless rubbish.
In his day Shakespeare was popular entertainment competing with now
long forgotten popular entertainment. Posterity, not today's regulators,
are arguably best able to judge what is quality programming.[9]

Future developments

The television industry is in turmoil. Chapter 2 opened with the idea
that the law of unintended consequences is applicable to television and
that the industry has a history of moving in a direction the experts did
not anticipate. Nevertheless it seems highly likely that supply will
continue to expand and develop. It will probably do so less rapidly than
forecast if the experience of the 1980s is anything to go by. Promises
of the widespread use of videotext, cable, and DBS satellites in the '80s
all went unfulfilled.

On the other hand rationalization in Italy and in the US cable sector
took place very quickly, so that it is necessary to keep a regulatory watch
on undue concentration in any sector. Economics argues that the
consumer is best served if there is competition. Neither private
monopolies nor public monopolies serve the public interest. As global
media conglomerates become increasingly important in the industry it
is vital that national and international bodies are able to implement a

policy of preventing undue concentration and collusion at a supranational level. Nearly twenty years ago the United Nations, recognizing the potential of international satellites, laid down the principle that 'Satellite Broadcasting shall respect the sovereignty and equality of all states'.[10]

The main thrust of this book has been for a major role for the market in an age of abundance in determining who will supply the consumer with television. This does not preclude a public sector, preferably to serve minority interests as opposed to being one among many pursuing profit. The market will likely determine how and which new media distribution vehicles will supply consumers with programmes and when. The preference option shows that most programmes will be light entertainment and that television is an entertainment medium. Profits have created the incentive for many new entrants to take big risks to find the most efficient means of delivery. Discussing Fox Broadcasting, Rupert Murdoch said, 'Sure it's a risk. But it's a high return. If we succeed, we're going to have an asset worth billions.'[11] The market, subject to regulation, will determine what mix of satellite, cable, broadcast, and video television the consumer enjoys in the year 2000.

The market may determine the quality of the picture the viewer receives. In 1989 HDTV was all the rage and consumer electronics firms around the world were seeking to establish standards, in the producers' interest. They sought to get their governments to promote various systems. The Japanese producers wanted the world to adopt their standard, European producers wanted their own, and the US industry was not sure what it wanted. In much of the discussion over what standards would be adopted it often seemed that the consumer was being forgotten as each region attempted to protect its electronics industry.

Improvement will undoubtedly come soon, bringing superb detail. Some experts believe that fast-moving computer technology will soon overflow into television, so that forecasts of homes linked by optical fibre, allowing computers to pick up television and information, are common. Forecasts of television which is shown on the walls around the viewer and which also sends the sensations of the performer are the material of serious magazines about the future. Economics warns that what is technically feasible is not necessarily commercially viable. Pay television and interactive television have already learnt that lesson; so may DBS and HDTV.

This book concludes with an anecdote about one of the fathers of television. It supports the view that runs through the book that the public is best served by a variety of rival services and limited government services. John Baird, who first showed television at Selfridge's in 1926, was an inventor and entrepreneur strongly moved by the profit incentive. He made his first small fortune selling socks treated with borax which he claimed were waterproof. Another venture, a jam factory, failed. However, when it came to television he was thwarted in his ambition to supply the product. Commenting on the event, he concluded, 'I hated the BBC monopoly. Without it we could have started our own independent television channel . . . but the government would have disbarred us from any such enterprise in those days'.[12] Baird would have approved of the age of television abundance.

Notes

1   The quotation is taken from M.L. Allen, 'What you see is what you get', *Canada and the World*, May 1987, p. 22.
2   At the time of going to press Time Inc. and Warner Bros. announced a merger to create what will be the largest or second largest media conglomerate in the world. Some commentators believed that the merger was a defensive move in anticipation of other mergers by the likes of Murdoch and Maxwell in Europe.
3   The cases of government interference in the respected BBC discussed in chapter 6 show why a state monopoly is as much to be distrusted as a commercial monopoly.
4   The book has argued that advertising is probably excessive and that consumers probably experience increasing marginal disutility from advertising. A progressive tax on advertising for more than, say, five minutes per hour would be the economist's likely remedy to this problem. A politically more acceptable solution might be a straight limit of so many minutes per hour, the approach many countries have taken.
5   Nothing sinister is intended in capture theory. In many situations of capture both parties genuinely believe that what they do represents the public interest.
6   *The Times*, 11 November 1988.
7   Jorg Becker, 'Social and economic consequences of VCRs in Third World countries', *Media Development*, January 1985, p. 11.
8   Giuseppe Richeri, 'Television from service to business: European tendencies and the Italian case', in Philip Drummond and Richard Patterson (eds.), *Television in Transition*, London: British Film Institute, 1986, p. 34.
9   David Graham, 'Public service and popular taste', *New Statesman*, 2 October 1987.
10   United Nations, 'Declaration of Guiding Principles in the Use of Satellite Broadcasting', Resolution 2916, New York: United Nations, 1972.
11   *Time*, 6 April 1987.
12   *New Scientist*, 10 December 1988.

Select bibliography

To list all the sources used to write a book on the world television industry would be virtually impossible. Every day an avalanche of new primary sources appears in the daily newspapers and weekly news magazines. The most important of the books, reviews, reports, magazines, monographs, news weeklies, and trade papers used are listed below.

Books

Ansal, Paul A.V., 'The role of the state in broadcasting in Africa', *Media Development*, 2 February 1985.

Arnold, Erik, *Competition and Technological Change in the Television Industry: an Empirical Evaluation of Theories of the Firm*, London: Macmillan, 1985.

Atkin, David, and Litman, Barry, 'Network TV programming: economics, audiences, and the ratings game, 1971–1985', *Journal of Communication* 36, 3, summer 1986.

Bagdikian, Ben H., 'Conglomeration, concentration and the media', *Journal of Communication*, spring 1980.

Bain, Joe S., *Price Theory*, New York: Holt Rinehart & Winston, 1952.

Baumol, W.J., Panzar, J., and Willig, R.D., *Contestable Markets and the Theory of Industry Structure*, New York: Harcourt Brace Jovanovich, 1982.

Baumol, W.J., 'Contestable markets: an uprising in the theory of industry structure', *American Economic Review* 72, March 1982.

Besen, Stanley M., and Soligo, Ronald, 'The economics of the network-affiliate relationship in the television broadcasting industry', *American Economic Review* 63, 3, June 1973.

Besen, Stanley M., 'The economics of the cable television consensus', *Journal of Law and Economics* 17, 1, April 1974.

Besen, S., and Crandall, R., 'The deregulation of cable television', *Law and Contemporary Problems* 44, 1981.

Bloch, Harry, and Wirth, Michael, 'The demand for pay services on cable television', *Information Economics and Policy* 1, 4, 1984.

Bork, Robert, *The Antitrust Paradox*, New York: Basic Books, 1978.

Bowman, Gary, 'Consumer choice and television', *Applied Economics* 7, 3, spring 1975.

Boyd, Douglas A., *Broadcasting in the Arab World*, Boston, Mass.: Routledge & Kegan Paul in association with the International Institute of Communications, 1978.

Boyd, Douglas A., and Straubhar, Joseph D., 'Developmental impact of the home VCR on Third World countries', *Journal of Broadcasting and the Electronic Media*, winter 1985.

Boyd-Barrett, J. Oliver, 'Western news agencies and the media imperialism debate', *Journal of International Affairs*, winter 1982.

Broadcasting in Asia: an Annotated Bibliography, Mass Communication & Research Information Centre, Singapore, 1974.

Broadcasting in Asia and the Pacific: a Continental Survey of Radio and Television, Philadelphia: Temple University Press, 1978.

Broadcasting in Pen, Malaysia, Boston, Mass.: Routledge & Kegan Paul in association with the International Institute of Communication, 1977.

Broadcasting Satellite Systems, Geneva: International Telephone Union, 1983.

Brown, Allan, *Commercial Media in Australia: Economics, Ownership, Technology, and Regulation*, St Lucia: University of Queensland Press, 1986.

Cassata, M.B., *Television – a Guide to the Literature*, Phoenix, Ariz.: Oryx Press, 1985.

Chu, James, 'The gathering of news about China', *Gazette* 33, 1984.

Coase, R., 'The economics of broadcasting', *American Economic Review* 56, May 1966.

Colvin, Geoffrey, 'The crowded new world of TV', *Fortune*, 17 September 1984.

Compaine, Benjamin M., *Who owns the Media*, White Plains, N.Y.: Knolegate Industry Publications, 1982.

Curry, Jane L., 'Poland's press: after the crackdown', *Columbia Journalism Review*, October 1984.

Cyert, Richard M., and March, James G., *A Behavioral Theory of the Firm*, Englewood Cliffs, N.J.: Prentice Hall, 1963.

Dawson, F., 'How safe is cable's "natural monopoly"?', *Cablevision*, 1 June 1981.

de Noriega, L.A., *Broadcasting in Mexico*, Boston, Mass.: Routledge & Kegan Paul in association with the International Institute of Communication, 1979.

de Stains, Ian, 'The medium and its message', *Japan Update*, autumn 1986.

Domowitz, I., Hubbard, R.G., and Petersen, B.C., 'Business cycles and the relationship between concentration and price-cost margins', *Rand Journal of Economics* 17, 1986.

Drummond, Philip and Paterson, Richard, *Television in Transition*, London: British Film Institute, 1986.

Drummond, Philip (ed.), *Television in Transition*, International Television Studies Conference, London, British Film Institute, 1984.

Editor and Publisher, *International Year Book 1987*, New York: Editor and Publisher, 1987.

Egbon, Mike, 'West Nigeria television service – oldest in tropical Africa',
Journalism Quarterly, summer 1983.

Ellickson, Bryan, 'Hedonic theory and the demand for cable television',
American Economic Review 69, 1, March 1979.

Europa Year Book, London: Europa Publications, 1986.

Fallows, James, 'Japanese yearnings', *The Atlantic*, June 1987.

Friedman, M., *Capitalism and Freedom*, Chicago: University of Chicago
Press, 1962.

Fukutake, Tadashi, *Japanese Society Today*, Tokyo: University of Tokyo
Press, 1981.

Galbraith, John Kenneth, *American Capitalism: the Concept of
Countervailing Power*, revised edition, London: Hamish Hamilton,
1957.

Gould, Johnson, Chapman, *The Structure of the World of Television*, Pion,
1984.

Great Britain, *Report of the Committee on Financing the BBC* (the Peacock
Report), House of Commons Session 1985–86, Cmnd 9824, London:
HMSO.

Great Britain, *Third Report of the Home Affairs Committee*, The Future of
Broadcasting, London: HMSO, 1987.

Great Britain, *Broadcasting in the '90s: Competition, Choice and Quality;
The Government Plans for Broadcasting Legislation* (White Paper),
Cmnd 517, London: HMSO, 1988.

Green, Diana, 'Cable television in France: a non-market approach',
Quarterly Review, August 1984, p. 16. A thorough discussion can be
found in Don R. Leduc, 'Policy patterns in Europe and the United
States', *Journal of Broadcasting*, spring 1983.

Greenberg, E., and Barnett, H.J., 'TV program diversity – new evidence
and old theories', *American Economic Review* 61, 1971.

Hardin, Herschel, *Closed Circuits: the Sellout of Canadian Television*,
Toronto: Douglas & McIntyre, 1985.

Hazlett, Thomas W., 'Competition vs. franchise monopoly in cable
television', *Contemporary Policy Issues*, 4, 2, April 1986.

Howell, W.J. Jr, *World Broadcasting in the Age of the Satellite:
Comparative Systems, Policies and Issues in Mass Telecommunication*,
Norwood, N.J.: Abbex, 1986.

Ito, Masami, *Broadcasting in Japan*, Boston, Mass.: Routledge & Kegan
Paul in association with the International Institute of Communication,
1978.

Jun, Suk-ho, and Dayan, Daniel, 'An interactive media event: South
Korea's televised family reunion', *Journal of Communication*, spring
1986.

Lent, John A., 'ASEAN mass communications and cultural submission',
Media, Culture and Society, October 1981.

Kahn, A.E. *The Economics of Regulation: Principles and Institutions*, New
York: Wiley, 1970.

Kariel, Herbt G., and Rosenvall, Lynn A., 'Factors influencing
international news flow', *Journalism Quarterly* 61, 3, autumn 1984.

Katz, E., *Broadcasting in the Third World: Promise and Performance*, Cambridge, Mass.: Harvard University Press, 1977.

Koutsoyiannis, A., *Non-price Decisions: the Firm in a Modern Context*, London: Macmillan, 1982.

LeDuc, D., *Cable Television and the FCC*, Philadelphia: Temple University Press, 1973.

Lent, John A., 'Mass media in east Malaysia and Brunei', *Gazette*, September 1982.

Lent, John A., 'Videos in Asia: frivolity, frustration, futility', *Media Development*, January 1985.

Liebenstein, Harvey, 'Allocative efficiency vs. "X-efficiency" ', *American Economic Review* 56, 1966.

MacBride, Sean, *Many Voices, One World: Report by the International Commission for a Study of Communication Problems*, Paris: UNESCO, 1980.

Mahan, Elizabeth, 'Mexican broadcasting: reassessing the industry-state relationship', *Journal of Communications*, April 1984.

Marks, David, 'Broadcasting over the wall: the free flow of information between East and West Germany', *Journal of Communications*, January 1983.

Masaki, Tomohiko, 'Focus on new media', *Economic Eye*, March 1985.

Matekera, José, 'Government support or commercialisation: the Japanese dilemma', *Media Development*, February 1985.

McLuhan, Marshall, *Understanding Media: the Extensions of Man*, New York: Mentor, 1964.

Merrill, John, *Global Journalism*, New York: Longman, 1983.

Meyers, William *The Image Makers*, New York: Times Books, 1984.

Minasian, J., 'Television pricing and the theory of public goods', *Journal of Law and Economics* 7, 1964.

Mishan, E.J., *The Costs of Economic Growth*, Harmondsworth: Penguin, 1969.

Muta, Hiromitsu, 'The economics of the University of the Air of Japan', *Higher Education* 14, 3, June 1985.

Needham, Douglas, *The Economics of Industrial Structure, Conduct and Performance*, London: Holt Rinehart & Winston, 1978.

Needham, Douglas, *Economic Analysis and Industrial Structure*, New York: Holt Rinehart & Winston, 1978.

Nippon Hoso Kyokai, *This is NHK*, Tokyo: Audience Public Research Bureau, 1985.

Noam, Eli M., *Telecommunications Regulation Today and Tomorrow*, New York: Harcourt Brace Jovanovich, 1983.

Noam, Eli M., 'Opening up cable TV', *New York Times*, 19 March 1981.

Noll, R., Peck, M., and McGowan, J., *Economic Aspects of Television Regulation*, Washington, D.C.: Brookings Institution, 1973.

Parker, Luane, 'A TV début in France', *Maclean's*, 3 March 1986.

Pearce, Edward, 'Dial M for Murdoch', *Encounter 2*, 1982.

Penacchioni, Irene, 'The reception of popular television in north-eastern Brazil', *Media, Culture and Society*, October 1984.

Penrose, E.T., *The Theory of the Growth of the Firm*, Oxford: Blackwell, 1959.

Pierinne, Jean-Marie, 'Monopoly and/or public service: the Belgian instance', *Journal of Communications*, October 1983.

Porter, W., *The Italian Journalist*, Ann Arbor, Mich.: University of Michigan Press, 1983.

Pragnell, Anthony, *Television in Europe: Quality and Value in a Time of Change*, Manchester: European Institute for the Media, 1985 (monograph).

Rainger, Gregory and Harvey, Jennings, *Satellite Broadcasting*, Toronto: Wiley, 1985.

Reizen, Joe, 'China tunes in on television and radio', *Journal of the Royal Television Society*, October 1985.

Roach, Colleen, 'The U.S. position on the new world information and communication order', *Journal of Communication*, autumn 1987.

Robinson, J., *The Economics of Imperfect Competition*, London: Macmillan, 1933.

Rogers, Everett M., and Antola, Livia, 'Telenovelas: a Latin American success story', *Journal of Communications*, January 1986.

Rubin, Michael, Huber, Mary, and Taylor, Elizabeth Lloyd, *The Knowledge Industry in the United States*, Princeton, N.J.: Princeton University Press, 1986.

Sanders, R., *Broadcasting in Guyana*, Boston, Mass.: Routledge & Kegan Paul in association with the International Institute of Communication, 1978.

Sandford, John, *The Mass Media of the German Speaking Countries*, London: Oswald Wolff, 1976.

Scherer, F.M., *Industrial Market Structure and Economic Performance*, second edition, Chicago: Rand-McNally, 1980.

Schmalensee, Richard, 'Do markets differ much?', *American Economic Review* 75, 1985.

Schudsen, Michael, *Advertising: the Uneasy Persuasion*, New York: Basic Books, 1984.

Schumpeter, J.A., *The Theory of Economic Development: an Inquiry into Profits, Capital, Credit, Interest and the Business Cycle*, London: Oxford University Press, 1961.

Schumpeter, J.A., *Capitalism, Socialism and Democracy*, New York: Harper, first edition 1942, third edition 1950.

Schwartz, A.T., 'Is cable doing enough in Manhattan?', *New York Times*, 8 November 1981.

Shepherd, W.G., *The Economics of Industrial Organization*, Englewood Cliffs, N.J.: Prentice Hall, 1985.

Shepherd, W.G., 'Contestability vs. competition', *American Economic Review* 74, 1984.

Sherrid, Pamela, 'Embarrassment of riches', *Forbes'*, 9 April 1984.

Shue, Vivienne, 'China's local news media', *China Quarterly*, June 1981.

Smith, Anthony, *Geopolitics of Information*, London: Faber, 1980.

Smith, Leslie F., *Perspectives on Radio and Television:*

Telecommunications in the United States, New York: Harper & Row, 1985.

Sparks, Allister, 'Forbidden television', *Channels*, May/June 1985.

Spence, M., 'Contestable markets and the theory of industry structure: a review article', *Journal of Economic Literature*, September 1982.

Stephens, Mitchell, 'Clout: Murdoch's political post', *Columbia Journalism Review*, July/August 1982.

Supple, Barry, *The Experience of Economic Growth: Case Studies in Economic History*, New York: Random House, 1963.

Sylos-Labini, Paulo, *Oligopoly and Technical Progress*, Cambridge, Mass.: Harvard University Press, 1969.

Television Digest, *Television Factbook 1987* 56, Washington, D.C.: Television Digest, 1987.

Traub, James, 'New Delhi gold rush', *Channels*, July/August 1986.

Tunstall, Jeremy, *The Media in Britain*, London: Constable, 1983.

Tydemand, John, and Kelm, Ellen Jakes, *New Media in Europe: Satellites, Cable, VCRs and Videotext*, London: McGraw-Hill, 1986.

Usher, Dan, *The Economic Prerequisite to Democracy*, Oxford: Blackwell, 1981.

Veljanovsky, C.G., and Bishop, W.D., *Choice by Cable: the Economics of a New Era in Television*, London: Institute of Economic Affairs, 1983.

Webb, G. Kent, *The Economics of Cable Television*, Lexington, Mass.: Lexington Books, 1983.

Wheen, Francis, 'No such thing as a free lunch', *New Statesman*, 17 May 1985.

Whitehead, S., *Broadcasting in Africa: a Continental Survey of Radio and Television*, Philadelphia: Temple University Press, 1974.

Williams, R., 'France: a revolution in the making', *Channels*, September 1985.

Williamson, Oliver E., *Markets and Hierarchies: Analysis and Antitrust Implications. A Study in the Economics of Internal Organization*, New York: Free Press, 1975.

Williamson, Oliver E., 'Predatory pricing: a strategic and welfare analysis', *Yale Law Journal*, December 1977.

Newspapers and magazines

Advertising Age, Africa, American Economic Review, Asia Week, Asian Profile, The Atlantic, Australian Financial Review, The Broadcaster, Broadcasting, Business Week, Cable TV, Calgary Herald, Canada and the World, Canadian Public Policy, Channels, Christian Science Monitor, Current Affairs, Democratic Journalist, Der Spiegel, Economic Eye, Economic Journal, The Economist, Encounter, Far Eastern Economic Review, Forbes', Fortune, Gazette, Globe and Mail, Harvard Business Review, Index on Censorship, Islands Business, Japan Quarterly, Japan Times, Japan Update, Journal of Broadcasting, Journal of Broadcasting and the Electronic Media, Journal of Communication, Journal of the Royal Television Society, Journalism Quarterly, The Listener, Maclean's, Guardian Weekly, Media, Culture and Society, Media Development, Mother

Jones, New Statesman, Newsweek, New York Times, The Observer, Omni, Pacific Islands Monthly, Quadrant, Quarterly Review, Radio Japan News, Report on Business, Satellite Entertainment Guide, Speaking of Japan, Sunday Times, Third World Communications, Third World Quarterly, Time, The Times, Times-Colonist, United Nations Chronicle, US News and World Report, Vital Speeches of the Day, Wall Street Journal, Washington Post.

Index

advertising: agencies 11–12, 64–6;
audit of 32; in Britian 121–2; in
China 31, 184, 187; conduct of
55; costs 93; demands for
24–33, 121–2, 170, 187, 188; in
Europe 150, 144, 145;
expenditure 28, 144, 145, 170;
and financing of television 31–2,
222–3; in France 156, 159; and
GNP, percent of 25; in Hong
Kong 214; in India 208–9; as
investment 27; in Italy 154; in
Japan 169, 170, 177; in Mexico
199; networks, choice of 94; and
news 99; and politics 72;
preference option 29–30; prices
55–6; revenue in Spain 165;
revenue, and viewer demand 29;
and sport 101–2; strategies for
65–7; in USA 63–9; in USSR
188; in West Germany 161
affiliated stations 10–11; and
networks 94–5
Africa: television industry in 202–5
Agnelli 153
Aird Commission (1929, Canada)
112
Algeria 41
All-Nigeria TV Service (NTV) 203
American Broadcasting Company
78; consumer demand 60; cost
cutting 86–7; news 101; and
Olympic Games 102; and sport
103
Amstrad 126, 130

Argentina 200; national share of
imported programmes 41;
receivers, growth of 19
Astra satellite 149
AT&T 6, 9, 10, 75, 82
Australia 11, 194; advertising as
percentage of GNP 25; entry to
industry 47; government demand
for television 34; national share
of imported programmes 41;
receivers, growth of 19;
similarities with Canadian
television 180; sport 42;
television industry 180–1
Australian Broadcast Tribunal
(ABT, 1977) 180
Australian Broadcasting Act (1942)
180
Austria 41; advertising expenditure
145; cable television 148;
demand, nature of 145; VCRs,
penetration of households 15
Awolowo, Chief 203
Azcarraja, Emilio 197

Baird, John L. 5, 6, 7, 227–8
Bakker, Jimmy 71
Belgium: advertising expenditure
145; cable television 146, 148,
149, 163; demand, nature of
145; international television 164;
national share of imported
programmes 41; restructured
television industry 149; satellite
broadcasting 147; VCRs,